MEDIATED *DOMINICANIDAD*

MEDIATED *DOMINICANIDAD*

DOMINICANS AND US MEDIA

KEARA K. GOIN

INDIANA UNIVERSITY PRESS

This book is a publication of

Indiana University Press
Herman B Wells Library
1320 East 10th Street
Bloomington, Indiana 47405 USA

https://iupress.org

© 2026 by Keara K. Goin

All rights reserved

No part of this book may be reproduced or utilized in any form or by any means, electronic or mechanical, including photocopying and recording, or by any information storage and retrieval system, without permission in writing from the publisher.

For customers in the European Union with safety or GPSR concerns, please contact Mare Nostrum Group B.V., Mauritskade 21D, 1091 GC Amsterdam, The Netherlands. Email: gpsr@mare-nostrum.co.uk

First Printing 2026

Cataloging information is available from the Library of Congress.

ISBN 978-0-253-07488-1 (hdbk.)
ISBN 978-0-253-07489-8 (pbk.)
ISBN 978-0-253-07491-1 (ebook)

CONTENTS

Acknowledgments vii

A Note on Terminology ix

Introduction 1

PART I: Rethinking the Dominican Relationship to Blackness

1. Theorizing Dominicanidad 32

PART II: (In)Authentic Dominicanidad

2. Dominican Celebrity Studies 52

3. Televisual Dominicanidad and MTV's *Washington Heights* 95

PART III: *Latinidades* and Hyphenated Identities

4. Competing Latinidades: *Orange Is the New Black* and Engagement with Latinx Specificity 134

5. Producing Dominicanidad: *Así Somos*/The Way We Are 159

Conclusion: "*Mi raza es dominicana*": Dominicanidad as a Unique Lens for Approaching US Racial Hegemony 187

References 201

Index 215

ACKNOWLEDGMENTS

There are many people I would like to thank who have been instrumental and provided unwavering support throughout the multiyear process that has culminated in this book.

First, and most importantly, to the countless Dominicans and Dominican-Americans I interviewed, spoke with, and engaged with in New York City, I am forever grateful and humbled by your insight. I only hope that this book is able to relay your voices and share your experiences. I would also like to thank the City University of New York Dominican Studies Institute (DSI) and the DSI Library for providing me with a home base for my fieldwork, being a source of information, and helping fund some of my time in the field. The wealth of scholarship you hold in your archives and the support through your initiatives are truly inspirational and were incredibly influential for this book. To Professor Sarah Aponte, I will be forever grateful to you for believing in my research and selecting me as one of the DSI research fellows. To Nelson Santana, thank you for being my cultural interpreter, key informant, and research facilitator. Without you, I would not have been able to complete my research, and for that, I will be forever grateful.

To my mentors—Mary Beltrán, Maria Franklin, Shanti Kumar, Janet Staiger, and Joseph Straubhaar—thank you for your comments, advice, and support along the way. Without your contributions, I would not have been able to craft and conduct this research project. To my colleagues, those at the University of Virginia Department of Media Studies and throughout the country, completing a book while teaching a heavy load is a long and arduous task; thank you for always supporting my efforts and believing in the possibilities of my work. I would like to especially thank my friend and academic soulmate Alfred Martin. Thank you for reading countless drafts, talking to me for hours, helping me work out ideas, and being my academic role model. I just hope that I can be half the scholar you are. To Pallavi

Rao, you have been my backbone and sounding board for many years now. Without your continued reassurance and insights, I might have given up long ago.

To Faith Hilliard, thank you for helping prepare my images for the book and working with me to create a wonderful draft for the cover. I truly wish I could have been able to showcase your artwork.

Finally, to my family, who to this day think my desire to be an academic is a sign of insanity, thank you for never doubting that this is something I could achieve. Thank you to my father and sister for proofreading things that you would normally have no interest in ever reading. To my partner, Chad Parker, thank you for lighting a fire in my heart and under my ass. This time has been a challenging one for us, but without you, I would never have known the level of joy I now experience every day.

A NOTE ON TERMINOLOGY

The confusion and contradicting discourses concerning the political name game of what term best represents and identifies people from or with heritage from Latin America or the Spanish Caribbean is often dismissed as trivial, but it is actually deeply rooted in the shifting sociohistorical reality and lived tensions for the people I refer to in this book as either Latinx or Latina/o/x or Latina/o(s). Popularly imagined—*imagined* being the key term here—as a homogenous "brown" race with a mixed ethnoracial heritage, the extreme diversity within the Latinx population is systematically flattened, ignored, and erased. A similar scenario arises when discussing groups of African descent. As I outline in chapter 1 of this book, African descent and Blackness are interpreted and articulated in a multitude of locational and culturally specific ways. As such, I want to clarify some of the terminology used in this book and explain some of the political alignments behind my rhetorical choices. Furthermore, as all these terms are contested, in both use and theory, one should assume an implied parenthesis whenever they are used.

Latino: According to Laura E. Gómez (2020, 9), "Latinos are people who currently live in the United States—whether or not they are American citizens and/or were born in this country—who are descendants of migrants or who themselves migrated from Latin America, and specifically from the former colonies of Spain in the Western Hemisphere." The genesis of the term *Latino* comes from both inside/below and outside/above. While originating in US politics of self-identification through the contributions of mainly Mexican Americans and Puerto Ricans, it has also become an imposed label. While still salient and self-ascribed by many, the term has nonetheless been taken up by commercial institutions and mainstream US society. However, when constituted within what Juan Flores (2000, 198) has referred to as the "Latino Imaginary," it points to "the 'community' represented 'for itself,' a unity fashioned creatively on the basis of shared memory and desire, congruent histories of misery and struggle, and intertwining utopias."

Latina/o: In a rejection of the gendered nature of language—specifically the masculine/feminine linguistic orientation of words—Latina feminist scholars introduce a subversion of masculine normativity and supremacy through inverting the gendered ending of "Latino/a" to "Latina/o." A simple rhetorical strategy, it highlights the gendered dynamics inherent in language and makes the Latina, feminine, and nonmasculine central. In solidarity with Latina feminist ethos, I, too, use this inverted construction of the term, particularly when the term *Latinx* is grammatically awkward. For example, I use "Latina/o" when referring to individuals or groups. As in: Many Latina/os have situational and fluid identities.

Latinx: Emerging in the last decade in both popular culture and academia, the term *Latinx* is a response to the homogenizing forces of *Latino*. In an attempt to be inclusive and gender neutral, it replaces the gendered *o/a* or *a/o* with the nongendered *x*. According to Maylei Blackwell, Floridalma Boj Lopez, and Luis Urrieta Jr. (2017, 129), whose scholarship has laid down the foundation for critical Latinx indigeneities, the term *Latinx* "reflects the shifting terrain of identification and the ongoing commitment to building unity through embracing the diversity of *Latinidad* by not erasing difference and specificity. Further, the term Latinx is an important tool to signal the colonial nature of the imposition of gender binaries and opens up the possibility for recognizing the diversity of Indigenous sex gender systems in the Americas, many of which included more than two genders." Many scholars and activists have argued that the term is inconsistent with Latin-based languages (Spanish, Portuguese, French) and can be difficult to pronounce. Others argue the term is an example of US linguistic imperialism. As a result, many prefer the term *Latine*. This term is more conducive to speakers of Spanish and retains gender neutrality, while also being able to refer to people in the singular or plural. While my relationship with the term *Latinx* is continually evolving—and as such might change—I feel that it best reflects the political ethos of feminist, queer, and intersectional thought and highlights a subjectivity rooted in the US. I would not use the term *Latinx* to refer to individuals who live in Latin America or the Spanish Caribbean. While I cannot claim to be the arbitrator of when a person transforms from *Latin American* to *Latinx*, my use of the term is intended to situate the subject(s) as part of a heterogeneous, radically hybrid (Valdivia 2020), intersectional, and dynamic population in the US.

Latin(o) American: María Elena Cepeda's (2010) analysis of the transnational identification of Colombians in the US uses the term *Latin(o) Americans* to emphasize the fluidity and multisituated nature of the transnational subject. The term allows for a continuity and connection to Latin America while acknowledging a connection to the US-based identity of *Latino*. To avoid divorcing the US-based self from the Latin American–based self, *Latin(o) American* accommodates for transnational, local, and contextual subjectivities. At times, I use this term to reinforce the transnational positionalities of US Latinx peoples.

Hispanic: The term *Hispanic* is rooted in a grouping constructed by external forces and, therefore, is generally not something US Latinx populations identify with (Flores 2000; Rodriguez 2000; Calderon 1992). Puerto Rican scholar Juan Flores (2000), in addressing the political semantics of the evolution of this terminology, suggests that while often seen as interchangeable, or at least possessing trivial differences, the terms *Latino* and *Hispanic* are loaded with different mythic meanings and, in reality, are steeped in history and the resulting power dynamics of US constructions of those people whom the dominant conventions of categorizing people in the US see as originating in Latin America or the Spanish Caribbean. Therefore, I only use this term when referring to hegemonic and dominant discourses or categorizations of Latinx peoples.

African American: I use the term *African American* when referring to people whose Blackness is rooted in the US sociohistorical context. The legacy of US Blackness is historically, socially, and ideologically specific and distinct from those found in other places and times. Usually situated in a narrative of historical enslavement, legal and social segregation, and social and institutional racism, the African American experience and identity are distinct from other populations of African descent.

Black: While the term *Black*, as with all racial categories, is a social construct rooted in European colonialism and white supremacy, it nonetheless carries significant and symbolic meaning. The term is used in this book to refer to any population of African descent, regardless of their location or positionality within the African diaspora. In the context of the US, the terms *Black* or *African descent* apply to "African Americans" but also apply to those whose heritage is not exclusive to the US (i.e., people who come from one of the dozens of other colonies/countries that participated in African enslavement or more recent voluntary immigrants from African countries). Therefore, Latina/os of African descent are Black, but they do not think of themselves, nor are they thought of by others, as African American.

MEDIATED *DOMINICANIDAD*

INTRODUCTION

I personally have a lot of respect for Felix [Sánchez]. I'll always remember 8 years ago when he participated in the games and won gold for the first time, the WHOLE country was paralized [sic] watching him run on tv [sic]. I was working in a bank at that point and both tellers and customers stopped what they were doing to cheer him on. When in the history of the DR have you seen anything similar? By Representing the DR, he's doing his DOMINICAN parents' heritage honor and at the same time inspiring generations of young dominicans [sic] into training and going for their dreams. I say kudos to Felix and may he continue to wear the bandera dominicana proudly for a long time to come.

—Poster on DR1.com

Félix Sánchez, a US-born and trained Olympic runner, decided that instead of representing his birth country in the Olympics, he would run for his parents' country: the Dominican Republic (DR). In many ways the epitome of the "American Dream," this successful athlete chose to represent Dominican pride rather than joining the thousands of US athletes who had lost their connection to the country their families came from.[1] I remember seeing Félix during the 2012 London Olympic coverage. He was exuding *machista* bravado and had a picture of his *abuela* (grandmother) pinned to his competition number.[2] I thought to myself, "Yes, this guy is ALL Dominican." To find out later that he had been born and raised in the US of Dominican-born parents only reaffirmed to me what I have always believed about Dominicans in the US: They not only prioritize a connection with the people they know on the island but also fundamentally identify as Dominican no matter where they physically live in the diaspora. Moreover, I believe that a shared consumption of media facilitates and sustains this transnational Dominican identity.[3]

The opening vignette illustrates five goals of this book: (1) demonstrate how Dominican-American identification maintains allegiance to the DR as more than merely an origin of heritage and emphasizes the significance and span of the Dominican imaginary within the US, (2) examine the embodied nature of *dominicanidad* (Dominican-ness) in terms of ethnoracial performativity and presumed Dominican cultural authenticity, (3) discuss the impact of media in establishing diasporic Dominican identification, (4) directly attest to the ways media is transnationally consumed and essential to maintaining shared identification, and (5) highlight the importance of media in sustaining dominicanidad regardless of geographic location or national citizenship.

Dominicans and US Media

My earliest research focused on the cultural impact of media on people living in the DR. Yet, throughout my 2008 fieldwork, it seemed all people wanted to talk to me about was the US. Yes, there was a US presidential election coming up that people were curious about, but they mostly wanted to talk about the people they knew who lived in the US, the times they had been there, and their plans for working or going to school there. Apart from my positionality as a *blanca* (white American) US researcher, their interest in discussing the US went a lot deeper. This curiosity was rooted in the historical connection Dominicans have with the US, their circular migration pattern between the two countries, and the open dialogue and cultural exchange they maintain with people living in the Dominican diaspora.[4]

In Santiago, I lived with a Dominican family. As we sat in their living room watching a Major League Baseball game on a US television channel, they repeatedly pointed out to me that each of the players who came up to bat were, in fact, Dominican (and there were many). As I asked questions about the Dominican players, they asked me questions about the US commercials that aired during the breaks in the game. It was not until the game was almost over that I realized how an unassuming night in front of the television had turned into one of the most revealing experiences of my entire fieldwork in the DR. As satellites transmit New York–based Dominican television stations to the island and Dominican-based stations transmit to New York, Dominicans in all parts of the diaspora take to the internet to stream media content, connect, reminisce, and maintain their cultural identity. It is through media that Dominicans, no matter where they are located, are able to establish a contact zone,[5] a cultural bridge, and an avenue for both preserving and challenging their identities.[6] Clearly, Dominicans on the island are not only interested but also fully invested in those Dominican communities off the island. On one level, this book is a response to all the conversations I had about my country while being fully submerged in another. Yet, more significantly, it is about Dominicans in the US, who are just as fiercely Dominican as those on the island. Additionally, because of what they watch, surf, and listen to, they are as connected with that island reality as they are with the streets of Washington Heights, New York City (NYC).

It is important to note that I am not Dominican. I have lived and conducted fieldwork in both the DR and the NYC Dominican neighborhood of Washington Heights. I was selected to be a City University of New York (CUNY) Dominican Studies Institute (DSI) Research Fellow. I have spoken at the Dominican Studies Association conferences and have volunteered to work at the Dominican Film Festival in New York City (DFFNYC). But these things do not make me part of what could be considered the Dominican community. I am a white, European-descended woman who never met a Dominican person until I went to college. While it is not uncommon to conduct research, especially ethnographic research, among a community where one is an outsider, it does create valid limitations on the authority the researcher can claim. Every ethnographer must recognize the power dynamics inherent in their research. I know that my academic and racial background, along with my predominant use of the English language, situates me as a person of privilege in relation to the Dominicans I interacted with. Yet I was also present in their spaces, those spaces where they have domain. To prevent concerns over invasion and mitigate my out-group status, my affiliation with the DSI, previous residence in the DR, acquaintance with many members of the NYC Dominican community, and sincere respect for Dominicans and Dominican culture(s) allowed me to establish a rapport with the people I interviewed and interacted with. Furthermore, there is an advantage to taking up the position of the Other in the research space. While true objectivity is impossible for any scholar, being part of the out-group does provide a certain analytical distance that would be difficult for an insider to achieve. As such, I can and hopefully do make a valuable contribution to Dominican and Latina/o/x Studies. However, I am careful to avoid speaking for Dominicans; instead, I see myself as a conduit through which they can speak.

I recognize that I am an outsider among the people this book is about. Ideally, such a project should be undertaken by a Dominican scholar, but this has yet to happen. It is easy to argue that my scholarship is valuable and addresses gaps in the literature based on the simple fact that so few scholars are doing work on US-based dominicanidad, especially in media studies. However, the argument that "nobody else is studying it" is not a sufficient reason to focus one's research on a particular topic. The reason I do research on and with Dominicans, and the same reason it baffles me why so few do the same, is that I find dominicanidad uniquely positioned to challenge US ethnoracial ideology. While the Dominican diaspora spans much of the globe, it is in the US that dominicanidad becomes most critically challenged and negotiated. The global influence of Hollywood media imagery and the relatively large Dominican population within the US contribute to the significant, observable, and transnational impact of US-based ethnoracial discourses within the negotiation of dominicanidad.

Dominicans, and other Afro-Latinx peoples in the US, struggle to maintain an identification that is distinct from both panethnic *latinidad* (Latino-ness) and Blackness as defined in the US. Often overlooked by both categories, people of Latina/o/x and African heritage in the US must attempt to negotiate and position themselves within a racialized system that fundamentally has no room for them. Miriam Jiménez Román and Juan Flores (2010, 1) suggest that even the term *Afro-Latino* is confusing to those in the US "because we are accustomed to thinking of 'Afro' and 'Latino' as distinct from each other and mutually exclusive: one is either Black or Latino." Furthermore, the various US English media avenues and industries misrepresent and underrepresent Afro-Latina/os in a way that marginalizes their identities and shapes how mainstream US society understands their racialization. Representations of Afro-Latina/os are extremely rare in US mass media and regularly limited to certain narrative locations (e.g., NYC). In Spanish-language media, such representations, while maintaining a more visible presence, are secondary, limited, and "negative," usually seen in their positioning as background characters or domestics in telenovelas, the trivializing of Caribbean interests in news coverage, and an almost total lack of cultural representation based in *afrolatinidades*.[7] As a result, those with an Afro-Latinx subjectivity are challenged to find representations that reflect their racial, ethnic, and national identities, often having to negotiate an identification with images that do not accommodate for their regularly ignored afrolatinidad.

To explain how Dominicans in the US navigate this identity politics minefield, this book draws on ethnographic interviews with Dominican Americans living in the Dominican communities of NYC and site-specific fieldwork in these neighborhoods, as well as the internet spaces where Dominicans participate. Examining media reception and negotiation by engaging directly with Dominicans in the US, I reveal those articulations of ethnoracial identity embedded in a diaspora sustained through mediation. In this book, *mediation/mediated* can be thought of in two primary ways: (1) as the result of being conveyed through an intermediary actor and (2) an understanding that media (whether film, television, print, musical, or digital) is itself an intermediary or filter through which various discourses are circulated. Through a critical cultural and reception study that investigates the consumption, interpretation, and production practices of Dominicans and Dominican-Americans, an online reception study that highlights the discourses involved in negotiating US-based dominicanidad, and a critical and textual analysis of those media texts that my study participants cited as having particular resonance to their identity as Dominicans/Dominican-Americans, I reveal how media influences the interpretation and experience of dominicanidad. Framing this overall project are the following research questions:

1. What types of media texts are Dominicans in the US consuming, talking about, relating to, and critiquing?
2. How do Dominican(-Americans) interpret representations of (or the lack of) Dominicans in popular culture, and are there certain representations of either latinidad or Blackness they connect with more saliently?
3. What role do ethnoracialized media representations have in their individual negotiations of self, and how do they operate across diasporic networks?

This book, therefore, investigates how Dominicans, an increasingly numerically significant Latinx group in the US, are navigating the media texts and the representations they include to negotiate the US ethnoracial landscape. Structured by the results of my fieldwork in NYC and online reception studies, the span of the media analyzed is primarily contemporary (media produced in the last twenty years or so) but multimedium. Interviewees included references to television, film, and print media, along with internet sources and other new media. To make this range of media more manageable, I focus specifically on the film *In the Heights* (dir. John Chu, 2021), Dominican celebrity texts, the MTV Dominican-American-centric reality show *Washington Heights*, the Netflix hit series *Orange Is the New Black*, and a group of Dominican filmmakers and other media creatives striving to work in the media industries. This book not only addresses a population in the US that is often ignored and marginalized within the literature but also complicates mediated ethnoracial identity negotiation processes within the US more broadly. For a book that is both highly positioned in NYC and diasporic, I conducted a triangulated study—an approach that aims to provide a more dynamic understanding by making the research multimethodological—to address how these negotiations are unfolding.

A Brief Dominican History

To better contextualize the experiences of Dominicans in the US, a succinct overview of the DR and Dominican migration to the US is in order. The island of Hispaniola was one of the first locations in the Americas to have a European settlement. Colonized by both Spain and France, the island's history has been shaped by the power struggles between those two imperial powers, the eradication of its Indigenous population, and the large-scale institutionalization of African enslavement. The plantation-based economic and social structure that dominated the first two centuries of European colonial rule on the island (whether by the Spanish or French) left deep scars on its peoples. The island referred to by the Indigenous Taíno people as Quisqueya became split into two separate but interconnected peoples along colonial divides that today are represented by the nations of Haiti and the DR. This division has historically been complicated and bloody.[8] After the Haitian Revolution (1791–1804), instigated by the revolt of enslaved and free Africans who made up the large majority of the French colony's population, the country's subsequent independence terrified the other colonial powers whose economic and political interests in the Americas were built on the foundation of enslaved labor. Concerns over similar revolts, European conflicts of the Napoleonic Wars, and the changing balance of geopolitical power (including the rise of the US as an independent nation and economic power) all manifested on the island of Hispaniola in a tug-of-war for dominance. Of particular note is the occupation of the Spanish colony of Santo Domingo, modern-day DR, by Haiti from 1822 to 1842. This contributed not only to the continuation of political instability on the island but also to a legacy of *antihaitianismo* (anti-Haitianism) within the Dominican national imaginary. By the mid-nineteenth century, both Haiti and the DR were nominally independent nations, but postcolonial interests in the island continued to provoke and exploit the peoples of both countries.[9]

The geopolitical struggle for dominance over the Caribbean came to a head during the Spanish-American War (1898) when the US wrested control over the last bastions of Spanish colonial holdings. This positioned the US as the dominant power in the Western Hemisphere and allowed for its extensive intervention in Caribbean and Latin American affairs. As a result, the US has intervened in the politics and economy of nearly all nations of the Americas at some point over the last 120 years (Gómez 2020). In 1916, acting in its own best interests, the US began an occupation of the DR that lasted until 1924. During the occupation, the US instituted a modern military state in the DR, establishing a militarist political environment (Krohn-Hansen 2013). However, this ultimately backfired when Rafael Trujillo (1891–1961), who rose to power in this militarist system, instigated a coup that ejected the US from the country and began his brutal dictatorship (1930–61).

Trujillo built a state and national consciousness in the DR predicated on antihaitianismo and rural populism (Torres-Saillant and Hernandez 1998; García-Peña 2016). According to Ernesto Sagás (2000, 45), the Trujillo regime "concocted the hitherto loose and unorganized ideas of antihaitianismo into a full-fledged ideology that perceived Haitians as inferior beings and enemies of the Dominican nation." This was then able to develop into a "dominant, state-sponsored ideology, and the parallel fabrication of an official nationhood by the Trujillista state." The culmination was the genocidal massacre (La Masacre del Perejil of 1937) of Haitians and Dominicans of Haitian descent along the DR's border with Haiti, as well as the political repression and disenfranchisement of the Dominican populace.[10] Trujillo's regime isolated the DR from much of the world and made it almost impossible to leave the country—although some refugees did manage to migrate to places like Puerto Rico, Florida, and New York. Trujillo was assassinated in 1961, which destabilized his political regime and policies. While Dominican politics and economics continued to be marked by corruption and instability—including a US intervention in 1965 caused by the turmoil resulting from the power vacuum created by Trujillo's assassination—the country has seen intermittent periods of growth.

Although people from what is now the DR have lived in what is now the US since the arrival of the trader Juan Rodriguez in the early seventeenth century (Stevens-Acevedo et al. 2013), the Dominican population in the US had been relatively small until more recently. The first major increase in the Dominican population coincided with the 1916–24 US occupation (Torres-Santos 2013). Following the rise of Trujillo, however, the growth of this population stagnated. After Trujillo's assassination and the 1965 US intervention, political unrest and US interest in the DR led to a significant rise in the number of people immigrating to the US (Krohn-Hansen 2013). Since the 1960s, the US Dominican population has grown exponentially, from an estimated population of 170,817 in 1980 to an estimated 2,216,258 in 2020 (Hernández et al. 2022). Because of continued political problems on the island and better economic opportunities in the US, Dominicans have become the fastest-growing Latinx population in the US. Most of this population settled in NYC at first—most notably the neighborhoods of Washington Heights, Inwood, the Bronx, Queens, and Brooklyn—but there are now Dominican communities all over the country (Hernández et al. 2022). The Pew Research Center's most recent survey found that, as of 2021, the total number of people in the US who identify as having Dominican heritage is 2.4 million, which makes them the fourth-largest Latinx group in the country (Moslimani et al. 2023). Around 50 percent of the population is made up of foreign-born individuals whose median income ($30,000 per individual) is in a similar range as other Latinx groups; this group also has a slightly higher rate of educational attainment than other Latinx groups (2023).

Dominicans in the US can be thought of as a transnational population. According to Jorge Duany's ([1994] 2008, 2) book *Quisqueya on the Hudson: The Transnational Identity of Dominicans in Washington Heights*, if transnationalism means "the construction of dense social fields across national borders as a result of the circulation of people, ideas, practices, money, goods, and information," then Dominicans in the US personify the transnational subject. Referred to in the DR interchangeably as *dominicanos ausentes* (absent Dominicans), *dominicanos en el exterior* (Dominicans abroad), or *dominicanyork*, they are nonetheless included within a shared Dominican national imaginary.[11] When compared to other Latinx groups, this group's population numbers might seem insignificant. However, one out of eight Dominicans lives in the US (Gómez 2020). Since 1994, Dominicans have been allowed to hold dual citizenship, and many have chosen this option. Therefore, Dominican transnationalism is not only sustained through informal networks but also created through a "deterritorialized transnational nation-state." As explained by María Elena Cepeda (2010, 61), "In a more official capacity, a transnational dynamic emerges when, in response to a large immigrant population, government officials in a nation set out to reconfigure the nation-state's borders in order to include even those residing outside the state's physical boundaries. The result, a 'deterritorialized transnational nation-state,' encompasses the immigrants themselves as well as their descendants." Such transnationalism is not exclusive to Dominican-Americans but is typical of many Latinx groups in the US. What makes their transnationalism distinct is "that few immigrant communities have developed such a large number and variety of transnational ties to their country of origin, and have maintained such strong ties over several decades" (Duany [1994] 2008, 8). In fact, Dominicans in the US can often wield more political and economic capital in the DR than those living on the island (García-Peña 2016). The lived daily experience of Dominicans in the US is one of perpetual oscillation "between Dominican and American cultures, between Spanish and English, and between 'here' and 'there'" (Duany [1994] 2008, 5). Due to circulatory migration, frequent return visits, and prolific media use, this transnationalism will likely remain undeterred, even as the population in the US continues to grow.

Regardless of the increasing numerical significance of Dominicans and Dominican-Americans, most people in the US have little familiarity with them or the DR. Furthermore, the extensive marginalization of these populations often renders them invisible and voiceless within the US imaginary, Latina/o/x homogenizing forces, and broader media representation. *Mediated dominicanidad* is a small step in rectifying this.

Methodological Approach

There is limited scholarship in the field of Dominican media studies. In many academic fields, Dominicans are mentioned only as one of the many Afro-Latina/o/x populations in the US. While a handful of Latina/o media studies scholars do address relationships between Latina/os and Blackness, it is usually to either briefly acknowledge the existence of Afro-Latina/o people or emphasize the in-between status of Latina/os within what is constructed as a Black/white racial binary.[12] Furthermore, much scholarly analysis on Latin American and Spanish Caribbean–based systems of racialization recognizes how these systems are grounded in an ethnoracial spectrum structure that is overall less dependent on phenotype and more dependent on class in terms of social stratification.[13] These are not studies of media representation or consumption, however. Moreover, it is these same scholars who suggest, as a promising research topic—just not one they want to take on—an examination of how these fundamentally different structures engage and interact with US racial thinking. Rooted in the contention that dominicanidad is uniquely positioned to challenge US hegemonic racial ideology, *Mediated Dominicanidad* operates as a foundational work in Dominican media studies and provides four critical interventions into the field of Latina/o media studies: (1) offers an exploration of the mediated representation and discourses contributing to a highly negotiated process of identification among Dominicans and Dominican-Americans, (2) reveals a more intimate and contested relationship between Blackness and latinidad based on how they are embedded within articulations of dominicanidad, (3) expands on the scholarship of latinidades by moving from the acknowledgment of infinite Latinx specificity to the empirical theorization of this concept in the Dominican/Dominican-American case, and (4) centers US media as integral to the negotiation of dominicanidad.

Because of the intricacies of Dominican ethnoracial negotiation and Dominicans' complicated history with their African descent, Candelario (2007, 29) stresses that "successful research on matters of race among Dominicans requires the establishment of a relationship between the researcher and the respondent." Here, she is advocating the necessity of a research methodology similar to hers, as well as mine: critical ethnographic fieldwork. In many ways, "the field" for my project on dominicanidad negotiation is a moving target, as it is in a state of constant flux and perpetual circularity. However, by using several methods, I can better saturate what can be uncovered from a diasporic field site. To provide a more complete picture, I took a triangulated research approach that combines participant observation and qualitative interviews with Dominicans and Dominican-Americans alongside internet, archival, and textual sources. Influenced by the audience studies conducted by Viviana Rojas (2007) and Jillian Báez (2018), I centered my efforts in the Dominican communities within NYC (e.g., in Washington Heights, which has the most concentrated population of Dominicans in the US) and conducted site-oriented fieldwork.[14] In conjunction with these more traditional forms of research, I also conducted an audience study via the internet that included reception methods such as textual and discursive analysis. These methods, in concurrence with each other, were the most effective and rigorous means to address my research goals.

New York City Fieldwork

The critical ethnographic component of my study strived to conduct fieldwork following in the vein of the scholarship of Purnima Mankekar (1999), who asserts that while hegemonic media discourses are not closed messages, these discourses nonetheless set limits on negotiated readings.[15] I draw from her work the notion of interpellation—the ability of certain media to "hail" certain audiences who are always spectators and who actively negotiate with these texts. Dominican-American audiences are also socialized through certain hegemonic constructions of ethnoracial identity, having two systems of socialization that they must reconcile. How are they navigating these two systems of identity, and, as in Mankekar's scholarship, is media consumption an extremely influential agent of socialization?

My research methods included in-depth interviews, informal surveys, and participant observation. It was more effective to build on each method after conducting an initial round of in-depth interviews, as these first interviews were integral to the project's direction. Moreover, it is from the in-depth interviews that the researcher is able to collect the details of everyday life. Each in-depth interview lasted from forty-five minutes to three hours, was conducted primarily in English, and followed an informal structure. Having only a short prepared list of open-ended questions, most interviews progressed in a conversational tone and were conducted in spaces that were familiar and comfortable for the interviewee, such as a local restaurant or coffee shop. This approach provided a sense of intimacy and allowed interviewees to drive the direction of the interviews themselves. Focusing most of my networking around community events, places of gathering (like salons, restaurants, and community centers), and contacts I cultivated from the CUNY DSI and the DFFNYC, I used a loose snowball sampling method to meet research participants. Overall, I conducted twenty-one in-depth interviews and, because I was living in the Dominican-dominant community of Washington Heights, was able to immerse myself within participant observation on a daily basis. Moreover, as a participant and volunteer at the annual DFFNYC, I could observe real-time media engagement among Dominican audiences and conduct several short, informal interviews.

In addition to my critical ethnographic study, I interviewed two Dominican-centric website producers, several Dominican filmmakers, and other media creatives. During my stints in the field, I conducted archival research at the CUNY DSI Library at The City College of New York. While the objective of this component of the research was to serve as auxiliary information—and for that purpose, its collections are incomparable—I also used these archival materials as part of a critical and textual analysis of Dominican media representation, negotiation, and production. The CUNY DSI Library houses extensive collections concentrating on Dominicans and Dominican-Americans, including written, visual, and audio collections concerning Dominican culture and people. The archival research informed both my ethnographic methods and those of my internet critical cultural and reception study.

Ethnographic Interviewees

To contextualize the many quotes and references in the following chapters, it is important to introduce the reader to some of my interviewees. This introduction is not comprehensive; I conducted several in-depth interviews and even more informal interviews that are not directly cited in this book. However, those uncited interviewees were nonetheless vital to my ability to make loose generalizations and enhance my understanding. While I cannot include the names and descriptions of all the people I interviewed, I can highlight those who made the most valuable contributions to this book. Each cited interviewee was given a pseudonym that reflects gender identity. I have also used endnotes throughout the chapters to identify the ages and immigrant generations of each person. Yet, to get a sense of the person behind the sentiments, it is my duty as the ethnographer to describe them. The majority of my interviewees are bilingual, millennials, upwardly mobile working and middle class, college educated, and NYC natives or near-natives.

Tina. The first in her family to be born in the US, Tina's parents are first-generation immigrants, her siblings are what is often referred to as generation 1.5—born outside but raised in the US—and she belongs to the second generation. She told me, "Even though my experience in New York is different from the DR, that doesn't make me any less Dominican." Coming from a middle-class family, she had more class privilege than some of the other interviewees. This privilege has allowed her to travel widely, and she shared some of her experiences with colorism while in Mexico and Chile. She loves to dance and listen to music, but she was highly critical of most mainstream media. A particular point of contention for her was the whiteness of movies and television. As a fan of Dominican writers Junot Díaz and Julia Alvarez, Tina has a hunger for Dominican/Dominican-American stories. Her broad interest in social justice and racial equality also informed much of our interview. Tina is very serious in personality and wanted to know more about me in order to feel comfortable being candid. To give my interviewees an opportunity to self-represent, I asked many of them, "Who would you cast to play you in a movie?" Tina's response was, "They would have to have curly hair. I would want her to be from the Bronx in order to be more accurate. It would need to be a person of color because a white actor would not be accurate. She would have to have similar personal characteristics in order to understand my specific privileges and inequalities. They should come from a Spanish speaking home so that her Spanish would have a natural flow to it." There are several critical elements in her response, and while some seem purely physical, they are nonetheless tied to Tina's self-identification. Of particular importance to Tina was the actor's background. While actors often play characters with very different backgrounds from their own, that would not be acceptable for Tina. To better express who she is, she felt a shared background would be essential.

Ana. When I interviewed Ana, she had only been in the US for six years, after moving with her family when she was in high school. While she lamented her lack of English fluency, I found her to be quite proficient. An amateur performer and media producer, Ana loves to sing and make videos. After she finished college, she wanted to be part of the entertainment industry. When I first met her, she asked me to appear in a low-budget documentary. With an upbeat personality, Ana was excited to be interviewed. Most of my interviewees watched Spanish-language television with their families, but Ana was also "really into" music competition programs. She especially appreciated the inclusion of Spanish-speaking performers, like Shakira, on judging panels. When asked about who should be cast to play her in a movie, she told me, "Someone who respects their parents. I would pick someone who is more into U.S. than Dominican culture in a social environment. Even though I identify myself as very Dominican. This is because of my parents imparting the importance of the culture. I would want her to be very close to her sisters and brothers. Should have 'puffy' or curly hair and be cute. She should use my accent." In addition to wanting the person cast to look and sound like her, a sense of family and an achieved assimilation into US culture was also important to Ana. For her, family is the embodiment of her Dominican heritage. Yet it was also important that this heritage did not mitigate her hard-earned assimilation into mainstream US culture. This internal contradiction is common among first- and second-immigrant generations. Cognizant of the prejudice and discrimination they face being perceived as "foreigners," emphasizing their "Americanness" to the outside world is a survival strategy. At the same time, maintaining their link to their heritage and culture reflects their reverence for their family.

Junior. Born in the US to parents from the DR, Junior identified as a Dominican-American. During our interview, I noticed that many of the topics I brought up were ones he had already considered and formed strong opinions about. In many ways a big kid, Junior is a voracious media consumer, especially of video games. From baseball to television to music, Junior had something to say. His desire to find even the smallest reference to Dominicans in mainstream media became very clear. He mentioned references to Dominicans in several rap songs and a few characters in the video games he was fond of. Junior also had an interest in Dominican films and had attended several screenings at the DFFNYC. Additionally, he was particularly keen to discuss the affinity between Dominican and African American culture in NYC. Unlike some of my other interviewees, Junior embraces the fusion of the two cultures brought about by geographic proximity and shared African descent. When asked about casting someone to play him, he responded, "Dominicans can look like anyone so what is important is the way that they speak. Being Dominican is all about the way you act and you speak. It is not really about how you look, anyone can be Dominican." For Junior, his dominicanidad was defined through the way he spoke Spanish, English, and the combination of the two. This linguistic basis of identity was shared by almost every person I spoke with. Moreover, it is not enough to just be able to speak these languages; one must speak them in a Dominican way.

Emmanuel. One of the oldest of my interviewees, Emmanuel was well into his thirties when we spoke, and his responses revealed more life experience. Born in the DR, he moved to the US when he was eighteen. He joined the US Army and secured US citizenship through his military service. He saw the army as a microcosm of US society and his deployments abroad as an opportunity to compare cultures. Even though he might be considered by many to be the embodiment of Dominican masculinity, he was highly critical of machismo and normative constructions of masculinity. It might be because of his military service that he felt secure in his assimilation to US culture and society, saying that he saw himself as a true "fusion" of Dominican and American. Training to be an officer, he was also working on a BA in Latin American Studies. This background provided him with extensive knowledge about the topics we discussed, enabling him to articulate his opinions during our interview. He was especially interested in speaking to me because he longed to discuss media and representation with others, as most people he knew did not share his interest in analyzing media texts. He said that the reason there was so little representation of Dominicans in mainstream media had to do with their relatively recent arrival as immigrants to the US. He thought it was only a matter of time until Dominicans were represented as frequently as Cubans or Puerto Ricans. Another question I asked many of my interviewees to enable self-representation was, "How would you like Dominicans to be represented in the US media?" When I asked this of Emmanuel, he told me, "They would have to go into the history in order to show what Dominicans became and how. By showing people not what we are now, what we were and how we became what we are. What is important to introducing people to Dominican culture is merengue, salsa, baseball players; it is not about the Miss Universe version of Dominican identity." Emmanuel sees Dominican identity as a process, one rooted in history and the blending of cultures: the Indigenous and the Spanish, the Spanish and the African, and the island with the diaspora. He did not want a representation of dominicanidad in US media to replicate that of the DR. His disavowal of the DR's Miss Universe contestants was particularly insightful, as these women tend to be very light skinned and come from elite Dominican society. To Emmanuel, they represent the lie the DR tells itself about who they are.

Luis. While lamenting that many people don't even realize he is Dominican due to his light skin and green eyes, Luis told me, "Being so involved with Dominican culture, I don't see myself as Dominican-American, just Dominican completely." Of those I interviewed, he probably made return visits to the island most frequently, returning two to three times a year. This geographical fluidity supports his self-identification, as does the significance he places on speaking Dominican Spanish, which is central to his rejection of a hyphenated identity. For people who do not "fit the phenotype of what a Dominican looks like," Dominican Spanish becomes the ultimate signifier of dominicanidad. Born and raised in the US, Luis is nevertheless critical of US cultural imperialism on the island and is vocal about its absence in his own sense of self. When asked how he would like Dominicans to be represented in mainstream US media, he told me, "People only know about the DR because of tourism. Everybody knows where Punta Cana is. Instead, I would like people to learn about Dominican cultural trends of music, food, and history. I would like to show them my face. I'm not the prototype, definitely not." Like many of my interviewees, Luis is frustrated with the one-dimensional representations of the DR and Dominicans. He is annoyed that people in the US are willfully ignorant of Dominican culture and history. At the same time, he is very vocal about his criticism of everything "American." His atypical phenotype makes him hold on all the more tightly to a national and cultural heritage he wishes more people would respect. Luis might be trying to reject his light-skin privilege, which would allow him to better assimilate into normative US society than many other Dominicans. In a way, he is implying that other Dominicans might deny him his dominicanidad because of his relatively higher social status. As a light-skinned Latino, fluent in English and possessing both a degree in accounting and a certification as a paralegal, Luis does not want to forget "who he really is," and he also wants to ensure his place within a larger Dominican imaginary.

Gabriela. Immigrating to the US with her family when she was thirteen, Gabriela is also part of the generation 1.5. Although her mother returned to live on the island, Gabriela maintains dual citizenship. When we spoke, she was pursuing a career in law enforcement, which affected many aspects of her life. This was reflected in her media preferences: she watched many TV police procedurals and action-oriented cop movies. Because of her interest in law enforcement, our interview felt more professional and formal than most of the others I conducted. Gabriela shared insight into the large number of Dominicans in the New York Police Department and was particularly concerned with how representations of Dominicans on the local news produced discourses of criminalization. She told me, "The only time people even hear about Dominicans is when they have committed a crime. The rest of us are invisible. This is a group [Dominican-Americans] that prioritizes success and community. But all people see are the negative and the good things are obscured behind that." Her criticism of representational tropes of Latinx/Dominican criminality is particularly relevant because of her job in law enforcement. Gabriela certainly was not the only person to complain about this, but she probably saw this criminalization as extremely personal. When asked about how she would like Dominicans to be represented, she explained, "The DR was the first step for Columbus. It established the first New World university and capital. The country is the result of the clash and combination of three different racial classes that fused together to create what is now Dominican. I would use the accordion, drums, and religion of African and native influences. The DR is not highly populated, and people like to relax and take their time there. It's something I don't have here [the US]; I have to work all the time. I think they live longer, but they have less money." Gabriela wanted to point out the significance of the DR in the Americas and highlight its contrasting worldview. She shares with many the desire to demonstrate a complex and dynamic understanding of what it means to be Dominican.

Carlos. As both a math major and a cinephile, Carlos is a man of dualities. He was part of a friend group that was always invited to free advanced film screenings. Spending most of his free time watching movies that epitomize US hegemonic culture, he also subscribed to several Dominican television channels at home. His media preferences divide neatly along his hyphenated Dominican-American identity. He was born in the DR but left with his family when he was only six months old. He used digital media to stay in touch with his family in the DR (he has sixteen uncles and aunts there), but he has not returned in years. Carlos told me, "I have two different lifestyles, one here and one there. I can fit in while in both places. Here it's fast paced, stressed, depressed. There it is relaxed and all happy. No awkwardness when there, even if I haven't spoken to people for an extended period of time." Partly due to his frequent consumption of Hollywood movies, Carlos is quite aware of the lack of representation of Dominicans. He believes that only people in the US who live near large populations of Dominicans are familiar with them. "In New York, people will know Dominicans, there are a ton of us here. But like in Nebraska, they might not even know of us. They probably think I am from Mexico." This lack of representation did not bother him as much as it did my other interviewees. Carlos found the lack of familiarity with Dominicans and the DR merely confounding. It did not necessarily bother him that people were ignorant of the Dominican community and culture, but it was vitally important to him. He found my question about who should play him in a movie particularly humorous, as if the thought of someone making a movie of his life was a boring thing to do. He said, "He would have to speak Spanish and be from Washington Heights, the ideal Dominican is always from Washington Heights. But he could look any way. People assume all Dominicans are dark skinned, but we are all mixed and all look different." He continued, laughing, "People are often unsure of what I am." Similar to many Dominican-Americans, Carlos felt he was just part of the "American story" whose life was little different from those of many other Latinx groups. His dominicanidad was important to him, but he also felt comfortable with hybrid cultural experiences. He thought it would be nice if dominant US society appreciated Dominican culture, "our music, our rice and beans, our plátanos," but he did not need external validation of his dominicanidad.

Diego. I formed the closest and longest-lasting relationship with Diego, who served as my key informant. He had a natural talent for connecting people, and his knowledge and wisdom were expansive. In addition to our several-hours-long official interview, I also spoke with him at least once a week. Born in the DR but mostly raised in the US, Diego shared an immigration story that was similar to those of many of the Dominicans I spoke with. And while most of his extended family have moved back to the DR, he has chosen to stay in the US and continue to engage with the many

Dominican cultural institutions in NYC. He has a particular passion for Dominican music; he attends live shows and writes about them online. He believes that the ideal way to introduce Dominicans and Dominican culture to the mainstream US is through a bachata documentary.[16] While Diego does frequently return to the island, even attending school there when he was a kid during his summer vacation from his US school, he says the magic of returning has slowly faded. As he got older, he became aware of some of the DR's problems and politics and grew to be critical of the hyperbolic nostalgia many Dominican-Americans have about life on the island. Diego's NYC-based dominicanidad is just as vibrant and meaningful to him as the idealized dreams others have about the DR. An educator and a scholar, he is connected to the lifeblood of NYC Dominican community and is a well-known personage at many of the cultural events I attended during and after my fieldwork. What surprised me most about Diego was his obsession with US superhero culture. He is a big fan of anything Marvel, with Wolverine as his favorite character in US media. He also seemed to be more comfortable using English in his everyday life, even though he was fluent in both Spanish and English. Diego embraces his hybrid cultural heritage and never lets that make him feel any less Dominican. When discussing the role of Dominicans in US society, he mentioned with pride the thriving Dominican-owned business organizations, such as the National Supermarket Confederation or the multiple taxi companies. Diego also felt compelled to defend famous Dominican baseball players whom he believed were being blamed for all that was wrong with professional baseball. Like many Dominican-Americans, supporting the visibility and success of Dominican professional baseball players is key to Diego's navigation of dominicanidad in the US. Yet, for Diego, a bodega owner is just as Dominican as someone who plays for the Yankees. Each is a window into the faces, spaces, and places that define US-based dominicanidad. Diego believes it is in the very connections between the DR and the US that the representation of Dominicans in US mainstream media is so important. When asked about who should play him in a movie, his response was revealing: "They need to speak Spanish the way my community of New York Dominicans do. But also speak fluent English. It is important that they know the history of the DR and Dominican immigration to the US and why it happened. I think it is particularly important to see the bridges and connections between the DR and US that pre-date the increase of migration in the 70s. Our immigration didn't start a few decades ago, we have been here for centuries. And the US has meddled with the DR for at least a century." Diego's discussion of the ties between the US and the DR might seem irrelevant to the question, but for someone to play him as a character, they would need to share a worldview that is not only hybrid but expansive. Understanding the intimate exchanges between Dominican and US culture was essential to Diego's sense of self.

Ciel. Born in the US to Dominican-born parents, Ciel, in many ways, represents the cultural and linguistic retention prominent among Dominican-Americans. Even so, she has often felt like an outsider on return trips to the DR. She is particularly insecure about the way she speaks Spanish, feeling that it marks her as a privileged "Dominicanyork." She uses social media to keep in touch with her cousins on the island, saying she "can live on the island through Facebook," but her visits every other year still feel somewhat awkward. This is a common sentiment expressed by Dominican-Americans, where each return visit challenges their perception of their dominicanidad. But at home in Queens, Ciel feels just as Dominican as anyone else in her family. The sense of "two-ness" experienced by many Dominican-Americans often manifests in their ties to Dominican culture and identity being situated in their home and with their family. In contrast, they tend to feel more "American" at school, work, or with friends. However, these Dominican-Americans typically do not see cultural and linguistic retention as a challenge to their integration in mainstream US society and popular culture. For example, Ciel was a big fan of major prime-time network shows like *Glee*, *How I Met Your Mother*, and *New Girl*. However, she does not identify with these types of media; she is merely entertained by them. Criticizing the fact that Dominicans are mentioned only in news reports about violence, Ciel would welcome any kind of representational inclusion that deviated from that. When asked about how she would introduce Dominicans to a mainstream US audience, she said that it was just a matter of showing the individual heritage and struggles of Dominican figures in the media. She said, "Why don't people know that Michelle Rodriguez is half Dominican? Why isn't she written a Dominican part to play?" Ciel believed that the invisibility of Dominican descent among Latinx figures in the media could easily be fixed. She seeks recognition and wants Dominican-Americans like herself to feel seen and acknowledged.

Dania. Born in the DR, Dania was ten when she moved to the US and does not have the same sense of NYC-centric identity as my other interviewees. When we met, she was about to start her fourth year at Brown University, and her experience in Rhode Island provided insight into the growing Dominican population in Providence. Many Dominicans in NYC feel that they define *the* Dominican-American experience. And while Dania spent some of her childhood in Queens, she did not feel her time there had much impact on her identity. Consequently, she was more in touch with the expanding presence of Dominicans outside of NYC. She was critical of people who felt that "real" dominicanidad belonged only to those who lived in Washington Heights or other Dominican enclaves in the city. I have heard this sentiment quite a bit from Dominicans who live in Florida; they complain that Dominicans in NYC feel their dominicanidad is the only type possible for Dominican-Americans. Dania was also highly invested in her African descent. She made a point to bring to my attention her natural hair and shared her frustration with the lack of representation of Afro-Latina/os—within both the US mainstream media and the Spanish-language media. When asked about who she would cast to play her, she told me, "They should have non-straightened hair and be proud of their Afro-Dominican culture. The hair is really important to me in representation and pride in being Afro-Dominican. They should have a similar or darker skin tone to mine, definitely not lighter because I don't want to erase that from my identity." Dania was not the only interviewee to express frustration with the marginalization of Blackness within constructions of dominicanidad, but she was by far the most passionate about and invested in celebrating her African descent. Unlike many of the Dominicans I have spoken with, Dania not only was comfortable acknowledging her African descent but also was empowered by its very acknowledgment. Keenly aware of the intersectional intricacies of dominicanidad, Dania told me the most students at Brown were completely blind to the Dominican community in Providence, even as members of that community took care of and cleaned their campus. For Dania, these invisible workers were very visible; she befriended them as fellow Dominicans and felt that they looked after her when she was on campus.

Leta. Although she claimed to know only a little about Dominican culture, Leta was a frequent return visitor to the DR, and most of her family still lived there. The youngest of my interviewees, she was born in the DR and moved to Washington Heights when she was three. Her tight bonds and constant communication with family on the island seem to contradict her limited knowledge about the culture. I believe she misinterpreted what I meant, as her young age made her feel like she did not have the right to claim any expertise in Dominican culture. She might not have known much about bachata, Rafael Trujillo, or why her cousins were identified as *indio* on their driver's license, but she had an acute understanding of her own experience as a Dominican-American. Moreover, I think her young age put her in a conflicted, liminal position. She felt both Dominican and "American" and was unsure how to negotiate the two. She told me,

> I go to the DR all the time. But sometimes I question myself whether or not I fit in. I might not have struggled the same way they have. But those that know me know that I was born there and am EXTREMELY proud to be Dominican. I love being in the DR. The one barrier is when me and my sister speak English to each other, which we do naturally. Every once in a while I feel excluded because I don't know what they are saying. Even though I mostly speak Spanish with my family at home and in the DR.

Leta is in many ways the quintessential second-generation teenager still navigating her sense of self. She feels pride in her dominicanidad and is intimately connected to the island and the people there, but she is insecure about her degree of belonging. She has yet to find a way to embrace her hybrid cultural heritage or understand where she as a Dominican-American fits into US constructions of latinidad. She is drawn to Latinx actors, performers, and celebrities but does not identify with them. This could partially explain her difficulty in articulating her experiences with me. There is no media mirror for her to see her reflection and recognize herself. While an avid consumer of mainstream US media, its resonance was always filtered through feelings of Otherness.

Alma. Born in the DR, Alma moved to the US when she was four. Her quiet and reserved personality made it difficult to talk about herself. After sharing some of her background and interests, she finally felt comfortable enough to share her thoughts about the NYC Dominican experience. Shy about herself and her media habits, she was excited to discuss the ways people can engage with Dominican culture in NYC. She mentioned how she was part of a text chain that notified her of impromptu "car meets." These were small gatherings where a group of people would park their cars in a random lot and throw a party. While she was embarrassed that these events were technically illegal, she told me, "It makes you feel like you are in the DR when you are there." Considering she had just returned from her most recent visit to the island a week before our interview, I found it particularly revealing that she wanted to describe the various ways she feels connected to the DR while in NYC. Alma also pointed out the handful of Dominican broadcast television channels available to NYC cable subscribers. She mentioned a commercial for one service provider that packaged those channels to target the Dominican-American audience. Watching the same televised content in NYC as on the island created a sense of connectedness that Alma wanted to highlight. Social events and imported media made her feel like she lived a life that was just as Dominican as those in the DR.

Carmen. Of all my interviewees, Carmen probably had the most strained relationship with her dominicanidad. She was born in the US to Dominican parents and grew up in a predominantly white suburb of Chicago. She had few chances to engage with other Dominicans until she came to NYC for college. Most of her friends are not Dominican, and in many ways, she is white passing. Her fair skin and unaccented English allowed her to escape the signs of Otherness that many of my interviewees discussed. She spoke about her discomfort during return visits to the DR, suggesting that she might feel better about those visits if she had grown up in NYC. Carmen's light-skin and linguistic privilege intersect with her class privilege; her father's profession as a doctor secured her family's position in the upper middle class. While it might be easy to dismiss her experiences as unrepresentative of Dominicans in the US, her negotiation of dominicanidad is just as valid as anyone else's. I think her insecurities around belonging also influenced her thoughts on how Dominicans should be represented in mainstream US media. She suggested, "I think the best way to introduce Dominicans to America is through a movie, as movies tend to have more control over the details of representation. I would make a movie that was a combination of separate stories, adding up to an entire movie. This would be the best way to show the different experiences of Dominicans. Not all Dominicans are the same! Of course, Dominican food and music should be used in the movie, those are the things that are important to being part of a Dominican family and what make me feel most connected to Dominican culture." Her desire to produce a movie consisting of vignettes rather than a single narrative reflects Carmen's belief that her life experiences differ from those of other Dominicans she has met. For Carmen, demonstrating the diversity within dominicanidad would make her feel seen and help her navigate her insecurities around belonging.

All of these interviewees serve as a crucial primary source for much of the analysis in the following chapters. Their insights are not merely an accumulation of data but a window into each person's understanding of their dominicanidad. Each one is an individual, unique in their experiences and outlooks. They represent the diversity and variety within Dominican communities in the US and are a testament to the lived realities of actual people and their everyday experiences.

Internet Critical Cultural and Reception Study

In the interest of diversifying my research methods and to better reflect Dominicans throughout the diaspora, I conducted internet-based research in the form of a critical cultural study that consisted primarily of a reception study and textual/discourse analysis. This portion of my research project was guided by the following questions: How are Dominicans/Dominican-Americans broadly using the internet as a medium of ideological exchange? Which media texts emerge as catalysts for such exchanges among geographical and digital Dominican communities? And what ethnoracial, cultural, and political economic discourses are being used within these spaces? As a rich resource for witnessing discourses in the process of negotiation, internet-based study is an efficient and textually "thick" way to approach research that seeks to discover how real people as parts of real audiences interpret and apply media messages in their everyday lives. Arguably, those who post online might be more invested than the majority of the popular audience; however, online comments and discussions are instructive in revealing the discourses that frame audience reception trends. Researchers can even learn from "troll" postings so common in digital forums. People tend to express their opinions more honestly online, where they can be more anonymous than in ethnographic interviews. Moreover, internet platforms are especially well suited for discursive expression and interaction, specifically in the case of those who have transitional, multiaxial, and multilocational subjectivities. Such spaces provide access for those marginalized groups that have historically been excluded from more mainstream forums. They also provide an essential way to communicate among those whose cyclical movements of immigration do not always coincide with where and how they position their identities.

On a conceptual level, it is important to clarify the difference between "space" and "place," as they are often conflated. In our modern, postcolonial, diasporic, and globalized world, rapid mobility and lack of territorial roots lead to the erosion of the cultural distinctiveness of places. Consequently, as the actuality of place/locality becomes increasingly blurred, ideas of space become more salient. This reality connects Benedict Anderson's ([1983] 1991) "imagined communities" to what Akhil Gupta and James Ferguson (1992, 7) refer to as "imagined spaces." As remembered places become symbolic anchors for dispersed peoples, "space itself becomes a kind of neutral grid on which cultural difference, historical memory, and societal organization is inscribed." Therefore, Dominicans in the US experience a conflicted association with *place* while simultaneously maintaining a strong connection to *space*. Essentially, an understanding of space as articulated here opens up the way to interpret a "Dominican imaginary." Online forums serve as spaces where Dominicans in the US (as well as in countless other countries) can engage in a sense of belonging that is usually associated with geographical or national frameworks. Digital spaces foster an imaginary: a space in which those who feel a sense of shared community come to interact and reaffirm their dominicanidad. As a group that builds their sense of self and community against traditional ideas of geography—suspended between two separate geographical locations yet positioning themselves in both—Dominican-Americans have carved out a *space* for themselves online while maintaining an ambivalent connection to *place*.

Internet-based discussions of dominicanidad are another way in which it becomes mediated. A medium in its own right, the internet was essential to every person I interviewed and with whom I spoke, serving as an indispensable bridge between themselves and their position within the Dominican imaginary. By examining how Dominicans/Dominican-Americans tap into this imaginary discursively within and through digital spaces, a more complex picture concerning how dominicanidad becomes mediated is revealed. My internet reception study was designed to reveal how people consume certain media, the different roles media plays for them, and the various discourses in which they participate. Based on her internet audience study, Molina-Guzmán (2010, 21) suggests that "blogs and discussion boards allow audiences from diverse gender, class, ethnic, racial, and national backgrounds to collaboratively produce alternative ideological spaces to interpret and reaffirm oppositional identity formations." Digital platforms create an ideal entrée into an investigation of Dominicans/Dominican-Americans as audiences that engage with various media texts through their attempts to connect to a Dominican imaginary. I conducted my internet research in two main ways: (1) a thorough exploration of websites based on dozens of keyword searches (and the inevitable rabbit hole of embedded links and follow-up searches) and (2) prolonged observation and interaction with several online forums, interviews with two Dominican-centric website creators, and the discussion of these websites within my fieldwork interviews. I not only analyzed websites textually but also interacted with them as a participant observer. More specifically, I was able to conduct a wider survey of Dominicans in several different locations and also access culturally oriented digital communities. By supplementing qualitative interviews and reception study findings with critical and textual analysis of the actual media texts being consumed, a more in-depth understanding of the practices of spectatorship and identification can be elucidated. Media is not merely a communication device; it is a space, a locality that articulates daily dominicanidad.

Chapter Summaries

This book's chapters are organized in a way that demonstrates the breadth and diversity of the relationship between media and dominicanidad. The book is organized into three parts: Rethinking the Dominican Relationship to Blackness, (In)Authentic Dominicanidad, and *Latinidades* and Hyphenated Identities. More than an organizational strategy, each of the three parts mirrors the predominant findings of my multimethodological research. Building to the conclusion, each part directly reflects how Dominican-Americans make sense of, negotiate, and navigate US media. I structure each chapter through a particular framework of dynamic mediated dominicanidad (cinematic dominicanidad, televisual dominicanidad, producing dominicanidad), meaning each chapter explores the concept of dominicanidad from a different angle.

Chapter 1, "Theorizing *dominicanidad*," builds a theoretical foundation for the subsequent chapters of the book. There are numerous discourses that inform and reflect the different ways of understanding negotiated dominicanidad, both mediated and individualized. This chapter engages the concepts—and those who study them—of latinidad, *mestizaje* (mixture), colorism, and other ethnoracial discourses (in the US and Latin America) in a dialogue with each other. It also articulates the position of Dominicans/Dominican-Americans within this dialectic. Using the film *In the Heights* (dir. Chu, 2021) to frame and contextualize, I explore the nuances of these often contradictory, problematic, and relational discourses.

In chapter 2, "Dominican Celebrity Studies," I examine Dominican responses to those few figures of Dominican heritage who are present in mainstream US media. Based primarily on interviews conducted during my NYC fieldwork as well as discourse and textual analyses, this chapter approaches these figures as star texts who have meaning both in greater US popular culture and within Dominican communities in the US. In this chapter, I address the questions: How are Dominicans living in the US responding to mainstream figures with Dominican heritage, and how is their dominicanidad being interpreted in terms of authenticity and relatability? What are the burdens of representation carried by these figures, and what factors have been used to justify their inability to satisfy that burden among US Dominican audiences? Furthermore, how do those interpretations reveal the directions of current struggles over the meanings of Blackness, latinidad, afrolatinidad, and dominicanidad? Taking an in-depth look at two Dominican celebrities, actress Zoe Saldana and baseball player Alex "A-Rod" Rodriguez, I argue that Dominicans in the US believe that they have gone through a process of distancing from their Dominican roots and a subsequent "Americanization." I conclude this chapter by asking: Is there a scenario in which a person of Dominican heritage could attain both mainstream success in the US and the support of the US Dominican community? By analyzing Dominican music stars Prince Royce and Aventura, I contend that mainstream stars of Dominican heritage can find US Dominican support and identification if they are seen as possessing an "authentic" dominicanidad.

Chapter 3, "Televisual *dominicanidad* and MTV's *Washington Heights*," analyzes fieldwork interviews and an internet reception study of Dominican responses to the MTV series *Washington Heights* (2013), a reality show shot in a neighborhood of NYC with the largest and most concentrated Dominican presence in the US. This chapter examines the following questions: What types of discourses appear in the reception of MTV's *Washington Heights* among Dominicans living in NYC, and how did they interpret the show's attempt at televisual dominicanidad? What industrial constraints framed the show as produced, and how might we understand the program in relation to the broader MTV reality television canon? I explore the reception to MTV's *Washington Heights* as not only the first mainstream Dominican-centric media text but also an inroad to active negotiations about the nature of dominicanidad. Beholden to both the constructed MTV brand and the functions of reality television more broadly, *Washington Heights* is positioned within a complicated vector of identification. Obviously facing an uphill battle against the burden of representation, the show was unable to satisfy Dominican expectations. Many lamented the portrayal of dominicanidad, insisting that the show was not an authentic representation of their lives and identity. Granted, *Washington Heights* had channel-specific industrial limitations due to practices of constructing programming for the MTV audience. Yet there is something to be said about the show's inability to resonate with the Dominican community it claimed to be featuring.

In chapter 4, "Competing *latinidades*: *Orange Is the New Black* and Engagement with Latinx Specificity," I conduct a textual and industrial analysis of Netflix's hit series *Orange Is the New Black* (*OITNB*) (2013–19) in relation to its use and articulation of latinidad, latinidades, and dominicanidad. As a series that helped cement the dominance of the streaming platform industry, specifically Netflix, *OITNB* is a different type of televisual text. In terms of both its production and consumption, different industrial and audience norms and expectations inform how such a text operates and is interpreted. The show is a subject of debate; scholars and audiences see it as either progressive and groundbreaking or as a neoliberal exploitation of the incarcerated—particularly women of color and those who are queer or poor. The show features a significant number of Latinas as part of its ensemble cast. Furthermore, since the show uses an axial character narrative strategy to fully develop each member of its large cast, individual Latinx stories are highlighted in a nuanced way that is all too rare in mainstream media. Focusing on the fourth season, when an influx of mostly Dominican inmates arrives at the fictional Litchfield Penitentiary, I argue that however problematic its Latinx representation might be at times, the show's careful attention to Latinx diversity and latinidades sets it apart from other media texts. Specifically, *OITNB* explores the nuanced negotiation of dominicanidad within the backstories of its Dominican characters—namely, Maria Ruiz (played by Jessica Pimentel) and Blanca Flores (played by Laura Gómez)—and the discussions throughout the prison of who Dominicans are and how they are distinct from the prison's other Latinx groups. Although the show's commitment to latinidades is not consistent over its seven seasons, there is a resurgence of this focus in the seventh, and final, season. Ultimately, *OITNB* is able to succeed where *Washington Heights* failed; it prioritizes Latinx specificity and constructs a televisual dominicanidad that has the potential to resonate with Dominicans in the US.

Chapter 5, "Producing *dominicanidad*: *Así Somos*/The Way We Are," is a response to the mediated exclusion of Dominicans in mainstream US media. This chapter investigates media production by Dominican/Dominican-American filmmakers and others in creative/production positions in media to illustrate Dominican responses to their own representation. By conducting interviews with Dominican/Dominican-American filmmakers who are part of the burgeoning Dominican-American independent film industry, I use their insights, aesthetic styles, and position as auteurs to construct an analysis of differentiation. Of course, each Dominican working in the media industries has a different understanding and relationship with their dominicanidad; however, three primary themes emerged from the interviews: responsibility, Latinx solidarity, and Latinx specificity. These themes are echoed in the chapter's discussion of the annual DFFNYC. As a participant and volunteer, I place the festival at the center of the analysis of Dominican media production. As one of the countless film festivals held globally every year, it might be easy to dismiss this one as merely a niche event. However, for Dominican audiences, filmmakers, and those in the media industries, it is a vital space for the self-representation of dominicanidad. This chapter also includes real-time reception findings from the attending audiences and filmmakers, something that is both highly informative and rare in audience studies. I conclude the chapter with a "Circuit of Culture" style analysis of the Dominican film *Veneno, La Primera Caída: El Relámpago de Jack* (dir. Blanchard, 2018), to investigate the making and negotiating of Dominican cinema.[17] This chapter's analysis argues that the auteurist vision of director Tabaré Blanchard, the nostalgia and popular significance of the film's focus, Dominican wrestler Jack Veneno, and the cultural capital of the film's star, Manny Pérez, indicate Dominican cinema is having a watershed moment.

The conclusion, "'*Mi raza es dominicana*': Dominicanidad as a Unique Lens for Approaching US Racial Hegemony," builds on my findings to explain how Dominicans in the US position their notions of self firmly within a sensibility of dominicanidad. Asserting their right to a unique identity that goes beyond US-based frameworks of identification, Dominicans in the US refuse to place themselves within a Black/white binary and instead continue to hold onto those paradigms that resonate with them. Facilitated by ever-advancing communication technology, frequent return visits, and the concentration of culture obliged by an enclave community reality, Dominicans in the US have avoided the traditional assimilation path that most US immigrant groups have followed. As shown in the preceding chapters, media consumption plays a significant role in how US-based dominicanidad is conceptualized as authentic, shared, and appropriately represented in US media. Whether it is through the criticism of celebrities of Dominican heritage, attempts at televisual dominicanidad, or the increasingly successful Dominican cinema, an examination of US media reveals that dominicanidad within the US is in a state of flux and constant becoming. Just as my Dominican interviewees refused to decenter dominicanidad within their individual subjectivities, this conclusion is a testament to the complex and problematic ways in which media attempt to engage with discourses of identity. I conclude this study with a discussion of the themes of the Dominican experience in the US that are most salient among the NYC Dominicans who are living them: the Dominican imaginary, a complex and shifting relationship with Blackness, and the hyphenated reality of being both "here" and "there."

Ultimately, this research will highlight an identity struggle that is seldom acknowledged while also making a significant contribution to the literature as a reflection on the processes of ethnoracial identity within the US. What it means to be Dominican while living in the US is a dynamic, active, and negotiated process that I reveal through the ways Dominicans interpret and consume media texts and formats.

NOTES

1. The term *American Dream* is a contested one that is rooted in constructs of normative whiteness, exclusive American nationality, revisionist history, and the marginalization of non-European immigrant groups. Stemming from the Industrial Revolution, it is a concept that is steeped in the hegemony of capitalism and the problematic assumption that the US is a meritocracy.

2. *Machista* is the adjective form of the concept *machismo*. In many parts of Latin America, the manifestation of ideal masculinity and patriarchal misogyny is perpetuated through machismo. It infers the dominance of men in society and relationships, heteronormative virility, and a celebratory attitude toward the performance of this articulation of masculinity.

3. See Ajurn Appadurai's *Modernity at Large* (1996). Postulating that the phenomenon of global flows in the modern world is an interactive system no longer sustained through a grounded connection to territory but a "rhizomic" one, Appadurai establishes his now-famous framework of global "scapes," of which ethnoscapes and mediascapes are informative of how I articulate Dominican diasporic engagement with media.

4. For more on Dominican migration flows and discussions of the Dominican diaspora, see Flores 2009; Brennan 2007; Candelario 2007; Duany 2006; Sagás and Molina 2004; Duany 1996.

5. See Rivera 2003.

6. Here I build on the scholarship of Michael Kearney 1995; Arjun Appadurai 1996; Nigel Thrift 1997; Allen Chun 2001; Louisa Schein 2002; Michael Curtin 2007; and Juan Flores 2009.

7. *Afrolatinidad* is a concept that recognizes the combined identity of being of both African and Latin American descent.

8. See Dayan 1995; Sagás 2000; Howard 2001; Candelario 2007; García-Peña 2016.

9. Dayan 1995; Sagás 2000; Howard 2001; Candelario 2007; García-Peña 2016.

10. See Torres-Saillant and Hernández 1998; Sagás 2000; García-Peña 2016.

11. See Hoffnung-Garskof 2008; García-Peña 2016; Duany (1994) 2008.

12. See Simmons 2008; Beltrán and Fojas 2008, 2009; Peña Ovalle 2011.

13. See Smith 1996; Dávila 1998; Torres-Saillant 1998; Howard 2001; Sagás 2000; Godreau 2006.

14. Rojas's (2007, 302) scholarship on Spanish-language talk shows in the US asserts that Latina viewers in the US are an active audience, positing, "Latinas don't just watch television, they watch it in a personal and social context that shapes their consumption and interpretations of television texts. Their ethnic, gender, and class identity permeates their evaluations." Báez's (2018) influential ethnography investigates how Latina audiences engage with media as a way to assess their position in US society and the "U.S. imaginary." Through a lens of symbolic/cultural citizenship, Báez found that, among her thirty-nine Latina participants

in Chicago, feelings of belonging were key to their interpretations and negotiations of both mainstream and Spanish-language media.

15. As part of this examination, Mankekar looks at notions of selfhood and subjectivity in terms of the concept of interpellation, a concept that acknowledges the intricacies of the relationship between ideology and subjectivity.

16. Bachata is a traditional Dominican musical style similar to merengue.

17. The "Circuit of Culture" model posits that in order to understand the meaning and workings of something, you must look at the links among the various positions of production, consumption, identity, regulation, and signification (Hall 1997b). While I do not conduct a formal circuit analysis, it does inform both my triangulated methodology and the organization of this chapter.

PART I:

RETHINKING THE DOMINICAN RELATIONSHIP TO BLACKNESS

1

THEORIZING DOMINICANIDAD

I am Usnavi and you prob'ly never heard my name
Reports of my fame are greatly exaggerated
Exacerbated by the fact that my syntax
Is highly complicated 'cause I immigrated
From the single greatest little place in the Caribbean
Dominican Republic! I love it!
Jesus, I'm jealous of it, and beyond that
Ever since my folks passed on, I haven't gone back
Goddamn, I gotta get on that
—(IN THE HEIGHTS, LYRICS BY LIN-MANUEL MIRANDA, 2021)

The cultural phenomenon that is Lin-Manuel Miranda has undeniably highlighted the visibility and recognition of the excellence and profitability of Latinx creative forces in US media. The Puerto Rican Miranda grew up in the New York City neighborhood of Washington Heights with an appreciation for his culture and a love of musical theater. After gaining attention and acclaim with his Tony Award–winning Broadway musical *In the Heights* (2008), Miranda became a formidable player in mainstream US culture and media after his successful reimagining of the story of "founding father" Alexander Hamilton. The 2015 Broadway hip-hop musical *Hamilton* was a major social event—coinciding with the second term of Barack Obama, the first African American president of the US—and became a cultural phenomenon. As a result, doors swung wide open for Miranda, including calls from Disney, and he became the face of Latinx cultural and media creativity and empowerment. And while he deserves much of the praise and hype, he is just one person. One person with one perspective, yet he seems to be responsible for speaking to and for all that is Latinx. He cannot always get it right—and he hasn't.

Miranda's massive success led to a renewed and broader interest in his first major work, *In the Heights*. The film version of the musical was released in 2021 after being delayed by the global pandemic. Highly anticipated because of its connection to both Miranda and Jon M. Chu, director of the surprise Asian American hit *Crazy Rich Asians* (2018), *In the Heights* was seen as a direct response to audience demands that Hollywood be more inclusive and encourage people of color to tell their own stories. In the lead role of Usnavi, portrayed by Miranda in the original stage version, *Hamilton* breakout star Anthony Ramos plays a Dominican-born bodega owner who hopes to return to the Dominican Republic (DR) to renovate his father's old bar.

Paying only lip service to the very real and ever-present challenges faced by the residents of this real-life neighborhood, the film's version of Washington Heights is more of a fairy tale than a gritty reflection of its reality. According to *In the Heights*, life is hard, but for those with a dream and drive, the possibilities are limitless. Visually spectacular and colorful musical numbers performed by beautiful actors are meant to celebrate the neighborhood's vibrancy. And while that might be the intention, the result feels more like an attempt to give the story the "Hollywood treatment." The major point of contention for a film expected to strongly affirm Latinx representation has been its lack of diverse casting. How can this be? How could a film starring a huge cast of Latinx actors, based in an area saturated with Latinx culture, and coming from the creative Latinx force of Miranda possibly fail to be inclusive and diverse? The answer is colorism: the buzzword used to focus the criticisms of this film and, in application, "the favoritism for lighter-skinned members of the same racial group" (Gómez 2020, 93).

While most of dominant US society thinks of "Latino" as a vague grouping of those who are "brown," Latinx peoples come from a rich variety of racial and ethnic heritages. This ethnoracial variety and heterogeneity is often sacrificed in media representation, especially regarding African descent. However, two recent Pew Research Center studies revealed that as many as one in four Latina/os identify as Afro-Latina/o.[1] Concerning Latinx groups from the Caribbean—the ethnic group featured in *In the Heights*—the percentage is significantly higher. Most Dominicans and Dominican-Americans have some level of African descent. Because the majority of the film's cast are light skinned or white passing, the film fails to adequately represent the community it claims to be celebrating. While this is certainly a contentious issue undermining Latinx representation more broadly, its import in Dominican representation specifically is a primary topic of this book. The homogenization into one group of the infinitely diverse and hybrid Latina/o/x peoples who make up the US-based category of "Latino" works as a process of reduction and normalization. As such, it is a marginalizing force sustained from both above/outside—based on the desire of dominant society to simplify and contain—and below/inside—rooted in what Frances Aparicio (2019) has called "horizontal hierarchies" among various Latinx groups.

There is no one way to be Latina/o/x. There is no single Latina/o/x identity or positionality, nor is there only one way to be Dominican. Dominican identities and positionalities are fundamentally dynamic. Does this reality mean that Lin-Manuel Miranda's version of the Dominican neighborhood of Washington Heights merely reflects his experience of it? Does the film reflect what he sees as an "authentic" representation of the neighborhood where he grew up and continues to live? Regarding the film's depiction of the neighborhood as a place and space, Miranda's articulation of it would resonate with those familiar with it, in contrast to the version presented in the MTV series *Washington Heights* (2013), which is discussed in chapter 3. But what about the people who live in this neighborhood? Are Usnavi and the film's other characters, as well as the actors who portray them, performing mediated dominicanidad? Is *In the Heights* a form of cinematic dominicanidad? To answer such questions, one must first understand dominicanidad.

Dominicanidad can be roughly translated to "Dominican-ness." However, as is true of many concepts that get lost in translation, dominicanidad is better understood as a sense of identity and positionality constructed by Dominicans that is negotiated within and against the various groups of Latin American, Spanish Caribbean, and African heritage. It is both individual and collective, normative and subversive, simplified and highly nuanced. But dominicanidad is more than a thing or experience; it can be used as a theoretical framework. For Lorgia García-Peña (2016, ix), dominicanidad is a "theoretical category that refers to both the people who embrace the label 'Dominican' . . . and the history, cultures, and institutions associated with them." Before discussing the relationship between dominicanidad and media, and to address the questions I ask about *In the Heights*, it is helpful to examine the numerous ethnoracial discourses that inform the construction of dominicanidad.

"Capital D" Dominicanidad Versus dominicanidad

Due to its colonial, postcolonial, and transnational history, the DR has evolved a paradigm of Dominican identity that is complex and mythical. For Ginetta E. B. Candelario (2007, 259), "Indo-Hispanicity was coupled with anti-Haitianism to give birth to Dominicanidad." While this argument is relevant to the various constructions of *dominicanidad* within the DR and the US, Candelario is actually referring to "capital D" *Dominicanidad*, which García-Peña (2016) distinguishes as being specific to the official narrative constructed by the Dominican state.

Despite the dynamic and negotiated *dominicanidad*, *Dominicanidad* (capital D) is the result of nationalist myth building by the DR's ruling and intellectual elite. The hegemonic grand national narrative of *Dominicanidad* reflects the desires, experiences, and positionality of the minority in the DR, those who trace their lineage to the colonizers. This myth was created in a neocolonial environment where many stakeholders sought control over and influence in the former Spanish colony of Santo Domingo (modern-day DR). *Dominicanidad* emerged in the nineteenth century when "Fear of Haiti combined with Dominican *criollo* colonial desire and the threat of US expansionism" compelled the ruling elite to see Dominicans as a "hybrid race that was decidedly other than black, and therefore different from Haiti's blackness" (García-Peña 2016, 7). This was expressed in many ways, often euphemistically, from claims that Dominicans were the "los blancos de la tierra" (whites of the land/island) to "el negro detrás de las orejas" (black behind the ears) (Gómez 2020; Candelario 2007). The explicit negrophobia embedded within the myth of *Dominicanidad* by the ruling and intellectual elite is rooted in two highly contextual understandings of Blackness: (1) the aforementioned association of Blackness with Haitians and (2) the conflation of enslavement with Haitian-ness and, therefore, Blackness. Consequently, when Dominican elites said they were not Black, they meant they were both not enslaved and distinct from the Haitians they saw as inferior. The neocolonial relationships they were building with Spain and the US—both countries dependent on enslaved labor and invested in its continuation—required them to distance themselves from a "biological," or essentialized, Blackness. Torres-Saillant (2010) argues that this produced a sort of limited deracialization of the Dominican people, who might be fully aware of their "biological blackness" but were able to separate it from the "cultural blackness" of Haitians and enslaved Africans (throughout the Americas). Extensive Dominican racial mixture was the foundation for the cognitive dissonance; they were mulatto, therefore not Black or white. However, these "racial gymnastics" (Gómez 2020) were not yet hegemonic; they were limited to elite circles. It was not until the rise of Rafael Trujillo in 1930 that these ideas would become institutionalized through the fiction of *indio* identity.

To consolidate the elites' sometimes facetious machinations of *Dominicanidad* into a coherent ideology and national imaginary, the Trujillo regime fabricated from the ambiguous notion of a "mulatto people" a mixed-heritage national narrative that subverted Dominican Blackness by replacing it with indigeneity. Even though the Indigenous people of Hispaniola had been eradicated during the early colonial period, in order to obscure Dominican Blackness, the Trujillistas invented a national narrative that attributed the non-Spanish heritage and features of the Dominican people to Indigenous descent. Therefore, those who thought of themselves as *mulato* began to be classified as *indio* (Sagás 2000). The formation of indio distanced the Dominican people from their colonial history and "created a mythological national past, with deep roots in the prehistory of the island, which gave the Dominican nation a sense of continuity" (35). Although the formal separation between "biological" and "cultural" constructions of race started in the nineteenth century, through the invention of indio, the DR developed what Wendy D. Roth (2012) calls a "nationality racial schema." Fundamentally, notions of race are conflated with nationality and culture, leading to the articulation of a *raza dominicana* (Dominican race). Such a racial schema, one that is based more on culture or nationality than on skin color or phenotype, is something the DR shares with much of Latin America and the Spanish Caribbean. However, while these groups share a similar type of racial schema, the schemas themselves are diverse. For example, in Mexico, this type of racial schema is embodied by a discursive *indigenismo* (Indigenous-ism) that historically claimed to celebrate the Indigenous past while also promoting assimilation to the mestizo norm in order to be considered a good Mexican (Blackwell et al. 2017; Ramírez Berg 1992). In the DR, the combination of a nationality racial schema and nationalistic myth building results in "the complexity of Dominican racialization [being] precisely linked to the fact that 'black,' as an ethnically differentiated segment of the population, does not exist in the Dominican imagination" (García-Peña 2016, 191).

However, it is important to acknowledge that as constructs, racial ideologies are not fixed or impervious to internal or external challenges. Such is the case in differentiating (capital D) *Dominicanidad* from *dominicanidad*. And this is where many critical race scholars err. Reduction of the Dominican relationship to Blackness as one of simple denial based on the negrophobia of the state not only ignores the consistent challenges to this ideology by Dominicans (on the island and from the diaspora) but also dismisses the agency inherent in the negotiation of *dominicanidad*. The patronizing tendency of those "who construe the reticence of Dominicans and other dark-skinned Latinos to make blackness their primary identity as a form of alienation" from their "true selves" works to dehistoricize their African descent (Torres-Saillant 2010, 53). Instead of acknowledging how the Dominican relationship to Blackness is historically and culturally distinct from that of African Americans or Pan-Africanism/Afrocentrism, they assume that Dominicans and other Afro-Latina/os are merely denying their African descent. And while there are certainly individuals who do so—such as the Dominican elites discussed above—this is not a universal condition. For most people, the relationship between dominicanidad and Blackness is complex, situational, and flexible. This becomes even clearer when dominicanidad is negotiated against, through, and with US constructs of Blackness.

US Blackness and Dominicanidad

Historically, US racialization has been structured in a Black/white binary opposition that designates any person with traceable or observable African descent as Black.[2] Referred to as *hypodescent* or, more colloquially, as the "one-drop rule," this racial paradigm is rooted in British colonial and early US African enslavement, where it shaped legal code and social understandings of Blackness (Khanna 2010; Davis 1997; Hall 1996). Furthermore, as with any hegemonic ideology, we see processes of negotiation involving this construction of Blackness where "to counter subjugation wrought by the one-drop rule, black Americans began to embrace this powerful rule as a way of resisting white racism. To do this, they began to invoke the rule as a tool of inclusivity to promote unity and numerical strength among the black community" (Khanna 2010, 99). As such, the concept of hypodescent not only is the framework for dominant notions of US racialization but also has been incorporated into self-racialization practices within the African American community. As a construct, therefore, it influences all US racial discourses, including those involving people not originally from the country. In practice, this means that a person "of African descent has little choice but to identify as Black" (Davis 1997, 317).

Therefore, when Dominicans and other Afro-Latina/os come into contact with a US system of racialization—one that is fundamentally different from those that have previously framed their racial identity—two things occur: First, they must renegotiate their self-ascribed racial identity, and, second, they must face the reality that US society places them within this system based on readings of the body and ethnic contextualization (Candelario 2007). US racial hegemonic ideology based on the normality of whiteness and strict binary opposition makes it difficult to clearly define those who do not easily fit into either category.[3] When Dominicans first encounter US racial ideology, they must reconcile their identities within a system that perceives them as Black.

When exploring how hypodescent and Black subjectivity discourses affect those people of African descent who do not align with the African American heritage narrative, it is important to note that Blackness in the US is based on assumptions of the "essential Black subject." Although this assumption has been widely contested, particularly by Stuart Hall, it is based on the belief that there is a fundamental quality within Blackness that has an almost spiritual resonance for all people of African descent. In other words, people of African descent, regardless of their individual history, heritage, and experiences, are often thought to share a kind of essentialized notion of what it means to be Black. When discussing Dominican and other Afro-Latinx racial issues, one should avoid the one-drop rule, as it inaccurately equates Dominicans with African Americans and could erase the importance of their latinidad (Latino-ness). This could result in the loss of the specific context and plight of Dominicans when they are misappropriated into US Blackness.

Stuart Hall argues that race is not a fixed and essentialized category but rather a floating signifier, and I see the potential for Dominican inclusion in constructions of Blackness as well as the inclusion of Black bodies in constructions of Latina/o/x that have categorically excluded them. Blackness itself is constructed in a relational manner. While historically, this relation has been an oppositional positioning of Blackness versus whiteness, it is still a fluid category that can and does bend. Hall (1996, 166) argues that "Black" is a "politically and culturally constructed category, which cannot be grounded in a set of fixed transcultural or transcendental racial categories and which therefore has no guarantees in nature." As such, the room for and, more accurately, the demand for negotiation become evident when Dominicans and other Afro-Latina/os in the US must navigate their racialization in a system that categorizes them within discourses of Blackness. Ginetta E. B. Candelario (2007, 8) contends that "Dominican identities are also embodied, displayed, enacted, and perceived according to their context," suggesting that at the heart of Dominican processes of ethnoracial identification is a Dominican racialized consciousness that is shaped in juxtaposition to an understanding of Blackness as existing elsewhere (e.g., in Haiti or the US). More importantly, there is an implied sense of flexibility of racialization because of the physical movement of Dominican bodies and the discourses that accompany them. Denise Brennan (2007, 210) claims that "the past few decades of migration from the Dominican Republic to New York and the transnational cultural and economic flows between the two places have informed a diasporic mentality in the Dominican Republic." Because of this diasporic mentality, or the relational nature of Dominican racialization, ethnoracial identity negotiation becomes a critical juncture in Dominican positionality within the US. Ultimately, "the Dominican case illustrates that identities can be situational, equivocal, and ambiguous" (Candelario 2007, 7).

García-Peña (2016, 190) describes what I call the negotiation or reconciliation of dominicanidad and Blackness as "'translating blackness,' referring to the experience of the Dominican migrant who navigates between various systems of racial identification, disidentification, and oppression." This occurs not only in the diaspora but also in a transnational process. Dominicans maintain strong transnational connections and identities (Duany [1994] 2008) that create a dialogue between ideologies from "here" and "there." Additionally, because of their circular migration and travel patterns, Dominicans throughout the diaspora contribute to the continual evolution and renegotiation of dominicanidad (Roth 2012). Whether it is because they "find a political language from which to articulate their own experience of racialization, oppression, disenfranchisement, and silencing" (García-Peña 2016, 191) or "because Dominicans cannot help but realize that in the United States race matters tremendously, [theirs] as well as that of others" (Torres-Saillant 2010, 52), dominicanidad becomes "challenged and re-created in this transnational space" (Roth 2012, 10). Yet not only Blackness but also transnational and US-based articulations of latinidad(es) engage in a conversation with dominicanidad.

Latinidad and Dominicanidad

If the relationship of dominicanidad to Blackness is fraught, it is no less so for latinidad. By their very existence, Latina/os actively challenge binary systems of racial meaning within the US; therefore, their in-between status renders them both ambiguous and hybrid. A Black/white binary broadly excludes Latina/os, making them invisible, which can be seen as a form of "symbolic annihilation" (Valdivia 2010). The Latino/a "body challenges the traditional binaries of racial representation, specifically the poles of whiteness and blackness" (Peña Ovalle 2008, 165). Afro-Latina/os and Latinx diversity reveals a fabricated visual system that randomly associates physical characteristics—such as darkness of skin color, hair type, eye color, and so on—with a perceived whiteness or Blackness (Candelario 2007; Valdivia 2007; Beltrán 2002). This means that latinidad in general and afrolatinidad in particular challenge the very legitimacy of such a binary. Latinx "in-between-ness" highlights the difficulty of drawing clear racial boundaries when reading racialized bodies of Latino/as and speaks to a history of ethnoracial mixture that becomes impossible to articulate in contemporary US racial politics regarding the body (Valdivia 2007; Peña Ovalle 2008). Dominicans in the US must negotiate their identities within this challenging situation. So, if latinidad operates outside and in contestation of hegemonic thinking in the US, what is latinidad?

Stemming from an identification with the term *Latino* and its variants, latinidad can be understood as the "processes where Latino/a identities and cultural practices are contested and created in media, discourse, and public space" (Guidotti-Hernandez 2007, 212). In practice, latinidad becomes a flexible and ambiguous association with Latina/o/x identity, culture, and community on both an individual and a panethnoracial level. Moreover, it operates alongside other paradigms of identity, most significantly national heritage. Subsequently, US Latina/os identify with various national-specific constructions—like *mexicanidad*, *colombianidad*, or US *pan-latinidad*—and a plethora of complex and hybrid racial and cultural identities, all of which are situational and contextual.[4] For example, a person born in the US to a Dominican-born mother and a Chicano (Mexican-American) father might identify as Latina/o, Dominican-Mexican, Afro-Chicana/o, Afro-Latina/o, Black, mixed-race, Dominican-American, Mexican-American, or "other." This person might be seen as embodying what Valdivia (2020) calls "radical hybridity"—a result of compounding hybridities. Alternatively, they could be described as an "Intralatina/o" (Aparicio 2019)—someone of mixed-Latinx background whose identities are multifocal and fluid. This example is not just a pointless exploration of the infinitely regressive nature of identity and identification. The point is that, like Blackness, latinidad is a floating signifier; there is no singular or monolithic latinidad. As carefully articulated by Valdivia (2020, 2), latinidad is a "broad multiplicitous and diverse category of ethnicity that is pan-national, multiethnic, intersectional, and transnational. Latinidad is a flexible and unstable hybrid construct whose mediated presence remains salient in the new millennium and indexes broader currents of population mixtures resulting demands, and backlashes from and through the mainstream." Latinidad, therefore, can be understood as a form of what Gayatri Chakravorty Spivak (2010) calls "strategic essentialism": the result of prioritizing commonality over individualism as a strategy in an environment that works to marginalize and oppress.

One could argue that the more nuanced articulation of latinidades better acknowledges the diversity and hybridity among those people commonly identified as Latina/o/x. Frances R. Aparicio and Susana Chávez-Silverman (1997, 15) assert that latinidad is not an all-encompassing category including all things related to Latin America but is a far more complex notion that is "contestatory and contested, fluid, and relational." They use the logic of latinidades to "describe the sets of images and attributes superimposed onto both Latin American and US Latino subjects from the dominant sector" (1997). It is through US homogenizing panethnic discourses that anyone categorized as Hispanic/Latino becomes grouped into one identity category: an identity category that fundamentally ignores and erases cultural specificity. Ultimately, there is no singular umbrella latinidad but rather multiple latinidades that are fundamentally constructed and often imposed. It is useful, therefore, to think of latinidades as able to "reach across national-origin lines but need not account in some comprehensive way for *all* . . . as one form of identity—among several—with which we can engage" (Caminero-Santangelo 2007, 215). But it is important to understand that dominicanidad can be understood as a further nuance to latinidades, framing the way Dominican-ness is understood and experienced in relation to both pan-Latinx and culturally specific forms of latinidad. Dominicanidad can operate as a discourse that simultaneously contradicts and reinforces articulations of latinidad(es) more broadly.

More hegemonically, Latina/os "as a population are supposed to provide a middle-of-the-road, acceptable, safe representation and presence of ethnicity in relation to the implicit paragon—whiteness—and against that which the mainstream refuses to assimilate—blackness" (Valdivia 2020, 119). Consequently, it is easy to see how Latinx Blackness becomes obscured by the concept of latinidad(es). The ability to both individualize latinidad and use it to promote pan-Latinx identification confounds and perplexes the mainstream (hegemonically white) US. Therefore, in popular and political practice, people of Latin American and Spanish Caribbean heritage are seen as belonging to the same ethnoracial identity category or panethnic group. Regardless of cultural or national specificity, in the US, those who are considered Latino/Hispanic and possess latinidad have been categorized in a way that both produces political solidarity and flattens Latinx diversity (Dávila 2001; Aparicio 2007; Mayer 2004; Molina-Guzmán 2010; Valdivia 2010). The construction of latinidad from above/outside refuses to acknowledge its dynamic nature and instead reduces the Latino subject—singular, as to avoid disrupting the simplicity demanded from US racial ideologies—as the following: possessing an identifiable "Latin look," Spanish-speaking, foreign/immigrant, and subsequently exotic/erotic/threatening (often all at once) (Caminero-Santangelo 2007; del Río 2017; Gómez 2020; Valdivia 2020).[5] The outcome of this is that Dominicans, and other Afro-Latina/os, are not included in what is "exemplary of US Latinidad. Dominican blackness does not fit the colonial fantasy that makes the light-skinned version of Latino/a . . . marketable in the United States," and therefore, "the diversity of Latino/a ethnicities, languages, and cultures are thus replaced with the 'repackaged' Latino/a—a concoction of stereotypes, fantasies, and historical figures associated with Spain and Mexico (bullfights and Cinco de Mayo)—that fulfills colonial desire for the foreign and exotic" (García-Peña 2016, 3).

Added to this scenario is anti-Blackness among US Latina/os, coming from below/inside. Intra-Latinx horizontal hierarchies—an example of which we have already analyzed in the negrophobia of the Dominican state—are the result of colonial, postcolonial, and transnational forces. Just because a group is homogenized into a monolith and subsequently Othered by dominant society does not mean members of that group cannot also Other those they see as inferior or too different to be considered one of "us." Consequently, when it comes to the borders of latinidad, "Who gets to be 'us' and who gets to be 'them' are questions under constant debate and revision" (Caminero-Santangelo 2007, 31).

Many of these horizontal hierarchies are the result of the position of *mestizaje* (mixture) within the inherent subtleties of latinidad(es). Mestizaje, or the process of racial mixing that occurred in most of Latin America and the Spanish Caribbean, produced ethnoracially mixed populations in the Americas. Carol Smith (1996, 150) describes this process.

> *Mestizaje* consists of at least three distinct, but related, processes: 1) the social processes (including rape, concubinage, marriage, inheritance and legitimation) used to procreate, socialize, and position people of mixed biological heritage (i.e., various combinations of Spanish, Indian, and African); 2) the personal identification of an individual or community—criollo, Indian, African, or actual biological "mestizo"—with mestizo

communities or the mestizo national subject (which are two different things); 3) a political discourse in which people (subaltern actors as well as intellectuals) argue about the racial, cultural, and political character of the mestizo in relation to other identity types (defined by the same kind of criteria) and what should be their relative positions in the society and polity.

The idea of mixture gives rise to the formation of a spectrum of racial classifications within the greater structure of mestizaje. This concept of mixture was embraced by much of Latin America and the Spanish Caribbean and used to create their systems of racial identity formation. Therefore, the notion of mestizaje serves as a critical lens through which to contextualize constructions of "mixedness" among those of Latin American and Spanish Caribbean heritage (Sommers 1991; Beltrán and Fojas 2008; Nakamura 2008). Significantly, there is a sense of solidarity in interpreting one's latinidad as part of a larger process of mestizaje, and, ideally, it also allows for ethnoracial specificity based on individual heritage. However, it also has served as a system of marginalization. Regardless of the fact of significant African and Indigenous descent among many Latin American and Caribbean populations, Blackness and indigeneity are obscured in multiple ways. Even in the acknowledgment—celebration, even—of a mixed heritage, it is the Spanish that gets privileged; a manifestation of erasure "via the guise of inclusion" (Blackwell et al. 2017, 131). The result of this is often the stigmatizing of the African and the Indigenous.

One of the most pernicious elements of historical mestizaje has been the promotion of *blanqueamiento* (whitening). As a political and social project typical of most countries that trace their history through mestizaje, blanqueamiento had the goal of "improving" the population by marrying or having children with someone with lighter skin or more traceable European ancestry. The desired result was that, over time, the "inferior" characteristics derived from Indigenous and African origins would be "bred out" of the population. The goal has been and continues to be prevalent in many areas, highlighting the fact that "in promoting mestizaje as national ideology, Latin American countries likewise promote anti-Indigenous and anti-Black racism" (Gómez 2020, 69). Probably the most prolific and influential example of this is José Vasconcelos's notion of *La Raza Cósmica* (the cosmic race). Around the mid-twentieth century, the Mexican Vasconcelos theorized that the mestizaje instigated by Spanish colonialism brought the "red, yellow, Black and White" races together to become the fifth and greatest race, "mestizos." Managing to be both utopian and racist, the concept of *La*

Raza Cósmica, by promoting mestizaje as the ideal state policy, worked to "mask white supremacy and conceal racial subordination in Mexico of Indigenous people and Afro-Mexicans" (Gómez 2020, 80). These ideas quickly spread throughout the Americas, even becoming influential in Trujillista *antihaitianismo* (anti-Haitianism) and state negrophobia. These ideas did not remain in Latin America and the Spanish Caribbean; they traveled.

Latina/os are not immune to heavily entrenched US hegemonic racial discourses. US-based discourses engage in a dialogue with those coming from Latin America and the Spanish Caribbean, like mestizaje. The result of the internalization of US racial ideology and the retention of heritage ideologies of race is a collective distancing among those in the pan-Latinx community from connections to Blackness (Cruz-Janzen 2010; Román and Flores 2010). In practice, this means that the Latinx community and its representatives often implicitly reinforce anti-Black racism through their hesitance to acknowledge the Afro-Latina/os who make up part of their community. According to Marta I. Cruz-Janzen (2010, 286), "The more Latinos become immersed in the racial ideology of the United States, ... the more powerful is their need and desire to free themselves of any and all vestiges of African ancestry." Without the explicit acknowledgment and inclusion of Afro-Latina/os in the Latinx community, it is no surprise that, as standard political and representational practice in the US, Latina/os are grouped under the label *Latino* and their heterogeneity masked by a generic representation. Although pan-latinidad has been beneficial in terms of alliance politics and solidarity, it favors certain experiences, representations, and identifications over others. Horizontal hierarchies are maintained among Latinx groups in various ways; skin color, accent, Spanish and/or English dialect all work to marginalize certain Latinx groups from the Latinx norm (Aparicio 2019). Certainly, many Afro-Latina/os claim a Latino/Hispanic identification; however, this identification is more appropriative or assimilationist than organic. Their association with this identity category is more nuanced than current articulations of *Latino* allow for and results in a desire to qualify where they fit within the ambiguous conglomeration that is latinidad.

The elasticity of latinidad(es) can, and hopefully will, expand to center Blackness. Afro-Latina/os are becoming more vocal in their demands to be seen and heard. Dominicans in the US also demand their inclusion and an end to their symbolic annihilation within the Latinx imaginary. Yet they still are victim to what García-Peña (2016) refers to as their "footnote condition." They continue to be a marginal afterthought within broader discourses of what it means to be Latina/o/x in the US. Therefore, when a film is set in the heart of dominicanidad in the US, it seems like a rare opportunity for this group to see itself represented.

IN THE HEIGHTS, DOMINICANIDAD, AND COLORISM

To conclude this examination of the contentious discourses that inform dominicanidad, it might be enlightening to apply these ideas to a tangible example, such as the film *In the Heights*. This chapter's introductory quote comes from the beginning of the film. This opening number establishes the setting (the world of Washington Heights) and introduces the characters of the story. As Usnavi leaves the apartment he shares with his adoptive grandmother, Abuela Claudia, he starts to hear the music of the neighborhood in the morning. The closing of gates, water hoses spraying the cement, the sound of graffiti being sprayed, the unshuttering of the corner bodega, and the piragua man calling out his daily flavors all create a symphony of Washington Heights. The neighborhood buzzes with the densely packed life on the move: cooking a breakfast of *mangú* (mashed plantains, fried eggs, fried salami, and fried cheese), braiding children's hair to tame it, hopping on the bus, greeting neighbors, stopping at the bodega to get your café con leche and daily lottery ticket, sharing the latest gossip (fig. 1.1). Looking into the small apartments, walls splashed with Dominican flags, murals of scenes from the island, and stickers reading "República Dominicana" surround the occupants sporting shirts and hats emblazoned with "Nueva York" and "NYC."

At its metaphorical center is City Mart Tropical Products, Usnavi's bodega. The inside of the shop feels almost like a shrine to the DR. A large flamboyant mural of the island and the Caribbean Sea occupies the wall, pictures and news clippings of the island and Washington Heights are displayed under the glass of the counters, Dominican brands and delicacies fill the overflowing shelves (figs. 1.2–1.4). To me, the film's first ten minutes are an explosion of dominicanidad on the screen. Accounting for the hyperbole and exaggeration of the musical film genre, the Washington Heights depicted in this opening is familiar to me, as I am sure it is for many others who have seen the film. But once the exuberance of the first few minutes is over, cracks in the cinematic dominicanidad begin to appear.

A film that is, quite intentionally, a spectacle of Latinx pride and vibrancy, nonetheless sidelines Afro-Latina/os to brief moments of visual inclusion. None of the large ensemble cast are easily read as Afro-Latina/o, and very few of them are even Dominican. Anthony Ramos, who plays

Fig. 1.1 Scene of morning activities in Washington Heights (*In the Heights*, dir. Chu, 2021).

Fig. 1.2 Usnavi standing outside his bodega while opening for the morning (*In the Heights*, dir. Chu, 2021).

Fig. 1.3 Mural on the wall of City Mart Tropical Products (*In the Heights*, dir. Chu, 2021).

Fig. 1.4 Images and clippings under the counter at City Mart Tropical Products (*In the Heights*, dir. Chu, 2021).

the lead character Usnavi, is (like Miranda) Puerto Rican. Vanessa, Usnavi's love interest, is played by Melissa Barrera, who is Mexican. Stephanie Beatriz, who plays the "Chile-Domini-Curican" Carla, was born in Argentina to a Colombian father and a Bolivian mother. Gregory Diaz IV, Usnavi's undocumented cousin Sonny, is Puerto Rican. The only two main characters played by Dominican actors are Nina Rosario (played by Leslie Grace) and Cuca (played by *Orange Is the New Black*'s Dascha Polanco). True, pan-Latina/o casting is typical of mainstream US media—as we shall see in chapter 4's discussion of *Orange Is the New Black*. But was this film not meant to reject the media industry's representation of Latina/os and latinidad? Furthermore, even though both Miranda and Ramos are Puerto Rican, the character of Usnavi is explicitly Dominican. Clearly, when Miranda was writing this character, he saw that the main protagonist of a story set in Washington Heights should be Dominican. If he was aware of the importance of Dominicans and dominicanidad to the soul of the neighborhood, why did he not apply this understanding to many of the other characters along with other aspects of the story and production?

As seen most explicitly in the musical number "Carnaval del Barrio," the film prioritizes a narrative of pan-Latinx solidarity and diversity over the opportunity to spotlight a Latinx group that is nearly invisible. "Carnaval del Barrio" attempts to show the similarities among Latinx groups while still acknowledging that they should "*Alza la bandera*" (fly the flag) of their perspective nationalities with pride (figs. 1.5 and 1.6). The audience is left with the impression that the culture in Washington Heights is a panethnic one, where Puerto Ricans, Cubans, Dominicans, and Mexicans

Fig. 1.5 Usnavi, Vanessa, and most of the cast of *In the Heights* (dir. Chu, 2021) performing "Carnaval del Barrio" while the flags of multiple Latin American and Caribbean countries adorn the courtyard.

Fig. 1.6 Lin-Manuel Miranda (*upper-right-hand corner*) on the balcony encouraging the cast of *In the Heights* (dir. Chu, 2021) to *"Alza la bandera"* (fly the flag).

all come together to celebrate their shared latinidad—that these distinct groups are more similar than they are different. While this is not a malicious description of what it is to be Latina/o in the US, it is an oversimplified one. Moreover, while it is true that the real-life neighborhood is not 100 percent Dominican, they are the dominant group. So why the pan-Latinx extravaganza?

The production of this film appears to have been affected by the hegemonic influence of Spanish/Hispanic normativity. I do not think Miranda and the others involved in the film believe that the Spanish heritage of Latinx peoples is superior to that of the African or Indigenous. Rather, the Eurocentric latinidad of *In the Heights* is the result of dominant ethnoracial discourses and their legacies. Aside from the film's saccharine-sweet approach to Latinx diversity, the audience must wonder: Are there only light-skinned Latina/os in Washington Heights? Yes, we see an extra here and there who appears to have African ancestry, and there are a few non-Latina/o African American characters and figures. But the bodies that matter in this movie, indicated by the fact they have more than a few seconds of screen time and are given lines of dialogue, do not deviate from normalized "Latin look" so familiar to mainstream audiences. It would be easy to blame Hollywood or Miranda for this oversight, but that does not address the ideological underpinnings that allowed the film's colorism to go unnoticed in the production process. These ideological underpinnings stem from multiple places and forces. On the one hand, "the idealized notion of *mestizaje* (itself a product of the racism inherent in colonialism) has obscured the lived reality of colorism and racism experienced by Latinos with visible African or Indigenous ancestry" (Gómez 2020, 172). On the other hand, "In the Latina/o diaspora, colorism . . . is clear evidence of the ways in which communities of color in the United States have also internalized [US] racial hierarchies" (Aparicio 2019, 88). What if the film had cast a dark-skinned Dominican-American for the role of Usnavi? Would that have introduced an element of "authentic" dominicanidad? This might merely rub up against US Black/white binary and/or (capital *D*) Dominicanidad, which might very well be the metric some audiences use for arbitrating authenticity. But the goal here is not "authenticity," as such a thing is based on individualized dispositions. The pursuit of cinematic dominicanidad should not be assessed by asking how "authentic" it is but how *dynamic* it is. It is clear that the film's colorism mitigates its ability to convey a dynamic dominicanidad. The various discourses covered in this chapter explain why and how this may have happened. By theorizing dominicanidad, one can dissect the ways dominicanidad is mediated and why we should care.

Notes

1. López and Gonzalez-Barrera 2016; Gonzalez-Barrera 2022.
2. I use the words *traceable* and *observable*, as there is a long legacy of racial passing where people of African descent have been perceived as white. These individuals who "passed" did so strategically as a device to combat US racism.
3. See Dyer 1997; McIntosh 1989.
4. Pan-latinidad is a form of panethnicity related to those who ascribe to a shared identification with latinidad.
5. Clara E. Rodriguez (1997) argues that US media has relied on a "Latin Look, which positions Latina/os as in between the poles of whiteness and blackness while at the same time prioritizing those features seen as European in origin."

PART II:

(IN)AUTHENTIC DOMINICANIDAD

2

DOMINICAN CELEBRITY STUDIES

In brilliant Technicolor, the tropical and exotic fictional island of *Cobra Woman* (dir. Robert Siodmak, 1944) was a romantic and primitive escape for a Western audience locked in a traumatic world war. Its star, María Montez, plays both the heroine and villain through the magic of Hollywood film. Beautiful, sexy, and mysterious, Montez was *the* "exotica" of 1940s Hollywood (Rodriguez 2004). She was the "white savage," "Queen Cobra," "Arabian belly dancer," "wild Gypsy," and "siren of Atlantis." Called the "Queen of Technicolor," her star image was marked by eccentricity and even narcissism (Méndez 2018). Often overshadowed by the "Brazilian Bombshell" Carmen Miranda in US popular memory, Montez was the first Dominican star in Hollywood. Referred to as "Dominican Dynamite" by Pete Martin of the *Sunday Post*, the racially white Montez was beloved among older generations of Dominicans, both on the island and in the diaspora (Capellán Pichardo 2015).[1] She embodied the Trujillista Hispanophile ideal and the Hollywood Latina spitfire (fig. 2.1). As an early example of mediated dominicanidad, "Montez's legacy is recognized from two very distinct angles, one recognizing her status as the first internationally renowned [Dominican] actress and the other considering her unstated privilege," namely, her whiteness and middle-class background (Méndez 2018, 127). Yet Montez was a flash in the pan, a celebrity who did not outlive her prime; she died at the age of thirty-nine. As a starting point of Dominican celebrity studies, her career is indicative of long-term Dominican involvement in mainstream US media. However, her obscurity in Hollywood popular memory and academic literature poignantly speaks to the continued invisibility of mediated dominicanidad.

My query to interviewees often felt like a trick question: "Do you know of any celebrities in mainstream media who are Dominican?" The most common response was something like "There are not many, if any." Dominican/

Fig. 2.1 María Montez in trailer for film *Cobra Woman* (dir. Robert Siodmak, 1944).

Dominican-American respondents in my fieldwork study suggested that Dominican representation in US mainstream media is limited, but at some point, almost every person I interviewed mentioned actress Zoe Saldana and baseball player Alex "A-Rod" Rodriguez. Many of them informed me, however, that Saldana and Rodriguez, along with other Dominican celebrities in the US public eye, have distanced themselves from their Dominican roots. They claimed these celebrities had "forgotten that they were Dominican" and "Americanized" themselves to become more popular and successful. Dominicans living in the US are often strongly connected to their cultural heritage and see these (off)white-washed celebrities as having squandered the opportunity to represent their community in a way that would resonate with them. Many see these celebrities as victims of the US media system, while others believe they have abandoned their roots.

The limited representation and mediated invisibility of Dominicans in mainstream US media does not go unnoticed by the US Dominican community. Consequently, they latch onto any figure with a link to dominicanidad and place a heavy "burden of representation" on them. Expanding on Stuart Hall's theorization of James Baldwin's "burden of representation,"

Isaac Julien and Kobena Mercer (1988, 4) contend that "if only *one* voice is given the 'right to speak,' that voice will be heard, by the majority culture, as 'speaking for' the *many* who are excluded or marginalised from access to the means of representation." This places an undue responsibility on those few individuals of a marginalized group who are granted tenure in US mass media and popular culture. Unlike white celebrities who are typically seen as individuals in and of themselves, Dominicans—mainly because of their limited representation—have to "represent the race" and are expected to be a reflection of the Dominican community as a whole. When these Dominican celebrities are made to represent an entire group of people, their individuality is lost, and they are turned into objects that can be interpreted as a cultural text in discourses of what constitutes dominicanidad.

This chapter examines an understanding of US-based dominicanidad, addressing the questions: How do Dominicans living in the US respond to mainstream figures with Dominican heritage, and how is that dominicanidad interpreted in terms of authenticity and relatability? What burdens of representation do these figures carry, and what factors have been used to justify their inability to satisfy that burden among US Dominican audiences? How do those interpretations reveal the directions of current struggles over the meanings of Blackness, *latinidad*, *afrolatinidad*, and dominicanidad?

In this chapter, I look at Dominican celebrity through the eyes of the Dominican community in the US based on my New York City (NYC) fieldwork findings and online reception research. I include responses from in-depth ethnographic interviews with Dominican-identified participants I conducted while living in Washington Heights. In these interviews, I addressed questions about their experience with Dominican representation, mediated identity negotiation and consumption, and views of mainstream US media. I also examined discussion forums on mainstream, Latino, and Dominican websites that featured pieces on Saldana and Rodriguez as part of an online reception study. Investigating how audiences interpret each celebrity as star texts, both forms of research focused on star-audience relationships—what scholars have referred to as parasocial relationships (Perse and Rubin 1988; Giles 2000; Rojek 2001)—and the role of such relationships in the articulation of dominicanidad. Building on star/celebrity studies scholarship (Dyer [1979] 1998; Negra 2001; Rojek 2001; Holmes 2005) alongside Latina/o media studies scholarship rooted in critical race theory

(Valdivia 2000, 2020; Beltrán 2009; Román and Flores 2010; Molina-Guzmán 2010, 2013; Gómez 2020), I contend that Saldana and Rodriguez have sacrificed potential Dominican-American identification and fandom for mainstream success. However, while Saldana and Rodriguez have not managed their burden of representation in a way that facilitates Dominican/Dominican-American identification, few stars of Dominican heritage have. To provide a counterexample, this chapter concludes with an analysis of Dominican-American music star Prince Royce and the bachata group Aventura, who serve as star texts that provide my research participants with a sense of shared dominicanidad.

Celebrities as Text

Celebrities' lives (however constructed those lives might be) become part of popular culture and its texts. Their films, television shows, magazines, and so on can be analyzed as cultural texts, but their personae—those parts of themselves that are performed and available for public consumption and interpretation—can also be analyzed and read as cultural texts. Celebrities are typically seen as representatives of our society, however inaccurate or problematic that might be.

The relationship between celebrities of Dominican heritage and the US Dominican audience becomes a synecdoche for the mediated invisibility of dominicanidad. By Su Holmes's (2005, 10) definition, a sociocultural phenomenon, celebrity is a *"system of representation . . . within which the celebrity self resonates within the public sphere."* The ways they resonate can be dramatically different based on the individual. Some of this is based on personal taste or preference, but it also relates to the fact that a celebrity is, on many levels, a fabrication. Richard Dyer ([1979] 1998, 3) posits that "from the perspective of ideology, analyses of stars—as images existing in films and other media texts—stress their structured polysemy, that is, the finite multiplicity of meanings and affects they embody and the attempt so to structure them that some meanings and affects are foregrounded and others are masked or displaced." Moreover, stars and celebrities are not seen as individuals in the same way that non-famous people are; instead, "stars are, like characters in stories, representations of people" ([1979] 1998, 20). Therefore, there are many aspects related to how the public reads a star, including their public persona, their private self, and the characters or roles they portray in media. Audiences understand celebrities through multiple perspectives, as the various media they encounter contribute to their specific interpretations. However, only certain elements of celebrities are promoted or highlighted to audiences, creating limitations and frameworks for how they should be read.

As texts, celebrities are ultimately subject to the interpretations of audiences regarding what they signify to them, often in highly personal and symbolic ways. As such, celebrity texts are useful in analyses of identity, for "it is *because* of the apparatus of manipulation and 'hype' that stars could operate as a site for the working through of discourses on the construction of identity" (Holmes 2005, 14). Put another way, identity is negotiated through the celebrity-audience relationship. Identity is often thought to be shaped by how audiences identify or disidentify, but audience interaction with celebrities as texts is usually more complex than this; Jeffrey Brown (1997, 123) refers to it as a "fluidity of identification." Members of marginalized groups often have more ambivalent relationships with media texts, and their interpretations should be analyzed in a nuanced fashion. Brown (1997, 141) contends that "we should begin to consider how the images themselves, the celebrities themselves, *and* our own fluid understanding of these texts (as informed by voices traditionally on the fringe of society) construct not a blank but a multilevel slate." Spectator subject position is therefore a critical element in understanding the negotiation of celebrity texts, especially for those in marginalized groups such as Dominicans.[2] The audience-star relationship between the Dominican community and stars of Dominican heritage is not merely a case of identification versus disidentification; it is a negotiated process based on how Dominicans in the US align their identities by challenging the star's authentic dominicanidad while also expressing a seemingly contradictory desire to see any signs of dominicanidad within the star text.

As outlined in the introduction, I draw on the insights provided by multiple interviewees. Their voices and opinions shape the content of this chapter. The individual and differing media consumption practices and tastes of these interviewees influence their interpretations of Dominican celebrities. Each shared their unique perspectives that are the result of their specific backgrounds. Taken together, they provide another way of mediating dominicanidad. Instead of a media lens, each interview was a mediation of one person's articulation of their dominicanidad for the interviewer, me, to interpret. I am careful to represent Dominican voices and have made an effort to understand my interviewees as thoroughly as possible; however, it is still my job as an ethnographer to compile and present the information. The sentiments shared by my interviewees in this chapter are intended to reflect the individualized process of media negotiation more broadly and their readings of Dominican star texts specifically.

US Celebrity and the "Americanization" of Ethnic and Racialized Celebrities

One of the major complaints shared with me during interviews was that Zoe Saldana, Alex Rodriguez, and other celebrities of Dominican heritage—such as baseball player Sammy Sosa, actor Michelle Rodriguez, and rapper Trina—have become "Americanized" and are therefore difficult to identify with based on a sense of shared dominicanidad. These charges of Americanization are often rooted in a conflicted relationship with assimilation or, more precisely, acculturation (Hernández and Sezgin 2010). The pursuit of socioeconomic upward mobility and even English-language fluency is not usually criticized by US Dominicans. This type of general assimilation into life in the US is seen as the result of living and surviving in this country. It is only when assimilation becomes acculturation do Dominicans in the US start to criticize it; the difference being that "acculturation is an issue of cultural *change*" (Roth 2012, 5; emphasis added). It is understood as a trade-off, where the lack of cultural retention and identification means that one is no longer Dominican but "American" instead.

The Americanization of the ethnic star text or star image is nothing new in US media. Diane Negra (2001) argues that Hollywood in particular is an "assimilation machine." Assimilation to US norms is seen as a fundamental step toward celebrity, and as these norms are often steeped in notions of whiteness, ethnic celebrities and their star texts are subsequently whitewashed in the minds of the US public. But there is still a noted Otherization occurring. Not read as quite white or even, at times, vaguely white—what Negra refers to as off-white—celebrities of color are expected to act like white Americans without being given any real inclusion into hegemonic white America. The ambivalence toward celebrities of Dominican heritage suggests that in the very achievement of mainstream success, Dominican stars are seen as Americanized. This isolates the celebrity not only from what might be considered their community of origin but also from meaningful inclusion into hegemonic white society, as they can never completely shed their ethnic skin. Seen as both traitors and outcasts, celebrities of color are put in a double bind whereby they must choose success and celebrity over the reification of their ethnoracial identity in an authentic enough fashion for their "home" communities. Saldana and Rodriguez, although repeatedly identified as Dominican by those in my ethnographic study, have not been able to manage their burden of representation in an authentic enough way to sustain support from US Dominicans.

Dominican celebrities are not only marked by ethnicity generically but also marked as Latina/o ethnics within dominant constructions of panethnic latinidad. Opportunity and success for Latinx celebrities have been framed by a preference for an accepted "Latin Look," but they are also based on the changing and contested racial status of Latina/os in broader US society.[3] Media industry factors frame Latinx opportunity in a way that both draws from and reinforces exclusionary and marginalizing Latinx regimes of representation. Ethnoracial analyses should avoid the diametric tendency to see representations in isolation, as if they were constructed within a localized vacuum.[4] Many scholars (López 1991; Shohat and Stam 1994; Beltrán 2009) support a more nuanced analysis of mainstream media representations, one that is useful for exploring many of the subtleties of Dominican-identified audiences in the US. Therefore, these representations of Dominicans in US media should be studied in relation to other Latinx and ethnoracial groups as well as the dominant Black/white paradigm in the US. Because dominicanidad in the US is not limited to—or even primarily concerned with—ethnoracial identification, cultural heritage and nationality become more salient vectors of identification, resulting in a contested relationship with Americanization.

Using this framework, I discuss the Dominican stars who were mentioned most frequently during my fieldwork: Zoe Saldana and Alex Rodriguez.

Zoe Saldana or Zoë Saldaña?: Cinematic Dominicanidad and the Hollywood Star

Born Zoë Yadira Saldaña Nazario on July 19, 1978, in Passaic, New Jersey, to a Dominican father and Puerto Rican mother, the actor known to the US as Zoe Saldana has all the potential to become an emblem of the Dominican experience in the US.[5] She and her family lived in Queens, New York, until the death of her father when she was only nine years old. After her father died, she and her sisters were sent to live with her father's family in the Dominican Republic (DR). There, her grandparents raised her and her sisters, providing Saldana with a physical and cultural connection to the island, which she speaks of often. It was in the DR that she first studied dance—a skill that helped her land her first major film role as a ballerina in the film *Center Stage* (dir. Nicholas Hytner, 2000). At seventeen, Saldana returned to NYC to

Fig. 2.2 Zoe Saldana at the *Avatar: The Way of Water* Tokyo Press Conference. Dick Thomas Johnson from Tokyo, Japan, CC BY 2.0, https://creativecommons.org/licenses/by/2.0, Wikimedia Commons.

pursue a career in dance and theater, joining the youth performance troupe FACES Theater Company and the New York Youth Theater. Following her first credited role in an episode of *Law & Order* (1990–2010, NBC) in 1999, Saldana has achieved mainstream US success by appearing in a myriad of films (fig. 2.2).

By surveying Saldana's roles, I place my audience reception study within a critical discursive and textual analysis of some of her films.[6] I discuss her first major film role in *Center Stage* as well as roles in *The Losers* (dir. Sylvain White, 2010)—one of the few films that cast Saldana as (Afro-)Latina—and the Black-cast African American niche industry film *Premium* (dir. Pete Chatmon, 2006). The range of Saldana's work demonstrates her strategic ethnoracial flexibility. She has been cast as Latina, Afro-Latina, African American/Black, and, interestingly enough, alien. This ensures a variety of film roles but makes it difficult for audiences to ethnoracially categorize her. By avoiding any particular ethnoracial label, some argue that Saldana might have forfeited her claim to dominicanidad and alienated some members in the Dominican community. Much like the criticisms aimed at Mexican-American boxer Oscar De la Hoya—as discussed by Fernando Delgado (2005), who examines how De la Hoya's masculinity and Mexican-ness were questioned because of mainstream success—Saldana's dominicanidad is also contested.

After examining the various roles in which Saldana has been cast, I argue that her self-fashioning as an ethnoracial moving target is seen by US Dominicans as a deliberate distancing from her Dominican heritage and an affront to their dominicanidad. Notably, a brief linguistic analysis (Baltes 1991; Bucholtz and Hall 2003) of the professional spelling of her name without the Spanish diacritics—Saldana versus Saldaña—highlights a more or less deliberate cultural distancing. However, although her indulgence in postracial discourses might have made her a mainstream star, her rejection of a specific ethnoracial characterization has created a distance between her and US Dominican communities. Saldana is ultimately unable to avoid practices of reading the racialized body that would associate her with Blackness in both embodied and representational ways.

Zoe Saldana's Cinematic Oeuvre

Saldana was cast as Eva Rodríguez, the rough-around-the-edges (Afro-)Latina ballet dancer, in her first widely distributed studio film, *Center Stage*. In this supporting but standout role, Saldana's character has a Latino name and occasionally speaks Spanish in the film. The film is set in the cutthroat world of a prestigious ballet academy modeled on the New York City Ballet's training institution, the School of American Ballet. In this world often defined by its whiteness, Eva is all the more noticeable against the backdrop of normative whiteness. In a scene at the beginning of the film, Eva arrives late to class with an attitude. She is not in dress code (pink tights and black leotard), and her hair is not styled in the mandatory bun. Her Otherness is written on her body through both her skin tone and clothing—Eva does not "belong" in this space. Later, the film associates Eva with Caribbean culture when she suggests some of the students take a break from their rigorous classes to go to a salsa club for "some fun." The audience is reminded that Eva not only is the Other because of her comparatively crude language and resistance to authority figures but fundamentally comes from a different cultural space. In what is supposed to be the scene where Eva is finally vindicated and shown in the full glory of her dancing abilities, the use of visual contrast marks her as Other. As the white dancers perform in black costumes, Eva, dressed in all white, who was not supposed to dance the principal role, surprises everyone when she walks on the stage. The difference in costuming shines a spotlight on Eva's body as foreign even as it displays her superior mastery of the European art form of classical ballet. Often regarded as Saldana's breakout role, it seemed to set the tone for how mainstream US audiences were guided to interpret her subsequent body of work: as racially Other—in this case, as (Afro-)Latina. However, *Center Stage* is one of only a few films in which Saldana has been cast as explicitly Latina—others include *The Losers* and *Colombiana* (dir. Olivier Megaton, 2011)—so its influence is limited regarding how audiences interpret Saldana's star text and the other characters she has portrayed.

The action-adventure film *The Losers* offers a rare opportunity to read Saldana as Afro-Latina. The film follows the gang of "Losers" headed by former military officer Clay (Jeffrey Dean Morgan) and their plot to seek revenge on and take down the CIA man who framed them for a failed mission in Bolivia. Assisting them is Aisha (Saldana), the daughter of the Bolivian drug lord involved in that botched mission, a fact uncovered toward the end of the film. As the daughter of a Bolivian, Aisha is clearly Latina, and because of her dark skin color, she can be perceived as having African heritage. This combination of factors acknowledges the possibility that a person can be both Latinx and of African descent. However, characters like Aisha are relatively rare among Hollywood narratives, and this type of racial mixture seems to be unique to Latin America, suggesting it might only be common there. Just as in Classical Hollywood (1930s–60s), the mixed-race actor is placed within exotic locales, anchoring such miscegenation firmly outside of the US. By placing the racially mixed figure in the realm of the Other, US media can enjoy the pleasure and excitement associated with the mixed-race body while also avoiding the complex issues such a figure brings into US hegemonic ethnoracial discourses. It is noteworthy, therefore, that location is the primary element that connects Saldana's various (Afro-)Latina roles; her mixed-race body is understood as Afro-Latina only because people in those parts of the world have an obvious history of racial mixture. Whether those places are in Latin America, the Caribbean, or NYC, a "safe" space for Afro-Latina/o subjectivity is created. This thinking is demonstrated through Hollywood's casting of Saldana; in those places associated with racial mixture, her afrolatinidad is unproblematic. But in those spaces where such mixture is invisible, exnominated, taboo, Saldana has been cast according to more rigid practices of hypodescent. She can assert her identity as Latina/*dominicana* as vigorously as she likes, but "Saldana herself is subject to an industry that prefers to cast light Latinas such as Jennifer Lopez for ethnic roles" (Valdivia 2020, 11).

Based on industry practices that still heavily rely on normative conceptualizations of the raced body rooted in a Black/white racial binary (Nakashima 1992; Dagbovie 2007; Beltrán and Fojas 2008), Saldana has been cast as Black/African American in roughly half of her roles. Some of my interviewees mentioned this casting trend. Ciel, for example, told me, "Zoe Saldana, she plays characters as if she wasn't a Spanish speaker, as if she was Black."[7] Ciel was particularly annoyed with the ignorance surrounding the Dominican heritage of people already present in the media. Films such as *Drumline* (dir. Charles Stone III, 2002), *Guess Who* (dir. Kevin Rodney Sullivan, 2005), *Death at a Funeral* (dir. Neil LaBute, 2010), and the Nina Simone biopic *Nina* (dir. Cynthia Mort, 2016)—which I address later in this chapter—place Saldana among primarily Black casts, within a genre of African American films, with characters whose names are not associated with a particular ethnicity. One such film, *Premium*, is the story of struggling actor Cool (Dorian Missick) and his attempts to win back the love of his life, Charli (Saldana), who is engaged to another man. Most of the characters can be read as African American, a fact made even more explicit through the film's critique of stereotypical African American representations. At one point, Cool, when talking about Charli and her fiancé being "two Black people in love," dismisses any question of Charli's racialization and, in doing so, confirms her racial reading as African American. Saldana's Caribbean background is completely erased, and the only racial markers are Black ones. This is consistent with most of Saldana's other films, where she can primarily be read as Black.

It is worth mentioning that Saldana has also been cast as an alien in several Hollywood blockbusters—*Avatar* (dir. James Cameron, 2009), *Avatar: The Way of the Water* (dir. James Cameron, 2022), upcoming *Avatar* sequels, and Marvel Comics' *Guardians of the Galaxy* (dir. James Gunn, 2014), *Guardians of the Galaxy Vol. 2* (dir. James Gunn, 2017), and *Guardians of the Galaxy Vol. 3* (dir. James Gunn, 2023). While scholars such as Daniel Bernardi (1997) have discussed the generic convention of using aliens in allegorical ways within science fiction, the frequency of these roles among Saldana's body of work indicates something more complex. The increasingly common trend of casting mixed-race and racially ambiguous actors as literally out of this world—as their existence in future and non-US/non-Earth–based realities seems to be less ideologically problematic—demonstrates Hollywood's continued discomfort with the positionality of actors who challenge dominant US racial thinking. The Hollywood imaginary of this world does not include nonnormatively racially situated actors; therefore, it makes perfect sense to place these actors in worlds and time periods that are not our own. LeiLani Nishime (2010, 36) posits that Hollywood has "simply rewritten the terms of the race debate and [has] taken cover under the umbrella of generic imperatives." It is not difficult to see why ambiguous bodies of color are more commonly represented within the science fiction genre, a genre that is intended to transport audiences into a fantasy world that does not explicitly challenge ideologies they are reluctant to reconsider. Saldana's ambiguity is more easily dealt with in a reality that does not have to explain her inclusion rather than in the current world as we know it. As Rachel Afi Quinn (2019, 59) has proposed, "Because her mixed-race body is already imagined as a surface on which racial meaning is unstable, it is not surprising that Hollywood now casts the Afro-Latina actress as characters that are blue or green in color with increasing frequency." An important question seems to be: How do Saldana's science fiction roles and, more importantly, her Black/African American roles, impact US Dominicans who would be compelled to identify with her?

Saldana and (In)Authentic Dominicanidad

While Saldana's casting history is reasonably diverse and has provided her with a fair amount of commercial success, her career has, nonetheless, done little to introduce Dominicans to a mainstream audience. Among my interviewees, Saldana's Hollywood success was not only criticized but also seen as a type of betrayal. In their analysis of the emotive work of celebrities, Heather Nuun and Anita Biressi (2010) discuss how stars attempt to rework their image when they are the subject of scandal. While discussing celebrities who have "betrayed the trust" of the public in terms of breaking *societal* norms or expectations, the same notion of betrayal can be used to understand those figures of Dominican heritage who break with *cultural* norms and expectations of their ethnic community. Nuun and Biressi (2010, 49) argue that "the celebrity figure spans the fields of the individual and the collective, the popular and the political, and thereby offers a model of personal success which reinforced the idea of individual achievement and social success as attainable by all."

Within the ideological dimensions of US stardom, Dominican celebrities' success comes at the potential loss of ethnic authenticity and community cultural trust. Some of my interviewees shared a similar suspicion with Gabriela, who suggested that it is not that there are no Dominicans in US popular culture but "for [her] they are basically invisible because those that are there play other characters . . . other races."[8] In Gabriela's daily life in law enforcement, she was surrounded by other Dominicans. She was disappointed that the history and influence of the DR was not recognized by people in the US. Gabriela believes that everyone in the Americas should be familiar with Dominicans, as the origin of the Americas is situated in the DR. Saldana's lack of vocal association with her Dominican heritage conveyed a lack of pride in the importance of the DR in exchange for mainstream US acceptance. Dominican celebrities, through the (off) white-washing of popular media assimilation, fail to carry out the expectations placed on them because they are a model of success that seems to be predicated on the loss of authentic dominicanidad. As reflected in sentiments expressed by my fieldwork interviewees and online forum commenters, Dominicans in the US are hesitant to identify with celebrities of Dominican heritage and feel a sense of cultural betrayal due to what many see as a failure to acknowledge their Dominican roots.

Many of the US-born Dominicans I interviewed insisted that they identify more with non-Dominican Latinx celebrities. Even though they might not share a national heritage with these figures, they more authentically represent latinidad within a pan-Latinx framework. Carmen told me, "I cannot think of any Dominicans in media I identify with, usually more Latinos in general. People like Shakira, Eva Mendes, and America Ferrera, those are the ones I identify with."[9] I contend that this type of pan-Latinx identification occurs for two reasons: (1) there are more non-Dominican

Latinx stars in both number and range of representation, lessening the burden of representation for each, and (2) some Dominicans align themselves with a more inclusive identity category that emphasizes cultural similarity and shared life experiences as a strategy to negotiate their identity in a context where Dominicans are scarcely included. This was particularly true for Carmen, as she was not raised around other Dominicans. Growing up in a predominantly white Chicago suburb made her try to find identification through *pan-latinidad* (pan-Latino-ness).

Latinx panethnicity is not merely a politically motivated process of homogenization; it is also an identity paradigm that is porous, flexible, and manipulative. On one hand, pan-latinidad works to generalize across diverse Latinx populations; on the other hand, its umbrella inclusivity allows people to opt in and opt out depending on what is most beneficial at a particular time. As Vicki Mayer (2004, 115) suggests, "Panlatinidad thus walks a line between describing the complex interweaving of cultures in economic, political, and social contexts and rendering these invisible." Therefore, while there may be few Dominicans among representations of pan-latinidad, there is a space within this construct for Dominicans in the US to carve out a sense of ethnic identification with celebrities who might not be Dominican but are seen as "authentically" Latina/o/x. This, however, is not a substitute for representations of dominicanidad. As Mayer warns, ethnically specific identity is at risk of being rendered invisible without representations of dominicanidad in mainstream US media that are seen as identifiable and "authentic" to US Dominicans. Therefore, stars of Dominican heritage, like Saldana, are held to a higher standard and are expected to express a form of dominicanidad that Dominicans in the US can identify with.

For Dominicans in NYC, Saldana's life and image are not relatable and even harder to identify with. For many of the Dominicans I spoke with, Saldana is not a member of their community; she is rather a celebrity entrenched in Hollywood glamour and mainstream US media culture. During one of my interviews, the matter-of-fact Emmanuel disparagingly suggested that "she is one of those" who might have Dominican roots but have become a product of the US cultural environment.[10] As someone who felt he could be both Dominican and American at the same time, Emmanuel believed that sacrificing one's dominicanidad was not necessary for US assimilation. Other Dominicans simply could not see themselves represented in Saldana, with Dania in particular maintaining, "That's just not me."[11] As someone who fully embraces her African descent, Dania might have been more inclined than others to identify with the darker-skinned Saldana. However, her class consciousness and the way she connected the US Dominican experience to working-class roots meant that Saldana's wealth and lifestyle were not relatable. From Saldana's glamorous appearance to her Hollywood lifestyle, the Dominicans I spoke with did not share with her the same dominicanidad. Still others were more critical of Saldana, accusing her of forgetting her roots and suggesting that she has intentionally hidden her Dominican heritage from her public persona, opting instead to sustain and encourage an ambiguous characterization. According to Luis, "She has fallen off into that Americanization. It could be of her own fault, or the pressures she has succumbed to. But for me, it kinda takes away the identity of who you are."[12] Luis himself was particularly invested in projecting his dominicanidad, criticizing the forces of US cultural imperialism in the DR and its diaspora. From disappointment to disavowal, my interviewees expressed a sense of distancing from Saldana as a potential representative of their community.

Isabel Molina-Guzmán (2010, 113) cites the similar case of actor Salma Hayek and her film *Frida* (dir. Julie Taymor, 2002) to posit that discourses of authenticity surrounding the film and its star "did not suggest, as [Molina-Guzmán] would, that authenticity is an impossible and problematic identity construction but instead [argue] that it is impossible for the US media to get Mexican authenticity correct." This suggests that the notion of authenticity, while it is elusive, is nevertheless a presumed tangible concept among audiences. Many of my interviewees reacted similarly to Carlos, who merely dismissed Saldana, saying, "I think she is Dominican . . . yeah she's Dominican. Maybe she will decide to one day play a Dominican."[13] Carlos, however, was not as concerned about Dominican recognition and representation as others I spoke with. He likes US media, and would keep engaging with it whether it featured Dominicans or not. He would have liked to see a Dominican character in the Hollywood movies he loves but was not too concerned about their absence. Other interviewees, however, did not share this sentiment. As the ambivalence toward the nationally rooted authenticity regarding both Hayek and Saldana illustrate, "the media and audience negotiations over the symbolic colonization of iconic Latinas inform how the bodies of ethnic women are used to discipline definitions of race, ethnicity, nation, and national identity" (Molina-Guzmán 2010, 115). This speaks not only to how, through Hollywood framing, Saldana's body is disciplined to fit within a Black/white binary racialization but also to how the Americanization of her star image disrupts her ties to dominicanidad.

There is, however, a strong argument that the issue is not Saldana's ethnoracial flexibility but rather her willingness to embrace Blackness, which is at the heart of why some Dominicans cannot identify with Saldana. As an Afro-Latino population that culturally constructs its identity in terms of a romanticized and fantasized connection to a colonial and Indigenous past, Dominicans position their subjectivity in opposition to those they see as embodying Blackness—namely, Haitians and other Black Caribbeans or African Americans in the US. While latinidad by its very nature challenges racialized binary thinking in the US, dominicanidad problematizes this thinking even further by complicating what becomes acceptably included within the boundaries of latinidad, Blackness, and/or whiteness. Although not the only reason for criticism regarding her authentic representation of dominicanidad, Zoe Saldana's frequent casting as Black/African American indicates a certain racialized aspect of how Dominican-American audiences perceive her star text. Many of the criticisms directed at her by my interviewees are clearly ones that a lighter-skinned Dominican-American would not face. For example, my interviewees criticized both Saldana and Alex Rodriguez for being overly Americanized, but the issue of race was brought up only regarding Saldana. Although the claim that Rodriguez is Americanized implicitly suggests that he has whitewashed his image and is therefore seen as "wanting to be white," it was only in discussions of Saldana that race was explicitly addressed. This speaks to the contentious relationship between Blackness and dominicanidad that is rooted in Dominican history and its complicated relationship with African descent.

Saldana's cinematic and personal connection with Blackness, both US based and otherwise, is seen as inconsistent with how dominicanidad is often articulated. Even though this is a slowly changing reality, where Blackness among Dominicans is both acknowledged and, at times, embraced, "to Dominicans, Dominicanness and Hispanicity are by definition *not black*, both in the United States and on the island" (Candelario 2007, 2; original emphasis). As explained by Luis, "The reason why Dominicans don't like to say they have African heritage is because it makes them seem primitive." He sees such a practice as a survival strategy to avoid the prejudice and discrimination faced by African Americans in the US. While it is certainly true that Dominicans have been accused of denying their African descent, the reality is far more complex and nuanced. As a leading scholar on Dominican racialized discourses, Silvio Torres-Saillant (2010, 461) explains, "Ironically, in the diaspora we find Dominicans demonstrating a greater propensity to classify themselves as Black than any other Latino subgroup."

In the context of the US, African descent is not necessarily denied, but it is qualified in relation to the Blackness of African Americans. In Candelario's (2007, 253) NYC ethnographic fieldwork, she states that inclusion in dominicanidad "is mediated by the historical relationship between blacks and whites in the United States, the current relationship between Dominicans and African Americans," and traditional ethnoracial ideologies.

In her explanation of the relationship between dominicanidad and Blackness, Tina told me that "when Dominicans say they are not Black they mean that they are not 'African American,' not that they are not of African descent."[14] Dedicated to social justice work, Tina was comfortable talking about her own African heritage. She articulated the complexity of the place of Blackness within dominicanidad in a way other interviewees were not able to. However, Tina's racial consciousness does not indicate that there is a lack of prejudice toward African Americans among the Dominican community. If anything, it points to the opposite. When Saldana plays African American characters, she is accused of not being Dominican enough by the Dominican-American community, even if this reasoning is done at an unconscious level. As a *latinegra*, defined by Marta I. Cruz-Janzen (2010, 282) as "Latinas of obvious Black ancestry and undeniable ties to Africa," Saldana's image among US Dominicans is a precarious one. According to Cruz-Janzen (2010), "*Latinegras* represent the mirrors that most Latinos would like to shatter because they reflect the Blackness that Latinos don't want to see in themselves." One might conclude that Saldana, as a latinegra, is a mirror to a reflection Dominicans would rather not see.

Because Saldana's Blackness is so readily understood by mainstream audiences, Dominican-Americans might not include her in their understanding of their own dominicanidad and are even less likely to accept her as a symbol of Dominican national identity. This illustrates the conflicted relationship between dominicanidad and Blackness that is playing out through Dominican media reception in the US and, more specifically, through Dominican reception of Saldana's star text.

What's in a Name?: The Connotations of Dropping the Enye (ñ)

In the context of Dominican authenticity, much can be learned simply by how Saldana's name is spelled. Many of my interviewees mentioned the absence of Spanish diacritics in her name as it appears in mainstream media. When discussing why Saldana did not represent dominicanidad, Tina said, "I think it is weird that nobody ever spells her name with an *enye*, you would think that would be important to her." The question of "to ñ or not to ñ" reflects how Saldana's subjectivity is interpreted within her star text. In the Dominican press, her name is usually spelled "Saldaña," but the US media spells it inconsistently. The *enye* (ñ) and other diacritics are often dropped from Spanish names and words by English speakers in the US because those accents are not part of the English language, and US fonts and printing types are typically not designed for their usage (Wood 1981). However, the ñ is both politically loaded and imbued with Latinx associations, so the choice of whether or not to use it reflects the writer's interpretation of Saldana's identity. What might be considered grammatical arbitrariness to some is actually a phenomenon deeply rooted in US hegemonic racial and ethnic ideologies. The politics embedded within language and semiotics are clearly observable in the confusion over the spelling of Saldana's name and, I argue, are purposefully manipulated depending on which media source is discussing her. For example, *Latina* magazine almost always uses the ñ when spelling her name, and more mainstream sources usually leave it out. It serves *Latina*'s purposes—whose primary audience is US Latinas and whose focus is on issues of Latina femininity—to enhance Saldana's claim to latinidad, prompting its readers to identify with her as a Latina. Mainstream publications have no such political agenda or mission.

Michael Aceto (2002, 603) argues that "many immigrants in the USA have anglicized their names or adopted Anglophone names for exclusive use among English speakers, while maintaining original or ethnic names for ingroup usage," but it is nevertheless difficult to suggest that Saldana uses the unaccented spelling of her name exclusively in English-speaking contexts. What is clear, however, is that the meaning inherent in removing the accent(s) from the spelling of Saldana's name in her professional life bleeds into Dominican and mainstream interpretations of how she self-identifies. Names, even individual proper names, signify certain connotations. Linguist Paul Baltes (1991, 75) posits that while proper names are primarily used to reference a specific individual, to denote them in semiological terms, they function on another level of signification where "names suggest descriptions regardless of their referential function." He discusses how certain names have a culturally produced connotative meaning—for example, "Bertha" implies a large woman, and "Vinnie" an Italian mobster—and, therefore, "stereotypes are subsumed under some representative name and then the name may be used to predicate specific features" (1991, 83).

I believe that accented names and the subsequent reasoning behind removing those accents belong in the same category. The use of accents visually and culturally marks the referent of that name and ties them both to a kind of foreign-ness in the US context and often a separate language identity—in this case, a Spanish-speaking one. Linguistic anthropologists Mary Bucholtz and Kira Hall (2003, 379) contend that "beliefs about language are also often beliefs about speakers," as names in a "marked" language—in this instance, Spanish is a "marked" language in a primarily English-speaking society—are both referential and contextual. Just as speaking Spanish marks the individual with certain cultural connotations, so does using the accented spelling of one's name. Bucholtz and Hall (2003, 382) further suggest that "language, as a fundamental resource for cultural production, is hence also a fundamental resource for identity production." It seems that names, and the choice to accent them or not, can influence how an individual is identified. By removing the accent(s) from her name, Saldana has made herself even more ambiguous, regardless of whether this was done for personal or professional reasons. "Through the varied spellings of her name, her ethnic identity shifts in public consciousness from African American to Afro-Latina and back again," allowing her to expand her film roles while remaining an ethnoracial moving target (Afi Quinn 2019, 54). Because Saldana has shaped her identity in this ambiguous way, the US Dominican community views her actions as a challenge to its desire to maintain and express a sense of dominicanidad.

"I Am Just Zoe": Zoe Saldana as a Raced Postracial Figure

Saldana told *Latina* magazine's Amaris Castillo (2013), "I'm not defined by sex, I'm not defined by race, I'm not defined by nationality, I'm Zoe." Saldana has made many similar statements, ones that allude to an unspecified racial or ethnic subjectivity while also disavowing any particular claim to identification. This is only one message that US audiences receive from Saldana: a refusal to be subsumed into any one category. However, my survey of her popular press coverage reveals that her real Hollywood strategy involves claiming all potential categories of identification (Black, Latina, African American, dominicana) in one publication and then turning around and saying she cannot be categorized in the next. This strategy may be an attempt to avoid Latina typecasting. As other scholars have discussed, many Latina roles rely heavily on the fiery Latina stereotype, revealing the intersectional connotation that aligns ethnic identity with a certain sexualized construction of Latina femininity (Rodriguez 1997; Ramírez Berg 2002; Beltrán 2009). Angharad N. Valdivia (2000, 92) posits that in the case of representational Latina femininity, "we get the sexually out of control and utterly colorful spitfire, an image quite specific to Latinas." But Saldana has made her subjectivity into a moving target, a seminal example of Stuart Hall's articulation of the "floating signifier" of racial or ethnic identity. A manipulability made possible, as Isabel Molina-Guzmán (2010, 6) argues, based on how Latinas are "ambiguously coded as ethnic and racial, providing for a more flexible performance of identity that does not always cohere to commonsense biological definitions of ethnicity or phenotypic definitions of race." In terms of a strategy for Hollywood survival, this approach seems to be working well for Saldana. Yet those who would identify with her subjectivity based on a shared sense of dominicanidad have something more at stake. And Saldana's refusal to project her dominicanidad in a way that might feel authentic for the US Dominican community often seems like betrayal.

Perhaps, this confusion and ambivalence are merely a result of postracial and color-blind politics. Molina-Guzmán (2013a) argues, "During a 'post-racial' moment where race and ethnicity are no longer supposed to matter, the casting politics surrounding black Latina/o actors produce a triple-burden across gender, ethnic, and racial barriers that is increasingly difficult to navigate." Saldana's own rhetoric is rooted in concepts of color-blind politics.

> I grew up in Queens and the Dominican Republic. It wasn't easy, s*** was going on. But the kind of world that we had indoors, that my mom created for us, makes more sense to this day than what is out there. I would come home from school and go, "Mami, what am I? You know, cause I'm getting all kinds of things and people are mean." And Mami would look at me and go, "You're Zoe." And I'd go, "I know, Mami, but what am I?" and she would look at me and say, "You're my daughter, your grandma's granddaughter, you're Zoe."[15]

Because of the ambiguity and confusion related to her racial and ethnic subjectivity, Saldana subscribes to her mother's childhood intervention and often insists on a color-blind career strategy. Ana, one of my interviewees, recognized this strategy when she explained, "She is protecting herself, as minorities are forced to cope with how Hollywood uses them." Ana herself felt that the best way to avoid discrimination was through assimilation when engaging in the public sphere, where cultural retention is reserved for the private sphere. Yet, for Saldana, this is only one side of the color-blind postracial coin. On the other side of ambiguity is flexibility, and, for Saldana in particular, this flexibility has proved highly strategic. Through strategic ethnoracial flexibility, which by its nature disturbs the

US dominant casting culture, "Saldana's willingness and desire to situate herself within US Blackness positions her within 'Americanness' and allows her the opportunity to increase her racial capital through cultural commodification" (Molina-Guzmán 2013b, 221). She is able to manipulate color-blind politics and promote an ambiguous or flexible star image that can favor one identification over the others, depending on the role she is playing at the time.

However, career strategy and postracial good intentions aside, just because Saldana says it is not important to define her race does not mean that audiences can no longer see it. Kristen Warner (2014, 14) contends that, "as a post-racial society, colorblindness and diversity exist in tension with the other and require both the seeing and the not seeing of race." Actors of color can identify themselves in the press however they choose. But similar to the argument that claiming society is now postracial does not equate to the end of racism, audiences will continue to read race onto the bodies of celebrities of color, regardless of how they self-identify. As Kent A. Ono (2010, 229) implores, "The strategic project of postracism, as unconscious as it often is, is to create a context in which messages that justify disavowal of racism undermine consciousness of racism and racism's historical effect." In her analysis of Saldana's star text, Afi Quinn (2019, 46) argues that "sociocultural bias and the stories we tell ourselves about race in the US and abroad (for instance, Black people aren't Latinx and Latinxs aren't Black) overdetermine what we actually *see* and how we read for race." Ciel told me that "there are very few representations of darker skinned Dominicans or Latinos" and, therefore, Saldana cannot fully escape being viewed through a racial lens by audiences. But she can exploit Hollywood's paradigms of postraciality—even if by doing so, she must sacrifice some of her claims to dominicanidad.

As an example of the type of discourse that surrounds Saldana, a stream of comments responding to an online article announcing the inclusion of two Dominican actresses in the megablockbuster *Avatar* reveals the levels of ambivalence to Saldana's dominicanidad. A brief notice on Dominicantoday.com, a news site based in the DR for English-speaking Dominicans, intended to highlight the significance of casting two actresses of Dominican heritage (Zoe Saldana and Michelle Rodriguez). Yet many of the responses focused on the computer-generated images (CGI) of the film, a result that angered some readers. This seems to reveal not only ambivalence to the two actresses of Dominican origin but also a lack of identification with the stars as members of a larger Dominican community. Reacting to the discussion following this announcement, one participant tried to turn the conversation by posting, "The spirit here is not to hail or denote the CGI, script, etc . . . the object here is to denote Dominican actresses or actors. period!" Another poster responded, "Nobody is criticizing any Dominicans in this thread." Those posting comments (many of whom are located in the DR) do not see a significant identification between their dominicanidad and Saldana and Rodriguez. This is just another Hollywood film to them, a Hollywood film with Hollywood actresses. It is not, presumably, a representation of their community or an expression of Dominican culture. It is only when they are reprimanded for missing the point of Dominicantoday.com's announcement that they even seem to acknowledge the significance of the casting. Although this discussion ends with a flippant dismissal, the broader discussion of Saldana's place in Hollywood and her (in)authentic dominicanidad continues on countless other websites.

Arguably, the best example of Saldana's contested ethnoracial identity is the controversy around her casting as African American musician and activist Nina Simone.[16] Although Saldana did publicly apologize for taking on the role, saying that Simone "deserved better . . . I thought back then that I had the permission [to play her] because I was a black woman. . . . And I am. But it was Nina Simone. And Nina had a life and she had a journey that should have been—and should be—honoured to the most specific detail because she was a specifically detailed individual," she had adamantly defended that choice for many years (quoted on BBC.com 2020). Most notoriously, in *Latina* magazine, Saldana is quoted as saying, "Let me tell you, if Elizabeth Taylor can be Cleopatra, I can be Nina—I'm sorry. It doesn't matter how much backlash I will get for it. I will honor and respect my black community because that's who I am."[17] This statement overlooks Hollywood's history and practice of using white actors in brownface, but it is nevertheless indicative of Saldana's approach to the roles she accepts and her flexible self-racialization. Yet, regardless of how Saldana justifies her choices to play a specific character, this does not always translate to audiences. In a Latina.com discussion thread including reactions to Saldana's casting as Nina Simone, posters share conflicting sentiments, demonstrating how Saldana's star text creates a space for negotiating racial and ethnic identity. One participant posted, "This is typical Hollywood. Even though Zoe is Afro Latina I can understand why African Americans are a bit upset at this pic. It is nothing personal but I think [there] are enough talented African Americans to play this part. Yes, Zoe is a Black Hispanic but African Americans feel their culture differs from Afro Hispanic/Latino culture" (Palomares 2012).

While most participants generally agreed with this sentiment, others mindfully contested it: "Zoe is black-latina just like there are black-Americans. I understand this double edge sword of being Afro Latino and it sucks socially having people not understand what a black Latino is or even beleive [sic] it. HOWEVER this shouldn't be a case about her culture it should be a discourse about whether she resembles [Simone] or not. Jennifer Lopez played a Mexican american, i love Zoe i think she can take on the physical look, she [is] an actress for goodness sake have we not seen other actors and actreses [sic] transform for the silver screen" (2012). This post demonstrates not only a recognition of racial and ethnic nuance but also an understanding of how this usually plays out within ideologies of the racialized body. However, another post elucidates how industrial practices and the politics of representation converge in this particular case: "Hollywood must think 'People think that Nina Simone and Zoe Saldana are both Black people. No one will ever notice they look very different'" (2012). This observation reveals how mainstream audiences conflate Blackness under an umbrella of skin tone, rooted in the normative logic of hypodescent.

There is a great deal at stake in this discussion thread, from contesting the idea of an inherent Black subject to industrial practices of colorism. Molina-Guzmán (2013a) takes on the complicated politics involved in Saldana's casting as Simone, contending, "It is Saldana's complex desire, willingness and ability to occupy and claim a Latina ethnic identity and a US black racial identity that is at center of the discomfort surrounding Saldana's performance of Simone." US hegemonic constructions of race and ethnicity place Blackness and latinidad in mutually exclusive categories. Therefore, when Saldana claims to be both, she is performing what Molina-Guzmán (2013b) suggests is a "radical identity." Saldana's identity is "radical" because it is a moving target, where she is all of these identities at once but also none of them. Because she rejects identifying along paradigms of racial thinking that are still informed by an outdated biological determinist mindset, she can justify portraying characters from across the racial spectrum as opposed to being limited to one ethnoracial label. Saldana is not stuck in one category; she travels among them with a fluidity made possible through her navigation of color-blind and postracial discourses. Whether this ethnoracial flexibility is strategic or radical, "positioning herself as *both* black and Latina—and passing for one or the other as needed—helps her reach a larger market" (Afi Quinn 2019, 53). Making visible the constructed nature of this categorization produces the type of messy identification and ambivalence illuminated within the discussion thread mentioned previously. Saldana's strategy to be all and yet none challenges preconceived notions of ethnoracial identification, yet it also isolates her from the Dominican community, a community that desperately desires to have dominicanidad represented in the US, but only if it is done authentically. What emerges from these examples is the precarious nature of practices of identification within the US, practices that are further contested in relation to the celebrity text of Alex Rodriguez.

Alex Rodriguez: A-Rod's Americanized Persona

In addition to frequent mentions of Zoe Saldana, Alex Rodriguez was brought up in nearly all of my interviews. Much like Saldana, Rodriguez has faced a contentious attitude from the US Dominican community, and his celebrity is just as polemical. Unlike Saldana, who has faced little negative mainstream feedback, Rodriguez receives criticism from both the mainstream and the Dominican community. Furthermore, while the activities of sports celebrities are similar in many ways to those of media stars and other mainstream celebrities, there are several nuances involved in sports celebrity that are important to acknowledge. Here I cite Gill Lines (2010, 286), who not only provides a literature review of sports-based celebrity but also explains sports star-audience relationships. In his review of the scholarship on sports celebrity, he explains that "the characterization of sport stars affords a central focus across both sports spectacle and narrative and celebrity sport stars images are communicated through a vast array of media products (Connel 1992; Rowe 1995; Whannel 1992, 1998b; Whannel and Wellard 1995). As their celebrity status grows, for some, the audience knows as much, if not more, about their personal lives as their sporting endeavours." The playing of the game is the primary source of spectatorship for sports stars, complicating how their celebrity works as they are framed within the notion of "real life" and not tied to associations of "scriptedness" or acting in the exhibition of their work. Even when their work is broadcast, it is rooted in a sense of realness that other media broadcasts are not so easily associated with. Lines (2010, 287) suggests, "Sports stars are real in the sense that they perform live under unpredictable sporting conditions over which apparently the media has little control. Yet, the nature of what the reader gets to see, hear and read about is determined and amplified by camera angles, replays, gossip columns, photographic images, chat shows and other such professional practices which ensure that the sport star image develops through selected constructions of reality." The

Fig. 2.3 Alex Rodriguez before Game 4 of the 2015 MLB World Series. Arturo Pardavila III from Hoboken, NJ, USA, CC BY 2.0, https://creativecommons.org/licenses/by/2.0, Wikimedia Commons.

actual work of playing sports is just one aspect of how audiences see these sports celebrities, however. Sports stars become figures and even icons in popular culture and various mainstream and niche media. It is not just their athletic performance that matters in audience interpretation of these figures; it is also their personal lives, their behaviors outside of the work of playing ball, and the manner and degree in which they receive coverage within and outside of the space of sports spectatorship. According to Lines (2010, 300), "What the audience know about and identify with certain sports stars is closely associated with the information that the media professional has selected to bring to their attention." Put simply, opinions of sports stars are not merely based on how well they play the game; they also involve audience negotiations of the intertextual representation of the star text.

The star text of a sports celebrity operates much like it does for other celebrities, wherein a narrative is built through the various media sources that cover their lives and careers. Moreover, sports stars are usually framed within the highly gendered narrative of the "hero" and are expected to uphold cultural constructions of ideal masculinity. Yet wherever there are heroes, there are also villains. The mediated narrative constructed within the sports star text uses discourses rooted in the hero/villain binary, where "while condemning bad behavior in sports stars, the media actually thrives on exposing it in order to ensure its commercial success and interest to its readers" (Lines 2010, 294). This is particularly the case for Latinx ballplayers, for whom there seems to be a "preoccupation with their actions as sports heroes, as men, and as a not quite legitimate population [i.e., foreign] that is often both lionized and vilified for being overly passionate and 'fiery' on and off the field of play" (Domino Rudolph 2020, 14). Furthermore, media narratives can easily transform the same sports star from a hero to a villain in one cover story or commentator's opinion. A sports celebrity is defined not only by their performance statistics but also by the stories the media shares about them.

Lines (2010, 288) posits, as a generalization, that "sports heroes are clearly promoted by the media as a source of national pride and function to represent national qualities, traditions and distinctions." And while this might be more true in some cultures than others, it is certainly true for both the US and the DR. The *Calgary Herald* (2011) published a piece on Dominicans and baseball, citing the significant presence of Dominican baseball players in the US: "[If] you've ever been to this sun-drenched country, you're likely not surprised. There are all levels of baseball played all over the place. It's a favorite sport and national passion. In fact, at any given time, there can be 800,000 kids playing organized baseball in the DR. That's quite a number, considering the country's population is only 10 million or so." A significant part of Dominican culture, baseball and its stars not only are sources of national pride but also provide potential exposure to Dominican subjects for a US mainstream audience. Dominican scholar Nelson Santana (2013) states that "after White Americans, Dominicans comprise the second largest group of baseball players—and the world is taking note. This year the Dominican Republic won the 2013 World Baseball Classic (WBC)." Baseball is integral to the Dominican experience on the island and abroad, making baseball stars household names. As Alan Klein (1991, 1) has argued, "Americans may love the game of baseball as much as Dominicans do, but they do not need it as much. For Dominicans, baseball is a wide-ranging set of symbols, every turn at bat is a candle of hope, every swing is a wave of a banner, the sweeping arc of a sword." Dominican baseball celebrities are assumed pillars of dominicanidad, and so their lives and careers are closely followed by Dominicans in the US. As such, they carry the burden of representing the Dominican community, a task that some are perceived to handle better than others.

Baseball has played a significant role in both historical and contemporary connections between the US and the Spanish Caribbean more broadly, and the DR more specifically. The reliance on Caribbean baseball talent has been fundamental to US baseball as an institution, and the sport has also been translated syncretically into Caribbean culture. Adrian Burgos (2005, 5) distinguishes the nuances within the relationships among baseball, the US, and Latin American and Spanish Caribbean players, contending that, unlike the associations baseball has in areas that might be considered part of the American empire, "due to the game's longer history in Cuba and other parts of the Spanish-speaking Americas, Latinos would infuse baseball with their own meaning[s] about nation, gender, and race that distinguished this scene." Pedro Julio Santana (a Dominican relating his experience of the US military occupation of the DR in the early twentieth century) expressed, "Baseball is the greatest thing that the U.S. has given us and other countries of the Caribbean. They have not given us anything else that, in my opinion, is of any value, but baseball!" (quoted in Burgos 1997, 75–76). Dominicans have not rejected the history of baseball in the US; rather, they have developed their own relationship with the sport independently from the US in culturally specific ways.

Caribbean and Latino ballplayers have long been crossing borders to pursue the sport, creating networks of migration and cultural exchange in the process. According to Burgos (2005, 23), "In the contemporary era even more Major League organizations have turned to the Dominican Republic and Venezuela in their search to find prospects as cheaply as possible and to offset the high cost of developing North American players and signing superstar free agents. These practices link the history of the hundreds of Latinos who have performed in the Majors in the integrated era with those who entered the U.S. playing fields during Jim Crow." Beginning during the era of professional baseball regulated by codes of segregation that prohibited Black players from Major League Baseball (MLB) and the subsequent creation of the Negro Leagues, Caribbean players would play in the US season and then return to the islands to play in the leagues there, cultivating careers that spanned transnational borders. Navigating between two separately defined cultural spaces, "these ballplayers empowered themselves through their networks that allowed them to make informed and calculated decisions as Transatlantic residents, thereby avoiding certain pitfalls and creating alternate means" (Burgos 1997, 80).

Fig. 2.4 Alex Rodriguez and Derek Jeter warming up in Yankee Stadium. Jeffrey Hayes, CC BY 2.0, https://creativecommons.org/licenses/by/2.0, Wikimedia Commons.

Alex Rodriguez builds on a legacy of Latino/x ballplayers who consciously navigated US racial ideology and practices to expand their careers, improve their status, and obtain privileges in the US. The way Caribbean baseball players have sustained a fluid process of identification suggests that conforming to US racial ideologies as well as national alliances and cultural identity was something uniquely available in the realm of baseball. Players would navigate the terrain based on their positionality to achieve the most success for themselves within baseball's transnational conditions.

A-Rod: The Damned Yankee

A much-contested figure, Alex Enmanuel Rodriguez (A-Rod) is both loved and resented by Dominicans in the US and the DR. Rodriguez was born on July 27, 1975, in NYC, where he lived with his two older siblings and Dominican-born parents until he was four years old. His family then returned to the DR, and that is where he learned to play baseball. When Rodriguez was eight years old, his family moved to Miami, where he continued to play baseball and achieve success on the field. Rodriguez's MLB debut was July 8, 1994, playing for the Seattle Mariners. After his stint with the Mariners, Rodriguez went on to play with the Texas Rangers before making his final move to the New York Yankees. His blockbuster trade to the Yankees in 2004 was not only big news in the sporting world but also a dream fulfilled for Rodriguez, who, like many other Dominican players, had always wished to play in NYC, the city of his birth.

As one of the biggest names in US baseball, Alex Rodriguez is a polarizing figure in the Dominican community. When asked to identify Dominicans known to mainstream US, Gabriela joked, "I would like to say Alex Rodriguez, but he says that he is American." More than anything, Dominicans in the US are disappointed with Rodriguez and his seemingly purposeful distancing from his own dominicanidad. Luis, the Dominican purist, expressed, "From what I have seen, they always try to make them seem more 'American.' . . . As he was coming up, even when I was younger, he was my favorite player. But what I didn't ever like was that I knew he was Dominican but they even went so far as to change his name to A-Rod. Cutting the Rodriguez completely out. But I understand it is a business thing. But it is cutting yourself out of who you really are. . . . This is what I think happens to all Dominicans that become popular." A particularly bitter subject for US Dominicans is Rodriguez's rejection of the Dominican National Team, who invited him to play for them during the 2006 World Baseball Classic. For many, this decision was emblematic of the baseball star's desire to distance himself from the Dominican community. Rodriguez's star image in mainstream US media reflects the paradigm of Americanization mentioned by my interviewees. Whether the "A-Rod" brand was self-created or a product of the US star-making machine, BMN News Team (2010) hits the nail on the head by suggesting,

> When the phrase "New York Yankees" is mentioned these days, it's pretty hard not to think of Alexander Emmanuel Rodriguez—third baseman for the New York Major League baseball team. Better known to his legions of fans as "A-Rod"—the Dominican baseball star is well-known for his lively reputation both on and off the field. Aside from his informal "brand" as a Ladies' Man, Alex Rodriguez is known for being one of the best all-around baseball players of all time. . . . Sure, you could say that A-Rod's amazing baseball record precedes any post locker room gossip. But it is more than likely the third baseman's saucy repute that has made him one of the biggest sports superstars in the world.

As "A-Rod," Rodriguez is a topic of interest for sports fans, media gossip enthusiasts, and swooning spectators. It is a combination of factors in his public persona that make Rodriguez more than your run-of-the-mill baseball player, setting him apart as a preeminent sports superstar—whether you like him or not.

However, Rodriguez's Americanized rebranding is often seen as an insult to dominicanidad, an insult that some can overlook and many others cannot. He personifies an assimilationist process that erases Dominican cultural identification in the quest for success in the US. Placing this Americanization within a historical context, baseball has long been an arena of ethnoracial identity negotiations and flexible subjectivities that ebb and flow with the currents of US ethnoracial history. As a central feature of what is imagined as "American" culture, "the baseball diamond therefore evolved into more than an athletic arena, it also became a cultural battleground where players and spectators waged discursive battles about citizenship, respectability, and racial equality" (Burgos 2005, 5). This means that ballplayers, of all backgrounds and heritages, have had to position themselves within discourses of American nationality throughout baseball's history (Domino Rudolph 2020).

One might say that the transition from Alex Rodriguez to "A-Rod" illustrates how this ballplayer navigated those nationalist discourses to further his career. Trading on these discourses, ones that privilege American identification within baseball as an institution, Rodriguez has continually reinforced the American over the Dominican. But even by doing so, Rodriguez has been unable to secure mainstream support, as he is seen as fundamentally unable to uphold the American values that frame the sport in US culture. In the US popular imagination, baseball heralds certain American values, including "individual responsibility to the larger community (teamwork), hard work (performing at your best), and collaborating for the greater good (winning as a team versus individual achievements)" (Burgos 2005, 2–3). A-Rod seems to flout these values with his active ego, womanizing behavior, and "selfish" use of performance-enhancing drugs (PED).

While Dominicans in the US question Rodriguez's ethnic authenticity, mainstream US media have made him the face of recent industry PED scandals. As "America's pastime," baseball holds an almost sacred position within US culture, where, "as a trope . . . baseball connotes a kinder, innocent past, where heroes could always redeem themselves and, by extension, the American dream" (Burgos 1997, 67). Rodriguez's series of PED accusations has left a stain on the "pure" and "All-American" sport. Rodriguez has become the unwitting poster boy for failing to uphold the values that the US instills into the sport. His self-accolades, high-profile romantic flings, and, finally, his sordid abuse of PEDs have made him an easy target for US media and baseball fans. Santana (2013) argues that "part of this steroids bias stems from this irrational hatred towards

Rodriguez," but PED use in baseball is more systemic than is discussed; the institution itself has created a culture of use and then scapegoats the players it set up for a fall (flowtv.org). As a transnational body, organized baseball has always been able to spin rampant PED use as the result of easy access to the drugs in the Caribbean and Latin America compared to their strict regulation in the US (Domino Rudolph 2020). Santana (2013) sees this phenomenon reaching further than just Rodriguez, suggesting that "in the 21st century Dominicans in baseball have become this era's Salem witches—the scapegoats of the steroid era, with Alex Rodriguez serving as the principal scapegoat." Whether due to Rodriguez's use of PEDs or his Americanized rebranding, baseball fans in both the US and the DR see his legacy as tainted.

A-Rod Is Not the "Yankee Type"

While Rodriguez's abilities on the field have received wide coverage, it is his personal life and career scandals that are frequently discussed in the popular press. Moving back and forth between hero and villain status, A-Rod has dated media celebrities like Madonna, Kate Hudson, Cameron Diaz, and Jennifer Lopez and has become a central figure in sports news forums as well as tabloid and celebrity gossip outlets. A CBS Sports column summed up Rodriguez's mediated image well when it suggested that "the indescribably talented 18-year-old kid who came out of Miami will henceforth be known now as the spoiled would-be all-time baseball great who felt the need to cheat the system to become better than the best. He was befallen to a rare combination of selfishness, ego and greed" (Heyman 2014). Unfortunately for Rodriguez, baseball fans' contempt for him did not begin with the most recent PED scandal; he has been fielding (no pun intended) criticism on multiple fronts. One need only look at the numerous A-Rod jokes on jokes4us.com, and others like it, to see how his public image has become the source of many a punchline. Here are some of my favorites:

> Q: What is an A-Roid cocktail?
> A: An overpriced drink that is best before October!
> Q: Why did Alex Rodriguez's wife file for divorce?
> A: Because she claims Alex abandoned her and she deserves to be treated better than the Yankees in October!
> Q: Why did A-Rod feel the need to take steroids?
> A: Every day he woke up feeling half-ass and he wanted to be ass-whole!
> Q: Why does Madonna and Alex Rodriguez make a good couple?
> A: They go well together since he hit 50 the same year she did!

Levity aside, these jokes are rooted in Rodriguez's perceived failure to uphold the core values of baseball and the nationalist discourses that inform expectations of baseball players. They lampoon Rodriguez on two fronts: his abilities as a ballplayer and his personal life.

There is no doubt that Rodriguez is one of the most-discussed sports stars in the US popular press. And similar to the case of Zoe Saldana, online discussions reveal the kinds of feelings and debates surrounding his public image. It is the rhetoric of A-Rod bashing and general dislike of the third baseman that seem to keep him at the center of media attention. For instance, RealClearSports.com (2013) commented that "while Alex Rodriguez may be one of the greatest baseball players to ever play the game, he is also one of the least liked people in sports." Many of the online baseball fans posting in anti-A-Rod discussion threads are not mere Yankees haters; they are Yankees fans who have developed a strong distaste for Rodriguez as part of their beloved team. After reading some of these comments, I wonder: Is there anyone who supports Alex Rodriguez? Not according to the *New York Times*, which stated that Rodriguez's peers have said that "Alex Rodriguez is a hypocrite and a 'prima donna.' He is not the 'Yankee type,' either, and he has 'monopolized all the attention' since arriving in the Bronx in 2004. Others have described his on-field conduct as 'bush league,' 'a little cheap,' an 'unsportsmanlike act of cheating' and more typical of 'junior high school baseball.' Tough crowd" (Shpigel 2010). What stands out to me the most among this litany of complaints is the accusation that Rodriguez is not "the Yankee type." The Yankees are seen as more than just one of the teams that make up "America's sport"; they are understood as "America's Team." From the iconic pinstripes to the roster of Hall-of-Famers, the New York Yankees are popularly imagined as epitomizing the American Dream through baseball. The pristine image of the Yankees, along with the connection between the term *Yankee* and notions of whiteness, renders Rodriguez's "bad" behavior on and off the field —based on their breaking with behavioral norms rooted in whiteness—seem as signs of disrespect to the sanctity of baseball.

Failure on Both Ends of the Hyphen: Neither American nor Dominican Enough

Alex Rodriguez is obviously not the ideal Yankee. Given the lack of support for Rodriguez from baseball fans, it seems that the US Dominican community would have his back, but they are just as critical, if not more so, of his persona. On the Dominican-American cultural website ESENDOM.com (2017), it was suggested that "for example, when a group of Dominicans carry on a conversation among themselves with Rodriguez as the protagonist, phrases such as 'disgusting traitor' are integrated into the conversation. Words of hate and ignorant statements spew out of the mouths of such individuals. The root of this ignorant way of thinking is simply envy." While this is a reasonable assumption, jealousy alone does not account for the frequent claims among Dominicans—several of which were shared with me in interviews and informal conversation—that Rodriguez is a "traitor." Reflecting on Rodriguez's early career with the Seattle Mariners, the *Seattle Times* published a quote from him—before he became A-Rod—that alluded to his ambivalent and conflicted relationship with his Dominican heritage: "'People used to ask me if I was Dominican and I'd say, "Yeah." But I had no idea what I was saying,' Rodriguez said last week in a quiet moment before his team was to play the LaRomana Asucareros [of the Dominican Baseball League]. 'Coming here meant more than working on hitting a curve or the backhand play in the hole. I came to find out where I'm from'" (Finnigan 1994). After his return to the States following his stint playing Dominican baseball, Rodriguez made numerous comments mentioning his discomfort living in the DR and feeling like an outsider there. While this experience is commonly shared among US-born Dominicans who return to the DR—including my interviewees Diego, Ciel, Leta, and Carmen—most Dominicans who live in the US use their visits to reconnect with their cultural heritage. They often acknowledge their insecurities around belonging but still express the importance of the return visits. Similarly, some US-born Dominicans believe that Rodriguez's aversion to being on the island is a missed opportunity to explore his cultural roots, which makes him a cultural "traitor." Some Dominicans in the US share ESENDOM.com's (2017) position that "Major League Baseball has never had a baseball player with the talent of Alex Rodriguez. Rather than judging him over every minor thing he does, Dominicans should celebrate the storied career of this prolific Dominican athlete." Yet others reject what they see as blind identity politics. They refuse to support someone just because their parents are from the same country and believe Rodriguez abandoned his dominicanidad for US success.

An example of the rhetoric surrounding Rodriguez's public image can be seen in the comments section of a 2011 Diva-dirt.com piece on his relationship with World Wrestling Entertainment star Torrie Wilson (Melanie 2011). The remarks ran the gamut of audience interpretations of Rodriguez's star text, some of them very similar to the ones I have mentioned here: "As a Yankees fan I have to ask... WHY A-ROD WHY?!?!? Stop dating and get ready for spring training so the Yanks can win their 28th World Series"; "I thought A-Rod's job was to end the Yankees season by striking out, like he has the last two years :)"; "I have a pretty major loathing for A-Hole, um, I mean A-Rod," and "Eww, A-Rod is gross. He looks like The Situation." One exchange between two commenters, one of whom was not familiar with A-Rod, covered his "ladies' man" image, with a post that asked, "I don't keep up with baseball at all so can anyone tell me what did the guy do to be considered a douche?" Another poster replied that "he cheated on his then wife with a couple of women and Madonna." If the discussion had ended there, this thread would not have stood out among the many I read. However, this particular thread directly referred Rodriguez's Dominican heritage as well as the Dominican-ness of two of the discussion participants. The first of these comments reflects a simple recognition of Rodriguez's Dominican heritage: "I don't like A-Rod even though we're both Dominicans, lol. Torrie is to [sic] good for him but if she's happy, I'm happy." However, it is the second comment that not only reinforces my claim that the US Dominican community believe Rodriguez has distanced himself from them but also shows that many Dominicans view this move as a betrayal: "I'm Dominican as well, and I'm not [a] big fan of A-Rod either ever since that controversy where it looked like he denied being Dominican." Rodriguez is seen as failing on multiple fronts; he is a failure at being Dominican enough, being a good enough baseball player, and sustaining the expectations of the sports hero.

Dominican Music Celebrities: A More "Authentic" Representation of Dominicanidad?

It may seem like media figures of Dominican heritage are being criticized on all fronts, and that is not entirely incorrect. Success in the US often facilitates, if not demands, a degree of acculturation into dominant norms—norms defined by notions of whiteness and middle-class status. People marked by ethnicity in the public eye must conform to perceived US norms while also being excluded from whiteness (Negra 2001). Similarly, by making concessions to US normativity, media figures are seen as overly Americanized to "authentically" represent their ethnic communities. Stuck in a sort of limbo, these celebrities are not considered to be true representatives of the communities they came from; neither can they fully assimilate into dominant white society. After examining the star texts of both Zoe Saldana and Alex Rodriguez, I ask what might seem like an obvious question: Is there a scenario in which a person of Dominican heritage in mainstream culture might obtain the approval of the Dominican community in the US?

This type of no-win framing, however, does not reflect how texts are negotiated. It is far more nuanced and complicated than merely assuming that one must fit into either the "American" or "Dominican" category. Even though we often think in binaries, that does not mean we are unable to think outside that paradigm. Elements such as hybridity and crossover success can allow for the cultural retention and respect for heritage that is demanded from the ethnic community while still allowing for mainstream and commercial acclaim in US culture. As exemplified by the cases of Zoe Saldana and Alex Rodriguez, this is a difficult situation to maneuver, and many, if not most, fail. My interviewees suggested that those figures of Dominican heritage who successfully balance mainstream success and Dominican authenticity are in the creative fields of music and literature, as well as many recently emerging Dominican politicians and advocates. According to my participants, these people have achieved mainstream success while maintaining respect and visibility for their Dominican roots. Dominicans in the US find it easier to relate to these celebrities than to those who become famous in US media but struggle to maintain an unproblematic image of dominicanidad.

Accustomed to looking for the smallest moments of identification in media, Carmen told me that "there are a lot more representations of Dominicans in music, in general. And, in particular, rap songs mention Dominicans a lot. Generally in terms of them being there, part of the environment." Whether it is rapper Jay-Z discussing his "Dominican homeboys" in NYC, or Dominicans singing about the streets of Washington Heights, the Dominican presence in the music industry is much more visible and diversified than in other types of media. Furthermore, these musical representations of Dominicans and dominicanidad are received more favorably by those I interviewed. Many interviewees believe that Dominican musicians do a better job of representing them and conveying the Dominican experience in the US. Junior, a college student I spoke with, told me that he would like to introduce Dominicans and their culture to the mainstream US through Dominican music: "More people just need to be informed about Dominicans. I would introduce Dominicans to mainstream US through music first, like bachata and Romeo, more mainstream crossover music like Aventura. They represent Dominican-American identity to me."[18] For Junior, dominicanidad was fundamentally linguistic. Because there is such physical variety among Dominicans, speaking Dominican Spanish confirmed that they were Dominican. It makes sense, therefore, that a fundamentally linguistic medium would better represent dominicanidad.

When Junior mentions Dominican-American identity, he is referring to the generational and transnational/diasporic construct of the "hyphen." Unlike Ramona Hernández and Utku Sezgin's (2010) findings, which detail how US-born Dominicans tended to hyphenate their identities (e.g., Irish-American, German-American, Mexican-American), my interviewees were resistant—or at least ambivalent—toward hyphenated articulations of self. (This complex relationship with the Dominican American subjectivity is further explored in the conclusion of this book.) However, while they avoided the hyphen within their personal negotiations of dominicanidad, they used it readily to describe their cultural experiences. In contrast to Juan Flores's (2000) view of Puerto Ricans in the US, whose ambiguous status as neocolonial US citizens means they live their lives "off the hyphen," the Dominican experience of the hyphen is more similar to that of Cuban-Americans. It is important to note that the Dominican experience is more broadly distinct from that of Cubans. Not only have Cubans been given a privileged position among Latinx groups because of their refugee status, they have also been politically racialized as white (regardless of the fact of significant Cuban African descent). This reinforces intra-Latinx horizontal hierarchies of race and language that would place Dominicans at the bottom (Aparicio 2019). In contrast to Cuba, Dominicans can travel freely to and from the DR and communicate with those on the island, sustaining a transnational positionality. Gustavo Pérez Firmat's (1994) scholarship on Cuban American hyphenated identity, however, helps elucidate the functions of authenticity diasporically. Particularly salient in the Dominican context is his notion of an "elastic" culture where "a sane biculturalism may consist in alternating cultures, rather than in trying to fuse them" (1994, 125). To be both "Dominican" and "American" at the same time provokes a reality where, "instead of being assigned separate roles, the two cultures rub together, creating friction" (1994, 130). But these are productive frictions, ones that become internalized, negotiated, and translated into what the Dominican-American experience is and the culture it fosters. Various relationships to the hyphen can be further understood through what Valdivia (2004, 2010, 2020) refers to as "radical hybridity." This theoretical framework positions Latinx hybridity as a space for negotiated subjectivity, identity, and culture. Just as the hyphen produces frictions, "Latina/o identity, as a hybrid form within US culture, remaps dominant hierarchies of identity and challenges popular notions of place and nation" (Molina-Guzmán and Valdivia 2004, 214). Those celebrities of Dominican heritage who can straddle the hyphen—those who can move fluidly from one side to the other—have been more successful at sustaining a shared sense of dominicanidad with Dominicans in the US (and often in the DR).

According to my interviewees in NYC and my internet reception research, among the most popular, successful, and discussed Dominican musical artists are the bachata/R&B/pop singer Prince Royce (Geoffrey Royce Rojas) and the bachata/R&B/hip-hop hybrid group Aventura (consisting of Anthony "Romeo" Santos, Henry Santos, Lenny Santos, and Max Santos). According to music enthusiast Diego, "Aventura paved the way" for Prince Royce to become "the voice of this generation of Dominican-Americans."[19] Diego told me he was comfortable in his hybrid/hyphenated identity and cultural heritage. He felt understood through the fusion of Dominican and US music styles, and the Dominican-American musicians who played such music. In the context of Prince Royce's and Aventura's abilities to seemingly shoulder the burden of representation among Dominicans in the US in a way that most feel is authentic to dominicanidad while also serving as models for success in the US, I conclude this chapter with a brief discussion of each.

In 2010, *Billboard* published a piece on Aventura and their success among Dominicans, Spanish-language music fans, and mainstream US fans: "[By] infusing its music with an urban sensibility—both visual and aural—Aventura connected not only with the music's hardcore fans, but also with a new generation of listeners that identified with the group's bilingual, bicultural makeup. This would prove to be a crucial factor in the act's continued expansion as it became attractive to both mainstream Latin media and mainstream media overall." The group's main musical genre, bachata, like much of Caribbean music, has historically not been popular in the US among Spanish speakers and non-Spanish speakers alike. However, the group's hybrid sound and style—what *Billboard* (2010) problematically refers to as its "bicultural makeup"—made them a standout in the industry. While bachata, merengue, and salsa are very popular among Dominicans and other Latino Caribbeans in the US, Caribbean music is followed mainly by this niche market, especially among older people and new immigrants. Aventura, by mixing bachata with styles popular in US urban music, has carved out a larger audience and fan base. Formed by the sons of Dominican immigrants, the group exemplifies the hyphenated reality of Dominicans living in the US while also appealing to a more mainstream market.

A 2011 National Public Radio (NPR) interview with group member Romeo Santos highlighted what makes Aventura successful as musicians and also able to speak to Dominicans in the US who have experienced exclusion from US culture. Santos tells NPR, "When we started Aventura, I think a lot of the reason why we became so successful besides, you know, doing good music, was also the fact that it was unique and different and never done. So this is what I compare this to: I've never seen something like this done before. And when I see movies and Dominican characters, they're not really Dominicans! I know what Dominicans sound like. I know their accent, I know their words, and they never get it. And now we have the opportunity to do it, and do it right." The members of Aventura seem to understand the US Dominican community's desire to see the group depicted and represented in a relatable way. In the NPR feature that called member Romeo Santos "the hottest artist on the Latin charts right now," Jasmine Garsd (2011) praised the group: "Aventura has sold 4 million records in the US and sold out Madison Square Garden in New York City several times. He may not be a household name among non-Hispanics yet, but Santos is determined to change that. His debut solo album, *Formula Volume 1*, aims to cross over into the English-language market and spread his brand of bachata to the masses." This self-identified Dominican-American group has developed a large and diverse fan base and achieved a level of crossover mainstream success that few other Dominican celebrities have.

This piece sparked a revealing discussion on NPR.org, a reputable mainstream media site. Posters not only talked about the band and how the Dominican musicians were covered in the piece but also engaged in discourses of dominicanidad. Moreover, some of the posts were in Spanish, the only instance of non-English comments I found on an English-only website. One poster demonstrated their support, saying, "Congratulations maestro Romeo! . . . congratulations to the people of the island, its rich culture, its good vibes. I discovered bachata music two years ago in a pizzeria in New York (the owners were Greek and French, I tell you!) From the first moment: wow! I live in the U.S. and Mexico and I always have my bachata music with me. Hooray bachata!" (Garsd 2011).[20] This participant does not identify as Dominican in the post, but their choice to comment in Spanish reveals a level of cultural solidarity that is both political and visual. It signifies that the members of Aventura have a level of cultural authenticity. Another form of cultural recognition came from a participant who is clearly a bachata fan: "Like a musicologist, Romeo seems to be preserving their natural voices for history. JLG, Aventura, Joan Soriano, el Mayimbe, Romeo and many others represent artists on a continuum named Bachata that's slowly been gaining recognition in mainstream circles. Let's respect their hard-won uniqueness" (2011). Many others shared their admiration for the group and identified themselves as fans.

However, among the praise came criticism similar to that faced by the other celebrities of Dominican heritage discussed in this chapter. One poster complained, "I really think the popularity of Santos right now is merely due to the similarity between his rhythm tracks and a lot of Mexican pop styles that have been around for a long time. That, and also the gimmicky new dance they've come up for it for the people in clubs who can't dance salsa" (Garsd 2011). Another poster said, "This report forgot to mention the artist who truly crossover the 'bachata' genre before Romero Santos, even if it was more of a pop version of this musical style. This artist is Juan Luis Guerra whose album 'Bachata Rosa' . . . was a huge hit all over the world in 1990!" (2011). These comments sound similar to the disavowals aimed at celebrities who are viewed as poor representatives of their Dominican roots. This discontent could be attributed to the sentiment "you can't please everybody." However, I argue that the negative comments reflect just how tenuous and difficult it is to manage the burden of representing dominicanidad.

Prince Royce received much less criticism in online discussions and is in many ways the darling of the industry—and Latina.com. Born on May 11, 1989, in the US to Dominican parents, Royce epitomizes the hybrid experience of Dominicans in the US. A native of the South Bronx, he has said, "I can't tell you if I'm Latino or if I'm American. I'm both. I speak Spanish just as much as I speak English and I write English just as much as I write Spanish" (quoted in Levin 2013). Breaking into mainstream Latin pop in 2010 with his bilingual cover of "Stand by Me," Royce had released three albums before his first all-English-language album in 2015 and came out with two hybrid albums following that. Epitomizing a life lived on the hyphen, Royce has made a name for himself and continues to receive acclaim from Dominicans and non-Dominicans alike.

He has a strong presence in Spanish-language media, mostly thanks to his role as a coach on the Spanish-language version of *The Voice*, *La Voz Kids*. Royce has also gained mainstream success, even performing a duet with one of the finalists on *The X-Factor*. Of that performance, Latina.com posted, "The Dominican superstar teamed up with Olivero in one

Fig. 2.5 Prince Royce being interviewed about his album *Alter Ego* in 2020. Tony Dandrades, CC BY 3.0, https://creativecommons.org/licenses/by/3.0, Wikimedia Commons.

of his final performances on the show Wednesday night. The final three contestants—Olivero, Alex and Sierra, and Jeff Gutt—all performed duets with pop stars in their genre. For Olivero, it seemed like an obvious choice to team up with Prince Royce, the bachatero he's often compared to" (Arreola 2013). Royce's voice and musical style have found a way to speak to the millions of Dominicans living in the US in ways that have alluded most others. According to Royce, his "music has attracted a lot of kids like [him], born and raised in the US, who still enjoy their Latin roots" (quoted in Levin 2013). Royce's ability to speak to those Dominicans in the US who are overlooked and underrepresented shows how he has managed to navigate an environment that has been inhospitable to other notable Dominican public figures.

Much like Aventura, Royce's music is a hybrid of Dominican bachata and US genres of hip-hop, funk, and R&B. He has said of his music, "It's very funky, going back to James Brown and Earth Wind and Fire with bachata. I definitely got creative while still keeping it commercial and down to the roots I really love" (quoted in Levin 2013). His brand of musical fusion has made him a breakout star in both the Spanish-language and mainstream music industries. By the age of twenty-five, he had already won numerous awards, performed with artists such as Enrique Iglesias and Pitbull, and recorded collaborations with Mana, Daddy Yankee, Selena

Gomez, and Thalia.[21] He has toured multiple times in the US and Latin America and has sold out venues like Radio City Music Hall in NYC and the Peacock Theater (formerly Nokia Theater) in Los Angeles.

Royce's most distinctive quality is his relatability to fans who believe they have a shared sense of not only dominicanidad but also the US Dominican experience. One fan told the *Miami Herald* that she "feels a connection with Royce and pride at his success. His parents are Dominican, he's from New York—it's my story. I had a customer the other day who said, 'Where are you from?' and I said, 'Dominican Republic,' and he said, 'Oh, like Prince Royce'" (Levin 2013). Like so many other young Dominicans born in the US, Royce spent summers in the Dominican Republic and felt the intense desire to connect with his cultural roots, but he never quite felt like a "true" Dominican. In the same *Miami Herald* article, Royce discusses his time in the Dominican Republic: "'It was poor but not that bad—we had electricity, we had furniture,' Royce says. 'Instead of hip-hop, he heard bachata,' which has grown from a raw, rollicking country music to a more melodic, romantic style that has usurped merengue as the D.R.'s dominant music genre. 'Those are the songs that really make me think of the Dominican Republic,' he says. 'Enjoying the natural things—the water, the beach, looking at trees. Getting bit by mosquitoes'" (2013). Like many Dominicans who were born in the US but still feel highly connected to the island culture, Royce prioritizes balancing the two cultures in the hybrid and hyphenated fashion discussed by many of my interviewees.

Conclusion

Music celebrities likely function differently from other types of celebrities. Musical expression can induce a certain affected emotionality among audiences and can reach people through different avenues than other types of media. Regarding the power of live musical performance, Mark Duffett (2009, 41) contends that "the market economy supporting popular music facilitates and realizes something much broader and less tangible than itself: a 'symbolic economy' of cultural power in which stars manage the emotions of their audience." Yet I believe these latest Dominican celebrities of Prince Royce's generation are more concerned about maintaining their hyphenated identity while navigating the celebrity machine. Whether it is because musical stars like Aventura or Prince Royce feel less pressure to Americanize, are less focused on being successful in the US mainstream, or insist on achieving their goals on their own (Dominican) terms, they have accomplished something most Dominican celebrities have not: earning the respect of the US Dominican community while initiating the integration of Dominicans into mainstream US culture.

Zoe Saldana has faced challenges in her career, and the way she has dealt with them has left a bitter taste in the mouths of the US Dominican community. Saldana has struggled to remain a moving ethnoracialized target and has done so at the expense of the support of the US Dominican community. For Alex Rodriguez, his presumed failure to embody the values associated with sports celebrity, especially as part of the "All-American" (i.e., white normative) New York Yankees, has left him vulnerable to criticism from both Dominicans and non-Dominicans.

Most significantly, however, I propose that, due to entrenchment in binary notions of racialization as well as the homogenization of Latinx diversity, the US mainstream media is fundamentally ill-equipped to include articulations of dominicanidad. Preventing the seamless introduction of Dominican subjectivities to a mass mainstream audience are the ideological frameworks that constitute the meaning-making abilities of the media as a sociohistorical institution in the US. Through its contradiction with dominant US ethnoracial paradigms, dominicanidad can only be precariously placed within what is imagined as "American" and must consequently be diluted into a palatable form. However, the determination of the Dominican community in the US to demand their mediated acknowledgment is poised to challenge how race and ethnicity are understood in this country.

Notes

A section of this chapter was published in Goin 2017 as "Zoe Saldana or Zoë Saldaña?: Cinematic *dominicanidad* and the Hollywood Star."

1. Martin 1945.
2. For more on reception among marginalized communities, see Bobo 1995; Rojas 2007; Báez 2018.
3. Clara E. Rodriguez (1997) argues that US media has relied on a "Latin Look, which positions Latina/os as in between the poles of whiteness and blackness while at the same time prioritizing those features seen as European in origin."
4. Ella Shohat and Robert Stam (1994, 6) argue, "Rather than speaking of cultural/racial groups in isolation, we speak of them 'in relation,' without ever suggesting that their positionings are identical. Rather than pitting a rotating chain of oppositional communities against a White European dominant (a strategy that privileges Whiteness if only as constant antagonist), we stress the horizontal and vertical links threading communities together in a conflictual network. Rather than recreating neat binarisms (Black/White, Native American/White) that ironically recenter Whiteness, while the 'rest' who fit only awkwardly into such neat categories stand by as mere spectators, we try to address overlapping multiplicities of identity and affiliation."

5. As discussed later in this chapter, Saldana's name is spelled inconsistently. "Saldaña" is used on her IMDb.com (Internet Movie Database) page and most frequently in her professional life. I use the unaccented spelling "Zoe Saldana" throughout the book to remain neutral on imposing a subjectivity onto her. I do, however, acknowledge that this decision is not entirely politically neutral and can be read as potentially problematic.

6. Dyer ([1979] 1998, 20) argues that characters played by stars and celebrities often have the most influence on how audiences interpret the star text: "The roles and/or the performance of a star in a film were taken as revealing the personality of the star."

7. Interview conducted on June 10, 2013, with a US-born woman in her mid-twenties.

8. Interview conducted on June 7, 2013, with a Dominican-born US citizen in her mid-twenties.

9. Interview conducted on July 10, 2013, with a US-born Dominican-American in her late twenties.

10. Interview conducted on June 6, 2013, with a Dominican-born US citizen in his early thirties.

11. Interview conducted on June 11, 2013, with a twenty-one-year-old US-born woman.

12. Interview conducted on June 11, 2013, with a US-born man in his late twenties.

13. Interview conducted on June 6, 2013, with a US-born Dominican-American in his early twenties.

14. Interview conducted on July 18, 2013, with a US-born woman in her early twenties.

15. Quoted in Hernandez 2013.

16. According to *Shadow and Act* (2014) the film was "in development for at least 5 years, Mary J. Blige was initially attached to star in the film, but she was eventually replaced by Saldana who brought more international box office gravitas to the production."

17. Quoted in Hernandez 2013.

18. Interview conducted on June 7, 2013, with a US-born man in his late twenties.

19. Interview conducted on July 11, 2013, with a DR-born but US-raised man in his late twenties.

20. Author's translation from the original Spanish.

21. Royce has received 16 Billboard Latin Music Awards, 13 Premio Lo Nuestros, 17 Youth Awards, 3 Latin Grammy nominations, silver and gold torches at the Festival of Viña del Mar, Billboard's Composer of the Year award, and, at the age of 22, Royce became the youngest recipient of Broadcast Music Inc's Latin Songwriter of the year (PR Newswire.com 2013).

3

TELEVISUAL DOMINICANIDAD AND MTV'S *WASHINGTON HEIGHTS*

"You are not showing the real Washington Heights. What is this community? This is just 6 people who could be anyone. What, just because they are Dominican it is representative of the Heights? This show had no legitimacy. Not really of the Heights, about the Heights. This is not representative of my community and I do not want it to be representative of my community."
—From an interview with Dania.

By the time my interviewee, Dania, shared her opinion of MTV's reality show *Washington Heights* (2013), I had already heard similar sentiments from many of my Dominican/Dominican-American interviewees. Dania spent her summers in New York City (NYC) and was typically critical of a monolithic representation of dominicanidad. Although she was not from Washington Heights, she was astutely aware of how that neighborhood was conceptualized as the heart of Dominican America. As my interviews were conducted soon after the season finale of the show and before it was canceled for low ratings, MTV's new take on its tried-and-true reality TV formula was fresh on the minds of Dominicans living in NYC. After establishing itself as an industrial leader in teenage and early adult reality television, starting in 1992 with *The Real World*, MTV seemed to find more success with its reality TV series than its original content platform of music videos. The network has become more skilled at creating reality programs that both are popular among audiences and influence US popular culture. MTV has formulated a certain reality brand, one that follows certain industrial conventions and adheres to a handful of narrative and production styles that can be recognized in each new series. While each new iteration of this MTV reality brand is not necessarily identical to the others, certain elements emerge when viewing the series as a canon. Therefore, for MTV, *Washington Heights* is just another example of exploiting an established formula with a new set of players. The Dominicans of Washington Heights, NYC, are merely a substitution in a perfected recipe that turned out to be a bad batch for the network. But Dominicans in the US do not see this as just another reworking of a proven MTV reality formula that happened to fail. For those who would align themselves with the cast of this show, Dominicans living in the US, much more was at stake than ratings.

In this chapter, I draw from interviews and online reception data to analyze the reception of MTV's *Washington Heights* as not only the first mainstream Dominican-centric media text but also as an inroad to active negotiations concerning the nature of dominicanidad. Tied to both the constructed MTV brand and the functions of reality television more broadly, *Washington Heights* is positioned within a complicated vector of identification. Like many of the shows in MTV's reality oeuvre, *Washington Heights* follows the lives of a group of early twenty-somethings who are more or less friends. The show depicts various segments of each cast member's life, including romantic tensions and "hookups," legal troubles, familial relationships, social gatherings, and the drama of everyday life—all against the backdrop of NYC. What makes *Washington Heights* stand out from other, similar reality shows is that its cast is almost exclusively made up of self-identified Dominican-Americans, with only one member of non-Dominican heritage. Like *Jersey Shore* (2009–12) and *Buckwild* (2013), *Washington Heights* capitalizes on the cast's marked cultural difference to create a narrative of Otherness through ethnoracial spectacle. Audiences are, quite purposefully, meant to interpret the cast and series' narrative within a framework of how MTV defines dominicanidad. But the show was canceled after only one season because its focus on Dominican-ness did not attract enough viewers for MTV to renew it for a second season.

Reality TV claims to be unscripted, so most audiences consider it a more "true" or unfiltered reflection of people's lives than scripted television. Put another way, shows categorized as "reality" do not have the safety net of a nonreal script. A script implies an authorial intervention, a premeditated narrative, a representation of the unreal—even if it is similar, or nearly identical, to the real world audiences inhabit. Authenticity, then, becomes central to how an audience interprets reality TV narratives, characters/figures, and representations. The fact that *Washington Heights* is a reality series increases Dominicans' scrutiny and expectations of its representations of dominicanidad. To investigate negotiations of "authenticity" that framed the reception of the show by Dominican audiences, this chapter addresses the questions: What types of discourses appear in the NYC Dominican reception of MTV's *Washington Heights*, and how did they interpret the show's attempt at televisual dominicanidad? What industrial constraints framed the show as produced, and how might we understand the program in relation to the broader MTV reality television canon?

This chapter looks at *Washington Heights* as part of MTV reality branding more broadly and responds to MTV scholar Amanda Klein's (2013) call to critically examine MTV programming: "So a poetics of MTV is, simply, an engagement with American identities as they [are] constructed, deconstructed and reconstructed.... It is our challenge to watch these programs and parse through the identity politics they present . . . MTV is doing what it has always done—it is filling a gap, in this case, our desire to figure out what identity means in a society that really wants to believe it is post-identity." Connecting the literature on reality television (Andrejevic 2002; Holmes and Jermyn 2004; Kraszewski 2010b; Ouellette 2010; Curnutt 2013; Klein 2013, 2021) with the work by popular cultural critics and contextualizing both through my interviews and critical and textual analyses of the show, I argue that *Washington Heights* was unable to find a large audience because it did not resonate with mainstream audiences and, more critically, many Dominican ones. My interviewees expressed many opinions about the show. Some were happy to see a show that featured Dominicans; others scrutinized every aspect for relatable moments. Yet the show was a disappointment to most of the Dominican community in the US because its portrayal of dominicanidad televisually and discursively was so diluted, it was unrecognizable to Dominicans/Dominican-Americans and failed to adequately represent their culture. MTV's primary audience was not interested in the lifestyle show of working-class Dominican-Americans; Dominican-Americans resented the exclusion of cultural markers and spoken Spanish; and most audiences (regardless of ethnic affiliation) found it hard to identify with *Washington Heights*' cast.

MTV, Reality TV, and the Spectacle of Otherness

As a principal network on the cable channel lineup, MTV has always been credited with innovative programming and the ability to redefine what is understood as television. First hitting the airwaves in the early 1980s, MTV has been *the* channel of Generation X and millennials. Even after abandoning its original format—music videos and other music-centric programming—MTV remains an important cultural broker in the US. Regardless of the network's shifts in programming, processes of rebranding, and attempts to stay relevant as new generations demand evolving types of media engagement, MTV has proven that "as time passed what had once been the pre-eminent medium for the broadcast of music videos became the pre-eminent medium for reality TV" (Jones 2005, 86). MTV began its foray into reality programming with *The Real World* in 1992, followed by *Road Rules* (1995–2007), a traveling version of the same format. As the signatures of the MTV reality canon, these series defined the MTV brand over the years and set the mold for most of the network's reality programs. It was not until *Laguna Beach* (2004–6) that the network's reality production style expanded to include more cinematic and highly stylized aesthetics. These two styles, one rooted in *The Real World* and the other in *Laguna Beach*, have supported MTV's reality brand that focuses on youth culture, vicarious lifestyles, and spectacles that depend on the casting of "normal" people placed in situations and environments that are connoted as societally, culturally, and/or unnaturally "abnormal."

MTV Reality Branding and Identity Production

Like any television genre, reality TV is susceptible to commodification and replication through the practices of branding. MTV has gone through several stages of rebranding over its four-decade history. From a programming schedule consisting entirely of music videos (yet only those that were in the rock genre and heavily white-centric), to exploiting the hip-hop generation, to reducing music-based programming for a wide range of youth-oriented programming, to the reality TV juggernaut it is today, each decade marked for MTV a rehabilitation and rebranding of its core programming. While the 1990s saw the MTV reality brand exemplified by *The Real World*, *Road Rules*, and those shows' various challenge and reunion spinoffs, the 2000s ushered in new shows with new themes operating within evolving political and cultural logics. Regardless of the decade, "the channel's mission is to define, brand, and sell youth culture to youth audiences. Although many different kinds of audiences have watched MTV over the last four decades, MTV's notion of 'youth' is limited by its own notions of its target audience: white, suburban Americans, of the ages twelve to thirty-four" (Klein 2021, 24). As it is currently branded, MTV produces shows that are issue-oriented in a way that highlights notions of difference without acknowledging the underlying systems that create these notions of difference. It also fails to encourage the kind of political debate that would make each new series feel less like a minority/marginalized flavor of the month—this month, Italian Americans; last month, rural Southerners; and next month, urban Dominicans in NYC.

Klein repeatedly contends that part of MTV's reality TV branding is its role as a broker of televisual identity. She has studied many MTV reality shows, examining each new addition to the MTV reality canon and noting how each contributes to the network's function as a platform of mediated identity construction. MTV not only creates programming for and about teenagers and young adults but also aims to focus on demographics of the youth population that seldom appear on television screens—and by doing so, to manufacture a sense of newness within a genre often criticized for its repetition. Klein (2013) suggests that "cast members of MTV's most highly rated reality shows (*Jersey Shore*, *Teen Mom*, *The Hills*, *The Real World*, and now *Buckwild*) willingly serve as synecdoches for their ethnic groups, their subculture, their class, their gender, their sexuality, their religion, or their region of the U.S." The participants on these shows are not only self-presenting their individual identities but also representing whichever group the show is exploiting. Although it might not have been MTV's intention, the network has paved the way for televisual dominicanidad by including *Washington Heights* in its roster of reality programs.

The MTV reality format has conditioned the youth audience, instructing them to be extremely self-aware and showing them that a key part of participating in the contemporary world is being able to verbally and visually articulate their identity. As US youth become increasingly engaged with new and evolving media technologies, the presentation of self becomes second nature. Any Millennial or Zoomer (member of Generation Z) can easily share how they conceive of themselves or create a social media profile. These generations have grown up with social media, reality show confessionals, and neoliberal individualism. Klein (2013) suggests that MTV has created a "new poetics of being-in-the-world," and that for youth audiences, MTV is "an identity workbook . . . that offered youth audiences . . . different ways to be and exist in an increasingly identity-focused world" (Klein 2021, 55). The network's reality programming allows participants to explore how they express and perform their identities as audiences concurrently negotiate against and along those televisual identities. Essentially, "the difference between the MTV of 1981 and the MTV of today is not simply the difference between music videos and reality TV—the difference is in the way MTV conceives of youth selfhood" (Klein, 2013). I would add that not only has MTV's conception of youth selfhood evolved over the years but this evolution is directly tied to its process of (re)branding. *Washington Heights*, with its cast of Dominican-American millennials, adheres to the constraints of the MTV reality brand of the 2010s.

Regardless of the era, one of MTV's central tenets is an overt identity project. And as Klein (2021, 9–10) attests, the network's reality TV offers "the fantasy of identity construction by creating pathways for understanding what it means to self-define or be defined, and what this process looks like on TV." However, part of this identity project is a simultaneous acknowledgment and disavowal of distinctive identity. On one hand, MTV makes visible a diverse range of identities; on the other hand, it then homogenizes them within concepts of postrace, postgender, postsexuality, and so on. The network focuses on creating identity for profit but overlooks how embracing these diverse identities could empower certain demographics by connecting with reality show participants. Those marginalized groups that are seldom represented in mainstream media (e.g., Dominicans) might have the rare opportunity to identify with televisual representations that resonate with them. Instead, to attract the largest mainstream audience possible, the representations of difference are diluted through the filter of the MTV reality formula to support the logic that, again, "we are all really the same." In 2014, Susanne Daniels, then head of MTV programming, substantiated this idea when she told *The Hollywood Reporter*'s Lacey Rose (2014), "My inclination is to cast as diverse and multiethnic as possible . . . I could see shows with African-American leads, Latino leads, Asian leads; ensembles that reflect the rainbow." Even as she acknowledges difference, Daniels places difference within the postracial discourses that celebrate the rainbow of multicultural America while simultaneously obscuring the reality of living life as an Other in a society still entrenched in white supremacy and normativity.

The televisual components of these shows—soundtrack, editing, cinematography, and so on—serve to instruct audiences how they should be interpreting the cast members. Although still adhering to formulaic narratives and aesthetics, "in most of MTV's reality series the aesthetics of each show condition the viewer's reception, inviting them to see each program's performance of identity as being tied to specific notions of taste and cultural capital" (Klein 2021, 137). MTV reality programming signifies difference through distinct production aesthetics that entice audiences to engage in identification, on the one hand, or a lack of identification on the other. Furthermore, many factors in MTV's reality programming compel audiences to disavow reality participants on certain shows by portraying them as clowns, buffoons, or idiots whom we should laugh at and mock. Instead of casting ordinary people who could be anybody, as MTV has done with *The Real World* and *Road Rules*, these other types of shows feature personalities who are so extreme that nobody could identify with them. To create fresh and original programming but still mitigate financial risk, "amid the terminal creativity, 'big characters' in 'worlds we haven't seen' has become the reality-TV programmer's mantra to producers" (Wallace 2013). These shows exploit a certain spectacle of Otherness, so before discussing *Washington Heights*, it is helpful to look at some other series that inform and engage with it.

MTV Reality TV as a Spectacle of Containment

The proliferation of reality TV in the contemporary televisual landscape not only is substantiated by impressive ratings but also is cost-effective for networks that would rather recycle proven and cheaply produced reality programming than risk the financial failure of a narrative series. The industry is obviously infatuated with reality TV, and in the highly competitive multiplatform, multinetwork, multimedia world, "the accelerated importance of the [reality TV] format is clearly also shaped by the 'risk-adverse' broadcast environment—the desire to minimise risk in the face of increasing competition" (Holmes and Jermyn 2004, 14). As a result, the television industry believes that reality programming has relatively low financial risk but can lead to a large payoff.

Although reality series may be lucrative, they are often associated with cultural deficit. Television, in and of itself, has historically been understood as a low-brow medium, and reality TV even more so. Programs such as *Here Comes Honey Boo Boo* (TLC 2012–14) and the Real Housewives franchise (Bravo 2006–present) might be popular, but they are also referred to as "trash TV." Moreover, these formats are copied, replicated, and reworked across different networks and media landscapes. Cultural critic Benjamin Wallace (2013) discusses this type of recycling and hypersaturation of the reality TV form, assessing that "if reality TV is an extractive industry, relentlessly depleting our cultural patrimony (geographic character, obscure vocations, piquant subcultures, sui generis personalities, human beings who don't conceive of themselves as corporate brands) for our amusement, it long ago exhausted the surface-minable goods. Thus the endless recycling of tropes (grab bag of sub-functional dead-enders thrown together in a McMansion, etc.), cast members (via spinoff shows, all-star shows), and people." Critics and audiences complain about the rehashing of formulaic programs that glorify "normal" people who often behave in ways we find deplorable, negative, desperate, and exploitative. Yet audiences still watch these (mostly) everyday people in often unextraordinary circumstances.

While MTV reality programs are not completely identical to one another, there does seem to be a large degree of carryover in terms of style, format, and theme. As a result, MTV's reality development strategy has been to recycle formats and recast the players from different US demographic groups or move the setting to locations they have not yet used. The basic formulas remain the same; they are slightly modified to seem original or, at the very least, not a complete reproduction of previous series. MTV has operated under the assumption that if *The Real World* is a proven formula, then shifting the setting by putting a cast of strangers on the road in a Winnebago will also be a success. And if *Jersey Shore* is a ratings smash hit, then replacing Italian Americans living in New Jersey with rural Southerners living in West Virginia in *Buckwild* should draw a similar audience.

Borrowing from Shari Roberts's (1993) conceptualization of a "spectacle of containment," I contend that, by recycling these identity-of-the-month series, MTV is exploiting difference in a way that makes it visible while simultaneously discrediting it. These programs highlight eccentric, exaggerated, and over-the-top characters, yet through the show, their performances of selves are transformed into masquerades of their "real" identities. This type of representation operates similarly to what Roberts (1993, 15) identifies as a "spectacle of containment" in her description of the US Good Neighbor Policy–era Brazilian starlet Carmen Miranda. She asserts that "masquerade mimics a socially constructed identity in order to conceal, but at the same time to indicate, the absence that exists behind the mask and ultimately to discover the lack of any 'natural'" identity or essence. Figures like Carmen Miranda and, I argue, *Jersey Shore* stars Snooki and The Situation, embody an excess of Otherness and therefore present a parody of themselves (López 1991; Roberts 1993; Shohat and Stam 1994). Their exaggerated personas, in and of themselves, mock the tropes that they are self-presenting through.

A poetics of excessive Otherness has also been noted by scholars of the representations of Blackness within reality television. For Racquel Gates (2013), anxieties rooted in double consciousness and the politics of respectability often lead to rampant criticisms of many of the reality shows that feature Black female casts. While these shows are extremely popular, there is often a process of shaming that cast members must negotiate based on criticisms of their behavior and personalities that make "Black people look bad." Their Black femininity is exploited by the television industry along with a preoccupation "with reconditioning African Americans into a version of Blackness that is acceptable by mainstream standards" (2013, 153). These dual demands result in efforts to both include and contain Black women as spectacle. In her scholarship on the Bravo series *The Real Housewives of Atlanta* (2008–present), Kristen Warner (2011) cites how the figures on the show embody Black femininity in a way that is both "too much and not enough." The show is "at once too much racialized spectacle and not enough post-racial reality (read: the types in play speak too much to the clichéd representations of black women as loud, brash, sassy, and angry)." What has been colloquially referred to as being "ratchet," the Black women on shows like *The Real Housewives of Atlanta* perform moments of excess that "depends on them being viewed as spectacles that . . . must be watched" (Warner 2015, 133). And while both Gates and Warner discuss these shows in relation to their potential for identification among Black female audiences—who find pleasure in their spectatorship—Black women are not the only ones watching these shows. Other audiences, regardless of ethnic or racial identity, can also find pleasure in the spectacle of excess that these shows both exploit and attempt to contain.

Also useful in examining these programs that use Otherness as televisual spectacle is bell hooks's (1992) scholarship on the commodification of Otherness. She posits that the seduction of difference, what she refers to as "a bit of the Other," adds spice to a mainstream culture that is interpreted as bland and is used to "enhance the blank landscape of whiteness" (1992, 29). What was authentically unique and different about the Other is consumed through its appropriation, which works as a destructive force that "not only displaces the Other but denies the significance of the Other's history through a process of decontextualization" (1992, 31). The world of the Other becomes a playground for white mainstream society where they can indulge in a reality that is exciting, intense, and threatening all at the same time. The combination of pleasure and danger that constitutes the represented world of the Other opens up a space for exploration among a generation of white youth who are in a constant process of identity construction and articulation. Series like *Jersey Shore*, *Buckwild*, and *Washington Heights* use the Other as source material to add variety to proven reality formats.

For much of MTV's reality programming, "location breeds identity" (Klein 2013). A trend established by shows like *Laguna Beach* and *Jersey*

Shore highlights the new direction of MTV reality programming by focusing on a location-based representation of identity—Laguna Beach becomes the epicenter of white affluent femininity, and the Jersey Shore is the home of the Italian American "guido." However, the affluent white women of *Laguna Beach* and *The Hills* are not presented as the same type of spectacle as are the casts of *Jersey Shore*, *Buckwild*, and, sometimes, *Washington Heights*. Klein (2013) explains, "The *Jersey Shore* cast members actively and self-consciously construct 'guido' identities for themselves while those on *Buckwild* tell MTV's cameras what it means to be 'country.'" This leads to the question: Aside from the off-whiteness (Negra 2001) associated with each cast, how is MTV turning *Jersey Shore* and *Buckwild* into spectacles of Otherness within its parameters of reality programming and branding?

Jersey Shore was not only a ratings hit for MTV but also a pop culture phenomenon. Loved by fans, hated and degraded by critics, *Jersey Shore* was similar to the numerous MTV reality programs that came before it: Take a group of twenty-something strangers, make them live together in a swanky house, and watch the drinking and fighting ensue. However, with *Jersey Shore*, MTV added a new ingredient to the formula: eccentric and exaggerated Italian American ethnicity.

Season one's cast consisted of eight self-identified "guidettes" and "guidos" who shared a house in the Jersey Shore town of Seaside Heights. 495 Productions' *Jersey Shore* filmed four of its six seasons on the Jersey Shore, with a season each in Miami and Italy. The cameras followed the cast members and documented their self-articulation of New Jersey–oriented "Italian-ness." Kraszewski (2010a) argues that the cast of *Jersey Shore* was "merely a bunch of Italian American stereotypes ripped from an understanding of historical ethnicities," which reinforced myths of white ethnic Otherness by suggesting that "Italian American identity can be reduced to blowouts, poofs, tans, and ripped bodies that look like Rambo's." From the very first episode, the cast members discuss with each other and the audience—through typical MTV confessional segments—how much they identify with their Italian American identity. A common Italian flag motif emblazes their clothes, phones, computers, and so on, and their weekly Sunday dinner together—which everyone was expected to attend, no matter how much they might be feuding at the time—all show how the series emphasizes an exaggerated Italian ethnic identity. The cast's performance of extreme ethnic Otherness is transformed into a spectacle of Otherness and a cartoonish masquerade, all of

Fig. 3.1 Cast of *Jersey Shore* (MTV 2009–12) drinking a toast during the fifth season of the show.

which create reality TV gold for MTV. On the one hand, audiences could take the show with a grain of salt and embrace it as "silly television . . . and by that measure, *Shore* is phenomenal," as *Entertainment Weekly*'s Tim Stack recommends (quoted in Kraszewski 2010a). Yet on the other hand, as Kraszewski (2010) explains, "Popular discourse surrounding *Jersey Shore* fixates on the cartoonish version of Italian American identity on the series; currently critics seem stuck on whether or not we should take pleasure in this cartoon." The show is ridiculed for depicting behavior that could reflect poorly on Italian Americans as a whole, yet it is this over-the-top behavior that draws the show's large audience.

Italian Americans and New Jersey have long been connected within the US popular imagination. Mobsters, wiseguys, greasers, and tough-broad Italian mothers have traditionally been represented as the bread and butter of New Jersey's Italian American population (Messina 2004; Giannino 2013). In *Jersey Shore*, the state of New Jersey and the excessive ethnicity of the cast members are conflated—New Jersey is portrayed as the home of the guidette/guido, an Italian American hothead whose primary interests in life are GTL (gym-tan-laundry), partying, and sleeping around. Public and critical outrage concerning how the show's cast might denigrate Italian Americans and foster "negative" stereotypes is not hard to find. While Italians/Italian Americans have long been stereotyped in US media, they are not necessarily underrepresented. Therefore, even though *Jersey Shore* might depict tropes of Italian American Otherness, it does not bear the same burden of representation as *Washington Heights*. For all the social criticism the series has faced, it never received enough opposition to mitigate its enormous ratings draw.

After *Jersey Shore*'s final season in 2012, MTV sought to replace it with something that could match its ratings. Along with a handful of *Jersey Shore* spinoffs—*The Pauly D Project* (2012), *Snooki & Jwoww* (2012–15), and *The Show with Vinny* (2013)—MTV greenlit reality series *Buckwild* and *Washington Heights* to air early in 2013. Hoping to reproduce the magic of *Jersey Shore*, *Buckwild* included an ensemble cast of young twenty-somethings partying, making mischief, and going "buckwild" in rural West Virginia. Instead of the boardwalks and clubs of the New Jersey Shore, the cast of *Buckwild* went "mudding," shooting, and engaged in general reckless, drunken behavior.[1] Zoo Productions sold the show to MTV as a "Redneck *Jersey Shore*." The producers, raised in West Virginia, imagined a series that "would follow a loose group of friends, and friends of friends, having the kind of cheap, resourceful fun they'd had themselves as kids. 'It was *Jersey Shore* meets *Jackass*,' says executive producer J. P. Williams, who grew up in nearby Morgantown" (Wallace 2013). Similar to the outrage *Jersey Shore* ignited, *Buckwild* received much media attention and ridicule for its depictions of rural America that aligned with the standing stereotypical tropes of the hillbilly, redneck, hick, and country bumpkin (Harkins 2005). Even before the show aired, "it got early buzz, after West Virginia senator Joe Manchin III, having apparently neglected to study how *Jersey Shore*'s critics had only helped power its success, called Buckwild 'a travesty' that trafficked in 'ugly, inaccurate stereotypes about the people of West Virginia'" (Wallace 2013). Furthermore, the show was, in fact, a hit. Even though it never reached *Jersey Shore* numbers, the network easily renewed it for a second season.

Taking over *Jersey Shore*'s vacated time slot, *Buckwild* recycled its format and fell right into place among MTV reality shows. The network's reality programming trades on spectacle, as "a significant function of MTV's reality identity series is, of course, to entertain audiences through the spectacularization of certain identities, turning them into displays of beautiful wealth (as is the case with *The Hills*) or into outlandish, comic figures" (Klein 2021, 127). Clearly defining much of MTV's formulaic reality programming, *Jersey Shore*, *Buckwild*, *Slednecks* (the network's follow-up to

Fig. 3.2 Cast of *Buckwild* (MTV 2012–13) "mudding."

Buckwild), and, in many ways, *Washington Heights*, exploit Otherness as a televisual spectacle, just in very different ways.

The Hills in the Heights or Quisqueya Shore?

MTV's show *Washington Heights* was the first mainstream television program to introduce Dominicans to a US mainstream audience that was fairly unfamiliar with this community. Gigantic! Productions creates "docuseries," including the NYC-centered *Washington Heights*, which premiered on January 9, 2013. The show follows the lives of axial figure JP (a.k.a Audubon) and his group of tight-knit friends. Reyna, Frankie, Ludwin, Jimmy, Rico, and Fred are all Dominican Americans who grew up together in Washington Heights. Taylor, the one white cast member, also grew up in the same neighborhood but serves as a figure of reverse tokenism among the otherwise all-Dominican cast. However, the real outsider in the group is Jimmy's girlfriend Eliza, who might be Dominican but grew up in New Jersey and not in "the Heights." The show's cocreator Beck Hickey stated, "We wanted to show a positive side to the neighborhood, and the people in it.... The neighborhood is beautiful and rich, but there are also these hardworking young adults with goals and aspirations" (quoted in Garcia 2013).

To Hickey's credit, the series did champion the struggles and successes of the cast and promoted neighborhood pride. However, this was done in a way that obscured the vibrancy of the neighborhood's Dominican culture in an attempt to produce an *American* success narrative.

The MTV audience was introduced to televisual dominicanidad in the first moments of the series when JP narrates, "These ain't the Hollywood Hills, these are the Heights. One of the last true neighborhoods left in Manhattan." With this statement, *Washington Heights* separates itself from the luxury and glamour of series like *The Hills* while at the same time inviting comparisons with those types of shows. Most importantly, it suggests that the representation of identity is largely unacknowledged; in *The Hills*, the backdrop of affluent whiteness is ever present but rarely mentioned, and in *Washington Heights*, Dominican-ness is immediately understood but then quickly subsumed into the repetitive association of being "from the Heights." Televisually, *Washington Heights* is more similar to shows like *The Hills* and *Laguna Beach*, but it also connects to the ethnic spectacle of containment seen in *Jersey Shore*.

Like most shows in a series, the first episode of *Washington Heights* served mainly as an introduction to the cast. It also established the narrative for each cast member, alluded to intragroup dynamics, and defined Washington Heights as a neighborhood. With JP's voice-over commentary structuring the flow of the episode, viewers were guided through the televisually defined neighborhood. Washington Heights became more than a location; it was portrayed as both the backdrop and the inspiration for the show's creatively inclined cast. Much of the discursive and televisual framing tries to explain what it means to be "from the Heights" in an almost mythical fashion.

Televisually, the neighborhood of Washington Heights is shown through sweeping outdoor establishing shots and brief appearances of landmarks that connote an NYC-centric theme rather than focusing on Dominican culture. The show portrays a city that is very familiar to the television landscape; this time, from the vantage point of the Uptown residents of Washington Heights. Quick shots of street signs, subway stops, and aerial views directed south toward the heart of Manhattan (instead of making midtown Manhattan the vantage point, as most films and TV shows do) tell the visual story of the neighborhood. The audience can visualize the neighborhood on a map of Manhattan (being shown the cross streets, the George Washington Bridge, and the subway stations), but little more is accomplished by these establishing shots (figs. 3.3–3.6). Aside from situating Washington Heights as an important neighborhood among the

Fig. 3.3 Shot of the 181st Street Subway Station.

Fig. 3.4 Vantage point shot centering the view from Washington Heights toward Midtown Manhattan.

countless enclaves in NYC, little in this footage explores or explains the Dominican presence.

The show then transitions to the story, with sweeping shots of the city and music centered on New York or Washington Heights (sometimes accompanied by untranslated/unsubtitled Spanish lyrics). But

Fig. 3.5 View of the George Washington Bridge connecting Washington Heights to New Jersey.

Fig. 3.6 Vantage point of the neighborhood pointing out the approximate area where each cast member supposedly lives.

these shots contain very few Dominican/Dominican-American cultural markers. They could be showing almost any working-class neighborhood in NYC. There are no storefronts displaying Dominican foods, products, or services; there are no billboards or signs in Spanish; and, apart from the occasional street sign that acknowledges certain intersections familiar to those who know Washington Heights, there is nothing in these shots that signals the Dominican-ness of this neighborhood. The only glimpses into the dominicanidad of the neighborhood are in the infrequent and brief—sometimes incredibly brief—flashes of the Dominican flag (fig. 3.7).

The virtual invisibility of dominicanidad televisually is reinforced by its discursive absence. While the majority of the show's cast self-identify and identify each other as "Dominican," this identification is never contextualized or explained. This suggests that being Dominican is similar to being part of almost any upwardly mobile immigrant group in a city filled with immigrant communities from almost every country. Instead of being represented in relation to the various experiences of the many ethnic enclaves in NYC and demonstrating what is unique about Dominican culture, this identification suggests that Washington Heights should be understood within the traditional NYC-centric immigrant narrative. In contrast to how my interviewees described the neighborhood—as a piece of the Dominican Republic (DR) positioned within NYC—the show frames the neighborhood as a piece of NYC that is inhabited by Dominicans.

Discursively, the most prominent element is the NYC vernacular English spoken with an NYC accent. A bilingual community, most of the Dominicans/Dominican-Americans in Washington Heights speak both English and Spanish fluently. They also effortlessly use "Spanglish" variants as well as code-switching between Spanish and English. In one of the only examples of this linguistic flexibility—a scene where Jimmy receives a phone call informing him that he has just made a baseball team that could lead to a professional career—the audience sees him using English and then code-switching to Spanish. After he receives the call, he first kisses his girlfriend, Eliza, and then immediately tells his grandmother, who lives in the same apartment, that he has made the team. This is a moment of Dominican cultural specificity that shows up rarely throughout the season. This scene highlights the importance of baseball for a young Dominican man as well as Jimmy's interaction with his grandmother, which would be familiar to many young Dominicans living in the US.

Fig. 3.7 Exterior establishing shot showcasing the display of a small Dominican flag, signaling the presence of people of Dominican heritage.

He calls to his grandmother in the kitchen, telling her in Spanish (with English subtitles on the screen) that he has made the team (fig. 3.8). In a matter of seconds, Jimmy goes from celebrating his success with his Dominican-American girlfriend in English to a touching moment speaking Spanish with his grandmother, who has undoubtedly played a large role in his childhood.

In addition to the dominance of English on the show, the progress narrative of the "American Dream" being shared—just with a Dominican accent—is central not only to the storyline of the first episode but also to the entire series. In the first episode, JP tells viewers that "we ain't got much in our pockets, but we have *big* dreams." Each episode moves the cast closer toward their individual goals, and by the season's end, the series has mostly fulfilled its story development. The season ends on an aspirational note: JP is on his way to success as a musical artist, Fred has been accepted to the prestigious Fashion Institute of Technology for fashion design, Rico is a working actor, Frankie is making a name for herself performing poetry, Reyna is gaining her independence by getting a job and moving out of her boyfriend's apartment, Jimmy is finding success in his baseball career, and Ludwin is moving to Boston to pursue his artistic dreams. Through his narration, JP affirms his desires for the show when he tells the audience, "When I say that I want to rep the Heights, that's what I mean . . . I want to

Fig. 3.8 Jimmy and his grandmother embracing after he shares the news of his success communicated in Spanish and subtitled in English for the MTV audience.

show people our voice." This statement defines the Dominican experience in the US in a way audiences are very familiar with. Rooting his progress firmly within Washington Heights and NYC ethnic enclave identification, JP helps non-Dominican audience members draw parallels between the experiences of the cast members and those of previous generations in their own families. However, by connecting the Dominican struggle in the US with the concept of the American Dream, *Washington Heights*—while possibly trying to reach a wider mainstream audience—obscures the specific and unique conditions of Dominicans in the US and subsequently dilutes dominicanidad.

The Dominican Darling of Mainstream Cultural Critics

Washington Heights likely avoided the mainstream criticism and disdain directed toward *Jersey Shore* and *Buckwild* because it promoted a progress narrative intertwined with the themes of the American Dream. Critics reviewed the show very favorably. The *Hollywood Reporter*'s Allison Keene (2013) praised the series, writing, "*Washington Heights* certainly shares more with series like *Laguna Beach* and *The Hills* than the travesties of *Jersey Shore* and *Buckwild* because the youth portrayed actually seem (at least to start off) sincere. Like *Laguna Beach*, *Washington Heights* has a primary narrator who is one of the group: In the former show it was (initially)

Lauren Conrad, and in this incarnation it's JP, a.k.a. Audubon, an up-and-coming hip-hop artist who seems to have genuine talent." Keene was not the only mainstream journalist to praise the show; much of the early entertainment press cited the show's high production values, cinematic style of filming and music score, and the "positive" progress narrative. Keene exemplifies the favorable media response to the show in her statement that "it feels both fresh and familiar—the scene is new, but the story is old. There's drama, but not as much trash. Which, unfortunately for it, may not make enough headlines to warrant the success it probably deserves." Praised for its *The Hills*–like production quality, *Washington Heights* received better reviews than shows like *Jersey Shore* and *Buckwild*.

Yet if *Washington Heights* has more in common cinematically with *The Hills*, why compare it to the sillier and more over-the-top, and therefore ridiculed, group of MTV reality shows? The show features brooding young people and their melodramatic relationships but barely acknowledges the cast's Dominican heritage. Unlike *Jersey Shore*, *Washington Heights* does not take every opportunity to capitalize on visual displays of ethnic culture. Instead of a spectacle of containment, *Washington Heights*, borrowing from hooks's terms, takes a "bit of the Other" and adds it to MTV's lifestyle-centric reality programming format. Playfully referred to as "*The Hills* in the Heights" by Dania, the show was set in what many consider the epicenter for Dominican culture and lifestyle in the US. One would assume, therefore, that some of this vibrant cultural expression would be portrayed on screen, but the show ignored many of the elements that make Washington Heights unique among other areas of NYC. The result was that the setting felt like it could be anywhere in NYC, from the South Bronx to Williamsburg. The show celebrated the hardscrabble life in NYC, and, in that respect, it was far more similar to the highly stylized and escapist series of *The Hills*. As seen below (figs. 3.9 and 3.10), the title cards of these four series demonstrate the visual similarity between *The Hills* and *Washington Heights* when compared to *Jersey Shore* and *Buckwild* (figs. 3.11 and 3.12).

Although *Washington Heights* does not mimic the glamorous lifestyle of *The Hills*, it does build on the conventions that show helped to institutionalize. Elizabeth Affuso (2009) explains, "While, both *The Hills* and *Laguna Beach* are ostensibly reality programs, they are seen as a new kind of reality, programs that are narrative based and are cast to appear like the fiction dramas that the shows are an outgrowth of." Criticized for the amount of scripting involved in what is touted as an "unscripted" series, *The Hills*, in particular, shares much of its aesthetic with film and high-quality TV

Fig. 3.9 and 3.10 Title shots for the series *Buckwild* and *Jersey Shore* demonstrate the similar production style among MTV programming trading in the spectacle of containment.

dramas. The show is filmed with a telephoto lens, uses cinematic lighting techniques, includes a great deal of staging and "character" blocking, and often uses nondiegetic music to enhance and shape the narrative. The editing of the narrative is also different from that on other MTV reality shows, where "in place of a confessional the show gives Lauren [Conrad] a voice-over narration to transition from scene to scene, aligning her with the protagonists of fiction shows and allowing her to provide some introspective

Televisual Dominicanidad and MTV's *Washington Heights* 115

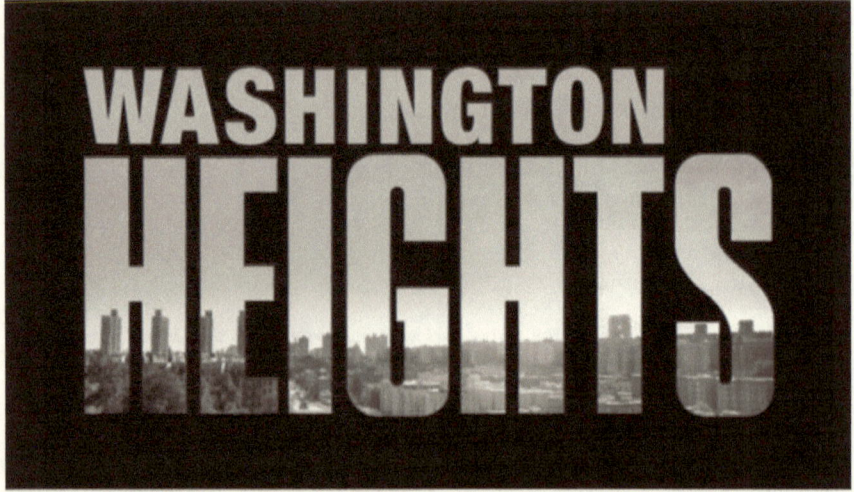

Fig. 3.11 and 3.12 The similarities between the title shots for *The Hills* and *Washington Heights* exhibit the locational and lifestyle-centric vein of MTV reality programming.

reflection on what is happening onscreen" (2009). The program's televisual cinematography and calculated mise-en-scéne—which also provide ample opportunity for product placement and endorsement—define a separate vein of MTV reality programming, one that deviates from the paradigm established through *The Real World*. Instead of the "shot on the fly" style that has characterized most MTV reality programs, "by mimicking the aesthetics of primetime serialized dramas and mainstream Hollywood releases, *The Hills* associates its subjects less with the 'authentic' world of reality TV and more with the world of fantasy" (Klein 2011). Sweeping establishing shots, beautiful people, opulent settings, and high fashion define *The Hills* to its audience.

From a production standpoint, *Washington Heights* is far more similar to MTV's lifestyle-focused programming. Essentially, the difference between *The Hills* and *Washington Heights* is that "*Washington Heights* is a docu-drama for the 2010s and the recession, where hair extensions are traded in for thick-framed glasses, tennis skirts for high-waisted shorts, and privileged white kids from the O.C. [Orange County] in their late teens through early twenties for their Dominican counterparts in a less privileged area of New York" (Keene 2013). *Washington Heights* does not offer the guilty pleasure experience provided by *Jersey Shore* and *Buckwild*. Instead, the show uses ethnoracial Otherness as a way to re-create MTV's cinematic lifestyle programming, just not one of white affluence (like in *The Hills*). *Washington Heights* failed to attract fans of shows like *Jersey Shore* because it did not, for the most part, depict the cast as exaggerated portrayals of excessive Otherness. The series also failed to attract fans of *The Hills* because, although it was very much a celebration of lifestyle, it did not portray the glamorous and aspirational lifestyle that appealed to fans of *The Hills*. As a hybrid of both types of shows, *Washington Heights* was unable to attract either audience. On one hand, *Washington Heights* tried to replicate an inclusion of Otherness used by *Jersey Shore*, the appeal of which, according to Klein (2021, 127), relates directly to "the classed (working or lower) and/or ethnic (Italian American) identities" of the cast, where Otherness is "made highly visible." Yet on the other hand, the show's production design was similar to the cinematic style of *The Hills*. *Washington Heights* combined the highly stylized feel of *The Hills* with the supposed ethnic specificity of *Jersey Shore*.

Before discussing how Dominican audiences reacted to the show, which was quite different from mainstream entertainment media coverage,

I want to examine a mainstream media review that provides a more nuanced examination of the series. Monika Fabian (2013), an ABCNews.com Fusion contributor, problematizes *Washington Heights* in relation to the overall MTV reality programming canon and suggests that just because the show features a Dominican cast, "that doesn't mean that 'Washington Heights' is the new 'Jersey Shore.' Stylistically, the northern Manhattan soap's slick production values and perfectly framed camera shots are more in line with 'Laguna Beach' and 'The Hills.' The cast of aspiring performers, artists, and athletes is much more glossy and self-aware than the guidos were in their debut season too." Fabian (2013) recognizes the immense burden of representation the show faced and questions whether or not MTV sacrificed Dominican authenticity for mainstream audience appeal: "What's missing from 'Washington Heights' is a true depiction of the rich, bicultural uptown Dominican (-American) culture." Unlike *Jersey Shore*, which inundates audiences with material elements of its portrayal of Italian Americans—Snooki's hair poofs, the GTL slogan, and fist-pumping dance moves, to name but a few—*Washington Heights* contains very few culturally specific references that could teach mainstream audiences about the Dominican-American experience or resonate with Dominicans in the US. Instead, "the unique local color is saved for sweeping establishing shots. Stylized imagery trumps authenticity on 'Washington Heights'" (2013).

Fabian (2013) speculates as to why, unlike *Buckwild* and *Jersey Shore*, *Washington Heights* does not exaggerate Dominican culture to the point of mockery, suggesting that a "lack of positive representations in mainstream culture seem to have weighted on 'Washington Heights' producers and the desire to create a positive portrayal to counteract drug-dealing stereotypes in hip-hop songs might've forced their hand. So we end up with a pasteurized version of uptown Dominican-American culture as a result. One that aims to be more palatable, but becomes innocuous and flavorless instead." To avoid using the narrow and stereotypical tropes of Dominican representation that do appear in mainstream US media, the show steered clear of most cultural references altogether. Apart from a random exchange in Spanish with elderly relatives and a few Dominican flags, there is not much in *Washington Heights* that reflects dominicanidad. Understandably, the Dominican community might be disappointed with this poor representation of their culture on a network that has branded itself through their identity project. However, as Fabian (2013) astutely points out, "No one expects a single show about white people to depict all of white culture. . . . Yet here we have a show . . . and we want them to get it totally right. Now that we've caught a glimpse of our blocks and brown faces on TV, we want to see all of ourselves and our lives on the screen."

"Finally! Dominicans on TV": MTV's *Washington Heights* and Dominicanidad

As the first Dominican-centric mainstream television show, *Washington Heights* was a hot topic among NYC Dominicans, and its airing was highly anticipated. However, the show's representation of Dominican-Americans and its limited inclusion of Dominican culture have proved disappointing to much of the Dominican community. During my fieldwork, I heard criticisms that ranged from those common to many reality series—it felt scripted, the cast did not have genuine relationships with each other, editors manipulated footage to ramp up drama—to outright rejection of the series as a representation of real Dominicans in NYC. Facing an uphill battle against the burden of representation, the show was unable to satisfy Dominican expectations. Many lamented the way dominicanidad was portrayed on the show, insisting that it was not an authentic representation of their lives and identity. Granted, *Washington Heights* faced channel-specific constraints because it was designed for the MTV audience—as I detailed above. Yet there is something to be said of the show's inability to resonate with the Dominican community it claimed to be featuring.

According to LatinoRebels.com (2013), *Washington Heights* was, predictably, a missed opportunity. The blog suggested,

> Here is the main problem with "Washington Heights": it could actually work in the media landscape if there was other programming that would balance it out. That is, if there were shows that DIDN'T try to push the stereotypes, then shows like "Washington Heights" would have to feel the pressure of trying to authentically portray what is in fact a very vibrant part of NYC. Instead, we get an MTV version of a neighborhood and now the whole world will think that this is what the real Washington Heights is all about. It isn't, and MTV failed, but hey, it's MTV, what are you expecting?

This post clearly understands the stakes involved in MTV's identity project. Recognizing that part of MTV's industrial strategy includes the exploitation of Otherness, the blog's major complaint is that MTV was fundamentally insensitive toward the show's potential burden of representation. Not surprisingly, MTV prioritized ratings over its duty as the first mainstream media outlet to prominently feature Dominicans. The problem is not that MTV used the concept of exaggerated Otherness to attract viewers (as was done with *Jersey Shore* and *Buckwild*) but that the network situated ethnoracial difference as the key component that made *Washington Heights* original and distinct, with no sensitivity to the fact that this would be the first opportunity for a mass mainstream audience to learn about Dominicans and their culture.

Plátano Wishes and Presidente Dreams: MTV's Approach to an Ethnic Enclave Community

As so vibrantly represented in the film *In the Heights* (2021) (discussed in chap. 1), Dominicans have reshaped Washington Heights in their image. Occasionally referred to as "Little DR" by some New Yorkers, Washington Heights looks and feels like a Dominican city. From the array of vendors lining every street to the salons specializing in Dominican blowouts, the area's enclave reality has created the perfect environment for Dominican cultural retention. According to Jorge Duany ([1994] 2008, 48), the "Dominican atmosphere, with its Spanish-speaking stores and employment opportunities for Hispanics, was a key attraction for many immigrants. The desire to preserve their cultural identity led many Dominicans to Washington Heights. The neighborhood thus became a transnational space, an American landscape reshaped by Dominican culture." Over the past four decades, Dominicans have created a thriving incipient enclave economy, building small business networks and shared cultural environments (Krohn-Hansen 2013). Although the Manhattan streets cannot replace the rural Dominican campo (countryside), in their homes, Dominicans display religious signs and images, Dominican flags and coat-of-arms, and folk art that "graphically recreated a Dominican atmosphere in Washington Heights" (Duany [1994] 2008, 41). In Washington Heights, products, foods, and news from the DR are never hard to find. During my fieldwork in the neighborhood, I could easily go an entire day without speaking English, and every nearby bodega sold Presidente, the Dominican national beer. Washington Heights residents are increasingly born in the US, but "many Dominicans in New York—or *Dominican-Yorks*, as their compatriots on the island call them—live suspended between two worlds, two islands, two flags, two languages, two nation-states" (Duany [1994] 2008, 27).

Unfortunately, MTV chose to ignore the cultural context of the show's namesake by excluding it from both the narrative and the mise-en-scéne. Dominicans who live in "the Heights" saw this as a glaring omission of the heart and soul of the area. Junior told me, "It wasn't really like the Heights... wasn't a faithful look at the Heights." Junior, one of the more media savvy of my interviewees, generally liked the references to Dominicans he had seen in other forms of media but felt that the show did not adequately depict the neighborhood he was so familiar with. Ciel, who represents the "two-ness" Duany described, said that watching the show was the "first time you see young . . . Spanish speakers of Caribbean descent being represented on TV. A lot of people criticized it. . . . Some of the realness was censored, I would like to see how they really would act. Like they might speak more Spanish." Many interviewees claimed the show had no substance, lacked the vibe of the actual community, and depicted few, if any, aspects of Dominican cultural life.

Julissa Bonfante of the *Huffington Post* was part of the website's online coverage of the premiere of the MTV series. She served on a talking-heads panel that offered critical responses to a show that many were apprehensive about. One of her columns was particularly inciting to *Huffington Post* readers, who used its comment section to hash out ethnoracial tensions concerning Dominicans as the newest dominant population in an area of NYC that has changed inhabitants over the generations—as one immigrant group develops roots and upward mobility in the US, another one replaces it in this economical neighborhood of an otherwise very expensive Manhattan. Bonfante (2013) wrote,

> Like many of my Dominican friends, we were glued to the premiere of MTV's *Washington Heights* last night. The introductory images, the landmarks, the legendary George Washington bridge, got us all sentimental and reminiscing about our childhood . . . I was born and raised there. . . . This is "one of the true neighborhoods left in Manhattan," says Jonathan "JP" Perez and "Audubon"—the group's peacekeeper and the show's producer—in the introduction, but I was disappointed not to see some of those true and unique aspects of this vibrant community. It was missing the authentic "Dominicanness" that characterizes the neighborhood. . . . The show has to strike a balance to appeal to the mainstream. But can the show be successful without sacrificing that Dominicanness that is synonymous with the neighborhood? Maybe this is just the new Washington Heights and I'm just old school.

This column evoked nostalgia and reflected the neighborhood pride that propelled the thematic arc of the first two episodes (aired back-to-back on premiere night) of *Washington Heights*. Yet, somewhat surprisingly, the first inflammatory comment in response to the self-reflective insight of Bonfante's (2013) column read, "I'm getting a little more than fed up with [this] nonsense. Dominicans did NOT invent, find, discover or create

Washington Heights. Before they landed there and ruined that perfectly good area 40 or so years ago, it was Irish, German, Jewish, Russian and Greek. And before them it was Native American, Dutch and whatever else . . . it irks me to no end that Dominicans swear up and down that they were the first ones that landed there." The comments spiral out of control into a racial and ethnic bashing of Dominicans. Like many of the ethnic neighborhoods in NYC, Washington Heights has certainly experienced many cultural changes and ethnic groups—including Jewish people, Irish, Greeks, Puerto Ricans, and now Dominicans—and currently faces a struggle with gentrification. Now that Brooklyn is becoming more expensive, the relatively low rental prices in Washington Heights and its significant decrease in crime rates over the last decade have enticed many young non-Dominicans to move there. And while there are small areas where gentrification has won the battle with Dominicans for control of apartment buildings and small businesses, the Dominicans of Washington Heights have fiercely resisted gentrifying trends. To highlight the flagrant intolerance of the post mentioned above, one poster commented, "Clearly people here are dealing with pent up, racial issues that have nothing to do with the show at all. For the person who said Washington Heights' time has come and gone, that might be the case for you and your personal memory of the good OLD days but the truth is, Washington Heights (just like Soho and Tribeca) is a NYC neighborhood that's here to stay. Who knows, 20 or 30 years from now it may once again be reminicent [sic] of what your memory of hood was but realistically speaking . . . I highly doubt that" (Bonfante 2013). The sentiments expressed by these two commenters continued to be discussed over the next few days, as shown in the column's comments section.

Adriana Maestas, senior contributing editor at Politic360.com, mentioned Bonfante's column to her own readers and noted the inflammatory response received by native Washington Heights resident Bonfante. The comments thread of Maestas's (2013) post redirects the discussion of the show from prejudice and xenophobia to a more problematized conversation about how best to represent Dominican culture to mainstream US audiences. One poster comments,

> The foods, the music, the sounds, the smells, the sights [are] what makes Washington Heights a Dominican neighborhood, or Irish, or Jewish; the languages portrayed, the locations used; all of these things were not true to what Washington Heights is . . . the Heights is not just fancy-ish restaurants, chilling on rooftops, poetry reads, and baseball. The heights is also loud barbershops, overstocked grocery stores, frio frio's, juice carts selling

Fig. 3.13 The cast of *Washington Heights* participating in one of their favorite pastimes: hanging out on the roof of an apartment building, talking, and drinking.

fresh squeezed OJ on the street, fruit carts, little boys and girls running around the block, grandma's yelling at their grand-kids, small apartments, Casa del Mofongo, Rice and Beans to go, cachapas, Nemos, Platanos (I mean how the heck did a mention to Plantains not happen within the first two episodes).

The poster goes on to insist that the show is not necessarily inaccurate, but it is not "fully accurate" either, as it portrays a version of Washington Heights that might only resonate with newer generations of Dominican-Americans. The comment suggests that it is pointless to criticize MTV for not staying true to the Dominican identity of a neighborhood that changes with each new group that calls it home. However, this comment also legitimizes the significant Dominican influence in Washington Heights and NYC more broadly. Most of the people discussing the show online are bothered by the fact that MTV is motivated more by the bottom line than the chance to showcase a vibrant Dominican community in NYC that the ever-expanding population of Dominicans in the US could identify with.

I Want My MTV: Negotiations of "Authentic" Dominicanidad

While most of my interviewees and online participants expressed disappointment with the show, some Dominican-Americans were ambivalent, and several were fans. Of course, media texts of every kind are interpreted individually, but the Dominican audience's reaction could be divided into three broad categories: affinity, ambivalence, and disavowal.

Of my Dominican interviewees and online posters who expressed an affinity toward the show, that sentiment aligned with one of the following reasons: (1) the show could be seen as a watershed moment for Dominicans to enter the mainstream US media; (2) those who enjoyed the show were already a part of MTV's broader target audience of teens and young adults; and (3) for some, the show was mostly a realistic portrayal of Dominicans born in the US who have a more Americanized sensibility. MTV targets teens and young adults, so if some of this demographic in Washington Heights prefers the American over the Dominican, then their approval and support of the show seems inevitable. Those who prioritized their identification with the millennial generation in the US over ethnic heritage would likely agree with what David Janollari, then head of TV programming at MTV, told thefutoncritic.com's Jim Halterman in 2012: "We are trying to reflect the lives of the core millennium generation, trying to connect with them by speaking their language and portraying characters and storylines that really feel resonant with them."

The association of the show with this "younger MTV generation" might have deterred some Dominican audiences who identify themselves separately based on notions of generation. However, it also attracted Dominican audiences who fit easily within the generational demographic that MTV targets. The importance of generation was exemplified by eighteen-year-old Leta, who revealed that she "expected there to be a lot of fighting and it wasn't going to be productive. I thought that people would be offended. Many people felt it was going to be bad, but I liked the story and watched it with my uncle, he is 25. I relate to the show in how everyone on the show seems to know each other and be interconnected. I also relate to the types of activities the show films them doing. Like the barbeques, [they] happen in the summer time."[2] Leta saw elements of the show that reminded her of her own Dominican-American experience. At eighteen, she is part of MTV's primary target audience, and it is telling that her response to the show was the most positive among all of my interviewees. The show resonated with Leta on both generational and cultural levels, while others whom I spoke with saw no elements of dominicanidad in the show. As the youngest of my interviewees, Leta had the most defined Dominican-American identity. She confessed that she "didn't really know much about Dominican stuff"; what she is intimately familiar with, however, is the Dominican experience in the US. The Americanized cast of Dominican heritage felt authentic to her and reflected the culture she grew up in.

Gabriela told me, "Almost everybody I know was talking about it. Heard that it is good because it is situated in a real environment and that a lot of people were excited for it to come out." She considered it a refreshing change from the depictions in the local news of Dominicans as criminals. As someone pursuing a career in law enforcement, Gabriela's main criticism of Dominican representation in US media was the stereotyping of Dominicans as criminals. Because the show mostly avoided showing Dominican criminals, its failure to explore Dominican culture was not as concerning to Gabriela, who merely appreciated the normalizing of Dominicans in NYC. The exposure the show provided to the NYC Dominican community was exhilarating for some Dominicans in the US who had long resented their mediated invisibility in US media.

There was also quite a bit of ambivalence expressed about the show. Junior told me that while he thought the series was not faithful to "the Heights" and many important aspects of the community were left out, his cousin liked the show for its originality. Even though Junior was unsure about the show because Washington Heights was not portrayed as the Dominicans who live there see it, he agreed with his cousin that the show "was a new idea on TV." Junior is not disavowing the show; he is merely suggesting that MTV could have done more to represent dominicanidad.

Like Junior, some viewers with mixed feelings about the show blamed MTV for any perceived shortcomings. Carmen, a Dominican American born in a white suburb of Chicago and the only one who watched every episode of the series, defended the show and criticized MTV for the show's inauthentic representation of dominicanidad. She was thrilled that a show featuring NYC Dominicans existed, but the way MTV framed the production and editing drew too heavily on regimes of representation that depict Latina/os as poor. She told me, "I liked that the characters were portrayed as artistic and creative. I also found it interesting that the white girl in the show served a token function, instead of the other way around." Painfully aware that the ethnoracial dynamics of US television ensemble casts usually work the opposite way, this cast member's whiteness was a rare treat for Carmen. Gabriela also blamed MTV for the series' problems, claiming that the way the show was edited removed aspects that could have made it more authentically Dominican. She expressed a desire for more inclusion of Dominican culture because, as packaged by MTV, she believed, "[At] certain times the show was more relatable than others, these are just Dominicans that are taking a different route. Like the scenes involving the brothers and their relationship and how the younger brother was in a bit of trouble. I do the same thing with my younger siblings, I try to look out for them and take care of them." For her, these brief moments of resonance were significant, considering that *Washington Heights* was the "first time [mainstream] U.S. has seen Dominicans as the focus."

One pop culture blogger who was a fan of the cast and the series' premise wrote of the show,

> *Washington Heights* on MTV is an example of a show that failed not because it wasn't good or didn't have a devoted, core audience. It failed because the network it was on didn't believe it would succeed and did absolutely nothing to promote it. MTV doesn't make reality shows about young people of colour, so *Washington Heights*, a show about Dominicans and Latino's [sic] living in upper Manhattan was a nice breath of fresh air. Instead of it being Jersey Shore with brown faces, it was about young people trying to make it and do something positive with their lives and their art. (White 2013)

Instead of criticizing the show's content, this blogger blames MTV for its cancellation and low ratings, believing that the network did not give the show the attention it deserved. Promoting *Buckwild* in its place, MTV did not give *Washington Heights* the airtime, publicity appearances, or promotion given to most of its programs. While it may be true that MTV did not adequately promote the show, the US Dominican community definitely noticed it. When I talked to Emmanuel about the show, he said he had not yet watched it but had heard other people's opinions about it. Emmanuel, who is older than most of my interviewees and travels widely due to his military service, was eager to hear what other people thought about the show. According to him, "The show was good because it has Dominicans that are trying to make something of themselves and it valued education. But I think it wasn't successful for MTV because it lacked the drama of some of its other shows." He concluded our discussion of the show by reassuring me, "I might need to watch that."

However, the very thing that made the show relatable to viewers like Leta—the emphasis of the *American* in Dominican-American—repelled others. As argued by Luis, *Washington Heights* "turned him off" because it was "too Americanized." This sentiment is not surprising, considering Luis is particularly hostile to the potential loss of Dominican cultural heritage due to Americanization. Yet he was just one of many interviewees who wanted to distance themselves from the show and vehemently rejected it. For Diego, a scholar who has dedicated much of his life to the preservation and celebration of US-based dominicanidad, *Washington Heights* in no way reflected the

Dominican-American experience. Taking particular issue with the show's portrayal of the NYC neighborhood he saw as the cultural center of dominicanidad in the US, Diego stated, "It is not authentic and I had hoped that the show would have turned out to be a bigger deal. But it lacked narrative conflict and the show's producers fundamentally misunderstood Dominican culture. In the end the show was a big letdown. Being Dominican is more than our music. It depicted the characters as dream chasers and was not a true reflection of Washington Heights." The show's failure to include aspects of dominicanidad clearly struck a nerve with him, as it did with many other Dominicans in the US. For a community that is underrepresented and often symbolically erased in mainstream US media, this show was a slap in the face. Finally able to see themselves represented in mainstream media and given the chance to introduce their culture to an uninformed mainstream audience, Dominicans in the US had high hopes for this show, but they were left frustrated with the final product.

The fact that the cast spoke very little Spanish was considered a major problem. Even younger Dominican-Americans, who largely identified with the lifestyle depicted on the show, criticized the lack of Spanish. Gabriela suggested that when cast members did speak in Spanish, those scenes were left on the cutting room floor because they might not be interesting or understandable to an English-speaking mainstream audience, noting that "all Dominicans speak Spanish to their families." For many of the Dominicans I interviewed in NYC, this was one of the main reasons the show and its cast were not relatable. Tina told me,

> I just didn't relate to the characters on the show at all. The conversations didn't seem to have a natural flow, we don't talk like that. Some of the slang they used was pretty Dominican, but their representation of families was distorted. More use of Spanish by the cast would have made it more authentic I think. There was a point that a lot of people in the Dominican community were talking about the show, but the topic died out pretty quick. There was a lot of hype at the beginning, but once it aired people thought it was a shit show and most people were disappointed with it.

A fan of Dominican American authors Junot Díaz and Julia Alvarez, Tina sought out representations of US-based dominicanidad. Her experience of growing up in a Spanish-speaking home shaped her understanding of her dominicanidad, and its absence from *Washington Heights* was a red flag. The show's limited bilingualism was a concern for most of my interviewees. In Washington Heights, bilingualism is the norm for the Dominican/Dominican-American population, which prioritizes retaining its heritage language over assimilation into US society. The fact that *Washington Heights* ignored the community's linguistic code-switching—which also includes the frequent use of "Spanglish"—showed Dominican audiences that the series had no intention of depicting an authentic dominicanidad. In my fieldwork interviews, I received similar responses to what Duany ([1994] 2008, 51) recorded in his research when he asked Washington Heights residents, "What makes one Dominican?": "The most frequently cited characteristic was the Dominican accent in speaking Spanish, followed by standard references to merengue and *comida criolla*, ethnic foodways." It might have been smart for *Washington Heights*'s MTV producers to ask a similar question of its cast members as well.

Affinity, ambivalence, and disavowal marked the mixed reception to *Washington Heights*. Regardless of which type of response was given, however, there was almost always some form of disappointment. This reaction of attraction, ambivalence, and disavowal from the Dominican audience is similar to what scholars have discovered about Puerto Rican audiences and their limited representation. One of the most influential texts on Puerto Rican representation continues to be the film *West Side Story* (dir. Jerome Robbins and Robert Wise, 1961). Much scholarship has addressed the regimes of representation in the film, but only a few studies have examined how Puerto Rican audiences react to the text. Relevant to my study, Kennaria Brown's (2010, 206) Puerto Rican interviewees found so few Puerto Rican stories in media, they "took what was available and found something to relate to despite the hegemonic context." Brown sees this action as rooted in a "hunger" for Latinx specificity in US representations of latinidad(es). Jillian M. Báez (2018, 76) uses the same term in her ethnographic audience study, where she argues that the reception toward the limited representation of Puerto Ricans "points to a 'cinema of hunger,' with audiences trying to identify with the few representations of their communities while yearning for more." Mediated invisibility and marginalization have created a hunger for representation as a validation of the Puerto Rican position in the US imaginary, where viewing practices are rooted in "hoping to belong and be recognized" (2018, 2). In her analysis of the reception toward the films *Chicago Boricua* (2004) and *Nothing Like the Holidays* (2008), Báez discusses how even though the films were criticized by those she interviewed—with claims of "negative" stereotypes and formulaic narratives—they sustained a contradictory yet concurrent response of celebration and distancing. There are many parallels between Báez's findings and my own regarding *Washington Heights*. Both of the films discussed by Báez's participants were set in the Chicago neighborhood of Humboldt Park, which, similar to the centrality of Washington Heights to dominicanidad, is seen as the heart of the Puerto Rican community in the city. Puerto Rican reception involved a certain "politics of localized recognition," but investing in *their* community's representation required them to negotiate between feelings of excitement and disappointment (2018, 76). I contend that "localized recognition" also influenced how NYC Dominicans responded to *Washington Heights*. There is a certain thrill associated with seeing your home portrayed on the screen, and this can explain why some interviewees enjoyed watching the show. Yet the show's failure to include Dominican signifiers and culture resulted in profound disappointment for others.

Conclusion: Televisual Dominicanidad as Trompe L'oeil Effect

What are the reasons for the show's mixed reception? Critics loved it, mainstream audiences ignored it, and Dominican audiences mostly saw its exclusion of overt dominicanidad as a disappointment or even an affront. For Klein (2021, 154), the show's failure could be explained thusly: "When nonwhite cast members appear in MTV reality series as separate from prominent stereotypes tied to their identities, they prove to be 'uninteresting' to MTV's mostly white, mostly middle-class audience. . . . They lacked catchphrases and could not clearly define (and/or commodify) what it is to be Dominican American in the way that *Jersey Shore* defined (and commodified) what it is to be a Guido." This assessment explains much of the reception from mainstream audiences. However, regarding MTV's application of identity as an organizing factor in its reality TV programming, it is important to recognize that "one of the drawbacks of packaging and commercializing authenticity is that it becomes increasingly hard to recognize the real thing" (Wallace 2013). Curnutt (2013) likens this phenomenon to the artistic effect of trompe l'oeil—a technique that uses hyperrealistic imagery to make a piece of art appear three-dimensional until one is up close to it. He contends, "Like *trompe-l'oeil*, the appeal of reality TV for media-savvy viewers comes from the ways in which its verisimilitudes call attention to television's representational limitations and, by extension, the medium's inability adequately to depict subjectivity" (Curnutt 2013, 301). Put another way, the fact that participants in reality television are "real people" injects an element of realism and thereby reveals the ways in which the program is staged. Drawing on psychoanalytical theory, Curnutt (2013,

304) states that "the participant's image exists within the televisual frame as something seemingly more authentic than the text itself. In this regard, its excessive realism functions as an internal signifier calling attention to the program's own representational constraints." It is not necessarily the participants or their world that are inherently inauthentic; it is the fact that they have been inserted into a reality program that makes it difficult to tell what is real and what is staged. Because audiences watch reality programs within a paradigm of suspicion, "in our haste to locate artifice, we run the risk of (mis)recognizing how truthful media that cater to a savvy viewpoint may in fact be" (Curnutt 2013, 309).

Audiences have become trained through the processes by which MTV brands its reality programming, leading them to interpret the narratives of these series in very particular ways. Reduced to its most basic function, "reality TV's *trompe-l'oeil* effect—its staging of its own fraudulent depiction of authenticity—is enabled by the actuality that its participants are, ultimately, what they appear to be" (Curnutt 2013, 306). However, the trompe l'oeil effect fails to take into account the influence ethnoracial discourses have on our ability as audiences to interpret a text. Yes, the grapes in the painting might seem like real objects from afar, but if we do not know what grapes are—if we have no cultural understanding of their essence—realizing they are merely painted on a wall does not reveal any truer knowledge about them. The same can be said for the representation of Dominicans within the media format of reality television; by looking more closely, audiences can see the staging involved in their depiction, but without an understanding of Dominicans, they are unable to interpret what is authentic and what is not. Furthermore, for Dominican audiences who are hyperaware of the meanings connoted by elements of the Dominican experience in the US, the fact that such representations are contained within a reality program makes their authenticity automatically suspect.

It is not surprising, then, that many Dominicans in the US criticize the *Washington Heights* cast for not having actual ties to the neighborhood in real life. During one interview, Alma told me that because she was suspicious about the cast's origins, the show was "illegitimate" in her eyes.[3] She further explained to me, "The promos for the show [she] has seen don't feel representative of [her] community," and, furthermore, she does not "want a 'lame' show [to] be the representation of Dominicans." Alma used consumption of Dominican-produced media as a way to maintain her sense of dominicanidad while living in NYC. When she compared the US-produced show to those she watched from the DR, she found it lacking. Furthermore, as someone who relies on community gatherings in NYC to maintain her connection to dominicanidad, Alma rejected the show because it did not reflect the Dominican character of the neighborhood it was named after.

Whether or not *Washington Heights* is a fair and accurate representation of Dominican American life in NYC is almost beside the point. As Kraszewski (2014, 241) illustrates, "Culture emerges not only through screen representations but also more complexly through institutional struggles and strategies to create certain representations, and by the way these representations interact with larger social trends." Regardless of how accurate the show's depiction of dominicanidad is, it introduced a growing population to the mainstream US consciousness. It might have been advantageous that this introduction was made through the medium of reality television, a medium that audiences already engage with through a skeptical lens. Furthermore, as the show never gained a large mainstream following, there may be better and more mainstream-visible opportunities to introduce dominicanidad.

The particular industrial, political, and cultural context of *Washington Heights* makes its appearance significant but contested. Similar to the exploitation of Otherness that continues to be the hallmark of much of MTV programming—not to mention in mainstream US television more broadly—the introduction of Dominicans/Dominican-Americans into the US media landscape is still threatened by the market's tendency to consume and decontextualize difference. The Dominicans I interviewed reflects the warning expressed by bell hooks (1992, 39), who contends that "the over-riding fear is that cultural, ethnic, and racial differences will be continually commodified and offered up as new dishes to enhance the white palate—that the Other will be eaten, consumed, and forgotten." The failure of *Washington Heights* to become a successful part of MTV's reality programming could, in turn, be an opportunity to reset the mainstream's introduction to dominicanidad. Or it could just as easily be the first of many media texts that trade on dominicanidad as a "bit of the Other."

Notes

1. According to Urban Dictionary (urbandictionary.com), *mudding* means to go "out in the mud in the back of a truck or jeep or other 4 × 4 vehicle and spin in the mud until all the occupants are covered in mud."
2. Interview conducted on June 5, 2013, with an eighteen-year-old DR-born woman.
3. Interview conducted on July 20, 2013, with a DR-born woman in her early twenties.

PART III:

LATINIDADES AND HYPHENATED IDENTITIES

4

COMPETING LATINIDADES

Orange Is the New Black and Engagement with Latinx Specificity

I enjoyed my backstory and the rebellious side of Blanca [Flores] and the other Dominican women, and most of all I love seeing how each character has a life of its own.
—LAURA GÓMEZ[1]

Originally, [Blanca] was a caricature... I had to create my own traits that I thought would work... her traits relate to a world that I understand and that I know.
—LAURA GÓMEZ[2]

A young Maria Ruiz comes home from school with a friend, both teenage girls wearing their Catholic school uniforms. As they chat and giggle, Maria notices her father is in the living room with several other men. Behind them on one wall is a large Dominican flag, and on the other is a group of five machetes mounted and displayed as if they were as important as the flag (fig. 4.1). Maria is embarrassed by her father and his obsession with maintaining his homeland pride. She does not share his distrust and animosity toward other Latinx groups. She knows she is Dominican, but she also knows that she was born and raised in New York. All her life, her father has varnished his illegal drug business with the facade of Dominican national pride. He tells her, "What, you embarrassed now? I made you, baby girl! You got my blood" (from the episode "Power Suit"). After she pulls her friend into her bedroom, thoroughly irritated with her father, Maria tells her friend, "They all front like, 'La patria,' but all they really do is sell drugs and drink Presidente, then complain about, 'Presidente doesn't taste the same

Fig. 4.1 Teenage Maria Ruiz's dad and apartment with decorative machetes.

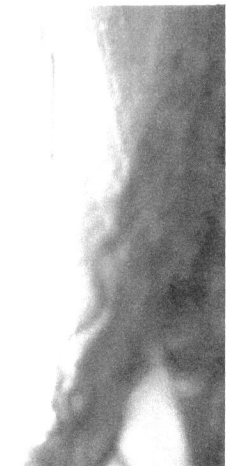

Fig. 4.2 Ruiz in her school uniform, complaining about her dad to her friend.

as like back home'" (fig. 4.2). But "home" for Maria is not the Dominican Republic (DR), and she just wants her father to be a "normal" father, probably like those she sees on television and in movies. Not only is she navigating her dominicanidad as a second-generation Dominican American, she is also doing so against her father's conflation of Dominican pride and his drug-dealing organization. There is a dissonance between Maria's US-centric dominicanidad and that of her father's, rooted in a nostalgic ideal of the DR.

Fig. 4.3 Ruiz walking up to Blanca, who is playing dominoes with the other Dominicans.

Fig. 4.4 Blanca looks up to see Ruiz approaching her.

As the song "El blue del ping pong" by Rita Indiana y Los Misterios—a radical merengue group known for their queer politics and use of Dominican slang—plays in the background, present-day Maria Ruiz saunters by Blanca Flores, who is playing dominoes with the other Dominican inmates (figs. 4.3 and 4.4). Several days before, Ruiz had stopped this group from retaliating after Blanca was attacked during a racially motivated assault, suggesting they need to be smart about how they strike back.³ Unlike

Blanca, whose dominicanidad was galvanized by the other Dominican inmates, Ruiz resisted identifying with them. Her childhood experiences traumatized her relationship with her own dominicanidad. Yet the attack on Blanca has shifted something in her. Ruiz sees how Blanca's Dominican solidarity has empowered her, even as she sits covered in bruises from her attack. Blanca represents for Ruiz a new way of being Dominican. The often-eccentric Blanca has always seemed a bit unhinged to Ruiz—whether due to her bushy hair, unibrow, predilection to talk to herself, or failure to adhere to gender norms—Ruiz now realizes that these characteristics are part of Blanca's self-possession, a self-possession that gives her strength. Nodding at Ruiz, Blanca tells one of the women playing dominoes to give her seat to Ruiz. As they look at each other, an unspoken acknowledgment arises (fig. 4.5). Ruiz is signaling that she is a part of this cohort, that she will now embrace her dominicanidad as part of both a survival strategy and a route to self-actualization.

In this chapter, I perform a textual and industrial analysis of Netflix's hit series *Orange Is the New Black* (*OITNB*) in relation to its use and articulation of multiple types of latinidad. Innovative in many ways, the show became a critical media text for scholarly analysis and gained popularity with a large mainstream audience. Of particular significance is its narrative structure that rotates the axial figure, allowing each member of the diverse ensemble cast to experience dynamic character development. While the cast includes many Latina characters, it was not until the show's fourth season that they drove the primary narrative, which was sparked by the introduction of a new group of mostly Dominican inmates to Litchfield Penitentiary. This shift in the prison's population allowed the mostly peripheral inmates Maria Ruiz and Blanca Flores—played by Dominican actors Jessica Pimentel and Laura Gómez, respectively—to each move into the critical axial role. Along with the backstories of Blanca's and Ruiz's lives before prison, the show focused on the discussion and negotiation of one more layer of diversity among the cast: latinidades.

As I have discussed in the previous chapters, the idea that all Latina/o/xs possess the same latinidad or that anyone categorized as "Latino/Hispanic" shares the same basic characteristics is a fallacy, yet it is a hegemonic one. The lived experiences and negotiations of identity and subjectivity among those within this category do not lend themselves well to homogenizing forces, even though that is exactly what dominant society has tried to do. Furthermore, as a form of strategic essentialism, latinidad has developed a growing salience among US Latina/o/xs. This could be the

Fig. 4.5 Ruiz and Blanca sitting opposite the dominoes table coming to an agreement to work together through a newly found sense of shared dominicanidad.

result of an internalization of hegemonic discourses, an act of solidarity to construct an empowered notion of a "Latino imaginary" (Flores 2000), or a subversion of and resistance to US Black/white binary racial ideologies. As argued by Frances Aparicio (2007, 40), "If identity is defined by the dialogic struggles between notions of the self and the constructions imposed from the outside (other individuals, institutions, and discourses), then Latina/o identities need to be understood at the interstices of both." As an alternative to amorphous latinidad, some scholars have advanced the notion of latinidades (Aparicio and Chávez-Silverman 1997; Caminero-Santangelo 2007; Blackwell et al. 2017), which allows for the possibility of Latinx specificity and acknowledges the immense diversity among this population. However, latinidades has rarely been successfully articulated through the US mainstream media. Audiences might get a glimpse into this heterogeneous reality—and are aware that Latina/os originate from many different nationalities and heritages—but this is rarely shown in most available media. In its fourth season, *OITNB* focuses on the individual Latinx populations within the prison, specifically those identified as Mexican, Puerto Rican, and Dominican. Not only does the show successfully represent latinidades, it also demonstrates this ability by featuring a level of Latinx specificity that has yet to appear in mainstream media. The show highlights and engages in discourses concerning Dominicans in the US, a group largely ignored by most media and relatively unfamiliar to most audiences. This chapter argues that *OITNB* not only attempts to engage with notions of latinidades but also presents Dominican identity in a way that makes it accessible to mainstream audiences and potentially identifiable to Dominican ones.

"To say that OITNB has struck a chord within popular culture would be a severe understatement" (Kalogeropoulos Householder and Trier-Bieniek 2016, 2). *OITNB* is far from a perfect show, however. Many people have criticized its use of ethnic and racial Otherness as plot devices, the centering of an idealized white female protagonist as a lens for viewership, the reinforcement of the connection between people of color and criminality, and a neoliberal approach to the plight of the incarcerated, to name but a few grievances. The show is a complex and thoroughly contested mainstream media text that galvanizes fans and critics into discussions that make people angry, uncomfortable, and, ultimately, self-reflective. Even through its problematic engagement with certain "negative" tropes of representation, *OITNB* has provided a mediated space for active negotiation of dominicanidad among and against its Dominican characters. The fourth season's exploration of latinidades is multifaceted and messy, just like the negotiation of identity is.

It's Not TV, It's Netflix

A thorough discussion of streaming and its redefinition of television as a medium is beyond the scope of this chapter; however, it is important to note how such a platform influences both consumption and interpretation practices among audiences.[4] The industrial parameters that control and direct broadcast television do not necessarily carry over to the streaming platform; therefore, the content, consumption, and interpretation of *OITNB*—and its role as one of Netflix's defining productions—require a brief exploration. In many ways, the show cemented Netflix's entry into "original programming" and "helped solidify not only the Netflix brand within the burgeoning metagenre of Quality TV, but also distinguished it clearly from American premium cable competitors like HBO and Showtime" (Hassler-Forest 2018, 368). Audiences can watch Netflix programming, both licensed and original, almost anywhere on almost any internet-enabled device. This has changed the way audiences consume television to the point that many scholars ask if we can even consider this television anymore.[5]

There is a marked difference between a television show broadcasted by a network or cable channel that relies on an advertising-based industrial model and one that is created by and for a streaming service that allows for freedom from advertising, conventions of scheduling, and content prohibitions. The two differ regarding both production concerns and those of audience consumption practices. For instance, "The freedom from advertisers in subscription-based programming yields different kinds of stories and storytelling" (Sullivan Barak 2016, 47). Producers do not have to worry about advertisers and are often encouraged to explore options for content not typically found on traditional television. This is fertile ground for innovative content creation, but it also reflects a change in how people watch television shows, namely, the now-ubiquitous practice of binge-watching.

Binge-watching provides audiences with a different relationship and level of engagement with the televisual text. Because Netflix releases an entire season on the same date, many audiences will watch multiple episodes in one sitting. This allows for a deeper understanding of the serial narrative and gives the viewer the chance to rewatch the show and further explore the textual complexity. Although the show is divided into one-hour episodes, each of which tells its own episodic narrative, releasing the entire series at once indicates a "shift in both industry and viewers' expectations of what constitutes a hit television show" (Symes 2017, 31). Moreover, *OITNB* engages in a metanarrative that "acknowledges its compulsion-inducing nature, particularly through references to media fandom, and does so in a way that emphasizes the intimacy of the televisual form" (Moore 2016, 160). Quite simply, *OITNB* and other series on Netflix offer audiences a more personalized and engaging way to watch television. Viewers participate in complex and personalized understandings of the televisual text based exclusively on its method of delivery. Combining this with a production strategy that caters to this type of consumption creates the potential to change how television impacts audiences, often in deeply meaningful ways.

Orange Is the New Black

As a foundational series for a successful string of "Netflix originals," *OITNB* not only is a popular mainstream show but also challenges much of the television industry's conventional wisdom. The show's journey to the screen is often credited to creator Jenji Kohan's clever "Trojan horse" approach, which used a normatively white protagonist as an entrée into an extensive and diverse cast. Based on the best-selling memoir *Orange Is the New Black: My Year in a Women's Prison* by Piper Kerman, the show outshines its source material and has become a true pop culture phenomenon. Not only is the show a success for Netflix (the network does not disclose its viewing numbers, but the seven seasons indicate a large audience), but it has also been awarded many industry honors. The first season alone received twelve Emmy nominations. And while the show's recognition has diminished somewhat since then, it is still held as a gold standard of the recent "quality TV" revolution.

Originally structured around the perspective of recently admitted inmate Piper Chapman (played by Taylor Schilling), the show attempts to represent a world that few viewers are familiar with and to do so in a way that is both politically aware and entertaining. Set in the fictional Litchfield Prison, the first few seasons follow Piper as she navigates the various, often racialized, factions that make up the body of the incarcerated population. Her time in Litchfield makes her question her sexuality, her sense of self, and her preconceived notions of the other prisoners. Piper is the typical white liberal who considers herself to be open-minded and progressive but has never considered her own white and economic privileges. She learns lessons the hard way and relies on those she sees as Others to educate her on her ignorance. As a character, she is easy to dislike. Luckily for those who do, she becomes increasingly less central every season. If Piper was Kohan's Trojan horse to get the series made, she could also be understood as a narrative device to encourage audiences to pay attention to and care about the rest of the characters, many of whom are women of color, queer, and/or poor.

What distinguishes *OITNB* from other large, diversely cast shows is its narrative strategy. Each episode highlights one or two cast members, making them the axial figure(s) of the episodic narrative. This strategy uses flashback scenes to show the characters' memories, helping the audience understand their experiences and dynamic development as prisoners. And while many shows use the flashback as a narrative strategy, "typically, only main characters receive this treatment, with other characters assisting on the journey of growth and self-reflection, but *OITNB* does not reserve this depth for Piper. Inmates have personality-shaping backstories that influence their identities, relationships, and roles in Litchfield" (Barak 2016, 53). This is a brilliant way to deal with a large ensemble cast, especially compared to similar shows that often have shallow character development. Not only do audiences get a better story, but, as Moore (2016, 166) argues, "flashback episodes work as a microcosm of what seems to be the show's mission: to look more closely at a range of women, and to see them on their own terms, rather than in some transition from Other to sameness."

The Politics of Representation on *OITNB*

Compared to much of contemporary television, the ethnoracial diversity of *OITNB* is breathtaking. To reflect all of the groups that populate the Prison Industrial Complex in the US, this diversity is necessary.[6] Does the setting minimize the show's impact on representational politics? Absolutely not; it just means we need to critically scrutinize how diversity is represented, especially in a space that is already hyperethnoracialized. Specifically, "the fictionalized depictions of incarcerated persons on *OITNB* cannot be adequately interpreted without attending to the ways in which race, gender, sexuality, and social class function not in isolation, but in tandem, regarding which categories of persons are always already considered criminal, regardless of actual behaviors" (O'Sullivan 2016, 404). How individuals navigate that space in *OITNB* is what makes its representational politics progressive—or not. Because most of the academic criticism focuses only on the first three seasons, it is necessary to examine the show as a complete televisual text.

Although *OITNB* has been praised for its diversity and efforts to project a sympathetic representation of incarcerated women, it is nonetheless a contested show. As Kalogeropoulos Householder and Trier-Bieniek (2016, 2) point out, "It has been both lauded for its original depictions of a diverse, mostly female, ensemble cast, while simultaneously playing up age-old archetypes of women and their sexuality that can be traced back to pulp fiction, 1960s exploitation movies, gender stereotypes in contemporary popular culture, and beyond." A show taking a sex-positive feminist approach, one that demonstrates the spectrum of sexual orientation among a diverse group of women, opens itself up to such critiques. Moreover, the way the relationships among the different factions at the prison are used as plot devices also minimizes *OITNB*'s potential as a radical intersectional text. However, the show's use of a narrative structure that makes—at some point throughout its seven-season run—almost each ensemble cast member the axial character of an episode is an ingenious strategy for rich character development. This approach also reminds audiences that an incarcerated woman is more similar to them than not. In season 3, *OITNB* begins to truly explore the women of color in the cast in a complex and critical way. And by season 4, this personal character complexity is extended to both inter- and intragroup dynamics.

A common criticism of the show is directed toward the use of the white, affluent, gender-normative Piper to entice white audiences to care about people of color and the Prison Industrial Complex more broadly. Many question whether this constitutes a "subversive use of whiteness" or a "normalizing of the white gaze" (Scott 2017). And while this is certainly a fair criticism of the first three seasons, does this remain the case for the remaining four? Responding to this question, Demers (2017, 411) asks, "When we look at *Orange Is the New Black*, does the protagonist ultimately become the lens through which we voyeuristically watch racialized struggles?" As the character of Piper becomes progressively sidelined in the overall narrative of *OITNB*, this becomes less and less the case. Demers goes so far as to say that the shift in perspective from Piper to a large group of women of color constitutes the type of "oppositional gaze" proposed by bell hooks.[7] Essentially, instead of being objectified through Piper's navigation of this ethnoracialized space, the characters of color start to "look back" at her objectifying gaze. Audiences start looking at the prison, the incarcerated women, and notions of race and ethnicity through the eyes of women of color.

The frequent use of flashbacks, which establish character development for a particular episode's axial character, facilitates this. It is the audience, not Piper, who has this background knowledge and who is shown the information from the perspective of the character who lived it (Barak 2016). As any intersectional feminist will attest, the personal is political. Through a consumption practice already understood as personalized to the individual viewer and a narrative strategy that dynamically individualizes most of its large cast, *OITNB* not only understands that the personal is political but also uses it as a paradigm for televisual storytelling.

On the intragroup level, the dynamics are thoroughly intersectional, where "sexuality, class, age, ability, and education overlap, complicating individual experiences in a group united by skin color" (Barak 2016, 52). In terms of their understanding of and relationships with those in their (racially) designated group, characters take on depth regarding one another and are therefore more complex and dynamic individually. Unfortunately, this does not always carry over to the intergroup dynamics in the first three seasons of *OITNB*. Both those in control of the prison and the show producers who use those characters to tell stories often pit the Latinas and African American women against each other. Not only does this reject coalition and alliance politics so central to intersectional praxis, it also reinforces racialized discourses of natural hostility among ethnoracialized groups.[8] And while this is a serious problem with the show, it only works to mitigate what is truly a significant effort to humanize and respectfully treat incarcerated women from a multitude of backgrounds. The details and intricacies of the lived experiences of those who are often invisible at best and symbolically annihilated at worst in *OITNB* make it a productive text. It is a text that makes people question what they think they know, talk to others, engage in debate, and, subsequently, rearticulate their worldview. Ultimately, "with this emphasis on the connection between lived experience and identity, the show makes an argument against essentialism, demonstrating how identity is always rooted in the intimate, embodied details of daily life" (Moore 2016, 165). What is more intersectional than that?

All Latinas are "Spanish": Seasons 1–3

Spanish. That is the term used to identify the Latina population in Litchfield. The term is used by administration, guards, incarcerated women from other ethnoracial groups, and, sometimes, the Latinas themselves. As Latinx people, these women likely have some degree of Spanish descent. Furthermore, the majority of them speak Spanish (as well as English). And while it is true that the term *Spanish* has been historically applied to people now referred to as *Latina/o/x*—both by themselves and by others (particularly in New York as an early twentieth-century translation of *Hispano*)—its use in *OITNB* both reflects these historical usages and, at times, reinforces their legitimacy.[9] While this might seem to be a trivial issue, Flores (2000, 191) posits, "With all the slippages and evident arbitrariness, though, what would seem a terminology free-for-all actually does mark off limits and contexts, and pressing issues of power." The term *Spanish* is used by the Prison Industrial Complex not just to reinforce segregation but also as a way to reject this population's rights to self-identify. This is one of the many ways incarceration strips people of their agency. However, just because the televisual Litchfield uses the term *Spanish*, that does not mean that the show cannot do so in a way that speaks to the politics of identification and also draws attention to Latinx peoples in complex and culturally specific ways. As I argue that the fourth season of *OITNB* is the watershed season for dynamic Latinx representation, I will discuss its representation of latinidad in two parts: seasons 1–3 and season 4 onward.

While not necessarily problematic, the first three seasons of *OITNB* make no attempt to distinguish the distinct latinidad among the Latina characters. This does not mean, however, that Latinas are not central to the narrative and constructed dynamic of the fictional prison. In fact, one of the first characters to receive the in-depth axial treatment is Latina Dayanara "Daya" Diaz (played by Dominican actress Dascha Polanco). *OITNB* makes her star-crossed love story with prison guard John Bennett (Matt McGorry) central to the overarching narrative of the first two seasons. Daya and her mother Aleida (Elizabeth Rodriguez), along with Gloria Mendoza (Selenis Leyva), are the Latina characters with the most screen time and character development. The fact that these characters are Latina is mostly inconsequential, outside of the fact that they can speak Spanish to each other and, therefore, escape from some of the all-encompassing surveillance that the incarcerated experience. The categorization of all the Latina characters as "Spanish," regardless of Latinx specificity, suggests that all these women are, or at least should be, allies and part of the same subpopulation of inmates. This manifests in enforced and voluntary segregation from the other racialized groups within the boundaries of Litchfield.

What is problematic is that in its first three seasons, *OITNB* rarely deviates from the hegemonic regime of representation of Latinas as oversexualized, hyperemotional, and victims of the men in their lives. As argued by Kalogeropoulos Householder and Trier-Bieniek (2016, 8), "Like so many Latina TV characters ... they speak broken English and are unwed mothers who have children by multiple men," typical of other shows where "Latina women make herbal potions for Santeria rituals, and they control the kitchen, promoting the stereotype of the 'hot and spicy' Latina that equates her with cooking." An episode that demonstrates this well, season 2's "Low Self Esteem City," lays out the backstory for the strong-willed leader of the Spanish inmates, Gloria Mendoza. Audiences learn that she has not always been so tough and in control of her life. The episode flashes back to Gloria working at her bodega, with her Tía Lourdes's (Olga Merediz) botánica at the back of the shop.[10] As she is running a food stamp scheme, Gloria gets into a fight with her abusive boyfriend, Arturo (Hugo Medina), who questions her about what she is doing (fig. 4.6).

> GLORIA: [Speaking playfully] Okay. And who are you to tell me how to succeed? You don't have a penny to your name ... (speaking Spanish with English subtitles)
>
> ARTURO: [Reaches across the counter and hits Gloria in the face] Don't fucking talk to me like that. I'm busting my ass trying to help you, raising your fucking kids like they're my own, and you gonna talk to me like that? (speaking Spanish with English subtitles)
>
> GLORIA: [Now scared and humiliated] I'm sorry. (speaking Spanish with English subtitles)

Fig. 4.6 Gloria has just been slapped and humiliated by her boyfriend.

When Arturo later hits one of her sons, Gloria refuses to take him back. He bursts into the shop to threaten her, and, as Gloria and Lourdes try to get him to leave, the police arrive. Both Gloria and Lourdes assume they are there to arrest Arturo, but they have come for Gloria. A dissatisfied customer of Lourdes's Santería services had turned Gloria into the police for her food stamp fraud, and she is arrested (fig. 4.7). Toward the end of the episode, in a scene that *Entertainment Weekly*'s Hillary Busis (2014) said, "seems beamed in from a telenovela," Arturo returns to steal the money Gloria was saving and knocks over one of Lourdes's Santería shrines. The candles from the shrine light the shop on fire, and Arturo is burned to death. When the episode transitions from the flashbacks to the present, Gloria is a powerful figure at the prison, asserting her authority to prevent others from taking advantage of her. As head of the kitchen, she holds the most powerful position an inmate can have. This episode could be interpreted as a valiant attempt to portray domestic abuse, but it does little to dismantle Latina regimes of representations. Gloria might be a central figure in the story; she might be able to wield a certain amount of influence within the prison system, but she is also just another example of an oversexualized Latina—as demonstrated through her multiple children from different fathers—who lets her emotions override her reason.

The sheer number of Latina characters on the show is noteworthy. Yet, if these characters' latinidad is homogenized, with little attention paid to national and cultural specificity, the first three seasons of *OITNB* fail at

Fig. 4.7 Gloria being arrested for fraud while her abusive boyfriend runs out the back of the bodega.

their goal of inclusivity and diversity. For instance, the character of Daya is not Dominican—like the actress who portrays her—but Puerto Rican. The same pan-Caribbean casting is used for the Puerto Rican character Gloria, played by the Cuban Leyva. As I argue elsewhere, Latinx peoples from the Caribbean are either homogenized into a pan-Latino group or associated with what I call "marginal latinidad."[11] As "'Mexican' functions as a metonym for all Latina/os in a classic deployment of the flattening of difference," people who are explicitly not Mexican are marginal to the normalized idea of what it is to be Latina/o/x (Valdivia 2020, 13). Because of either African descent or a heritage rooted in the Spanish Caribbean (as opposed to Mexico/Latin America), marginal latinidad is "a form of Latino subjectivity and representation that, while included within US pan-Latinidad, is positioned outside of how Latina/os in the US are popularly imagined" (Goin 2016). As such, a mainstream audience and those casting for a mainstream text often do not recognize or consider the distinction among people of Dominican, Cuban, and Puerto Rican heritage. Therefore, pan-Caribbean casting is still a common practice. While such practices do not create the same type of backlash as does the casting of Puerto Rican Jennifer Lopez as the slain Mexican American singer Selena Quintanilla-Pérez, for example, they do reflect the general industrial dismissal of cultural specificity and the reliance on whether or not the actor "looks like" someone who has the ethnoracial background of the character.[12] As I argue in the following section, while this is combated by the great care given to Latinx specificity starting in season four, pan-Caribbean casting and the interchangeability of Caribbean Latina/o actors mitigate the potential extratextual impact of heterogeneous Latinx recognition.

Dynamic Latinidades and Dominicanidad: Season 4

Two of Litchfield's notorious meth addicts, Angie Rice (Julie Lake) and Leanne Taylor (Emma Myles), sit in the auditorium before being addressed by the prison administration (fig. 4.8). There have been many problems brought on by the overcrowding of the prison due to its recent privatization. The new inmates, most of whom are Latinx, spark the following conversation between the two ("Power Suit"):

> ANGIE: There's so many Mexicans now. It's like a Home Depot park'n lot in here.
>
> LEANNE: Dominicans. If you're gonna be racist, you gotta be accurate, or you just look dumb.
>
> ANGIE: Is Dominicans the ones that wear gold chains and smoke cigars and swim to Florida?
>
> LEANNE: No.
>
> ANGIE: Is it the coffee and the coke and the "Hips Don't Lie"?
>
> LEANNE: No, they talk a lot and play baseball, and they're always like, "I'm super not black," even though Haiti is the exact same island.
>
> ANGIE: That's right. Yeah . . . I hate them.

While this somewhat casual exchange about racism is meant to be comedic, it does reflect an understood depth of Latinx specificity from a character whose primary narrative function is to provide a presumed uneducated white Other for audiences to laugh at.[13] Leanne's familiarity with the multifaceted racial politics of Dominican identity is one of the few mainstream acknowledgments of the ethnoracial complexity of the DR and Dominican Americans. I discuss the complex relationship between dominicanidad and Blackness later in this chapter.

Although problematically framed, this asinine exchange nevertheless demonstrates a level of Latinx specificity that is not only rare but almost always mishandled when attempted. In the fourth season, not only do the Latinas get the upper hand among the incarcerated population, but the idea that Latinx peoples come from different nations, heritages, and races is openly discussed by both Latinx and non-Latinx characters. The radical visibility

Fig. 4.8 Racist inmates Angie (*left*) and Leanne (*right*) discuss the differences among different Latinx groups while waiting in the auditorium to be addressed by the prison administrators.

of Latinx specificity is abundantly clear in an exchange between Daya and Aleida, both Puerto Rican, and Dominican Blanca and Ruiz (fig. 4.9). As they work their usual kitchen assignments, which they have done together for nearly three seasons, the tension erupts as Ruiz puts down a stack of trays to be washed ("Power Suit").

> DAYA: How many fucking trays can there be?
>
> RUIZ: Whoa!
>
> DAYA: It was bad enough before these fucking plantain-eating Dominican bitches came.
>
> RUIZ: Everyone's gotta eat.
>
> DAYA: They're fucking everywhere! They're taking over the TVs, blocking the bathrooms, and commissary's all out of VapoRub. Like, no offense, but it's the truth.
>
> BLANCA: You see what I'm talking about. (speaking Spanish with English subtitles)
>
> RUIZ: [to Blanca] Just leave her alone, okay. She tried to do the right thing. Her baby got snatched up, and—
>
> BLANCA: [interrupting] Being sad made her racist? (speaking Spanish with English subtitles)
>
> ALEIDA: She ain't racist. She's just saying racist things.
>
> RUIZ: See? (speaking Spanish with English subtitles)
>
> BLANCA: How are you okay with this? [to Ruiz] (speaking Spanish with English subtitles)

Competing Latinidades 149

ALEIDA: Besides, we're Puerto Rican. We're supposed to give you shit.

BLANCA: Ah. [crosses arms and looks at Aleida]

DAYA: And Puerto Ricans are not the one[s] clogging the drain in the Spanish bathroom with all that kinky hair.

RUIZ: Oh!

ALEIDA: That would be the Dumb-inicans. Am I right?

DAYA: Dumb-in-a-can.

ALEIDA: [to Ruiz and Blanca] Not you guys. You guys are cool.

BLANCA: Fuck you, Bacardi bitches.

ALEIDA: Ah.

Up to this point in the episode, Ruiz has tried to stay away from the Dominican factionalism that has been manifesting. However, as she is reminded of the anti-Dominican sentiment harbored by many Puerto Ricans—due to both a growing population of Dominicans in Puerto Rico taking low-paying jobs and Dominican immigrants' dominance in the formerly Puerto Rican areas in New York—she finds herself being convinced by Blanca into siding with the Dominican faction.[14] This is a turning point in *OITNB*'s shift from pan-latinidad to thoughtfully constructed latinidades.

Inherent in latinidades are intergroup dynamics. As covered in chapter 1, the relationships among Latinx groups are often rooted in nationality. These nationality groups maintain Latinx specificity as well as horizontal hierarchies (Aparicio 2019). This can and often does manifest in "a national origin hierarchy that largely corresponds to White skin privilege. Those with greater Spanish ancestry have higher status than those with more visible Indigenous and/or African ancestry" (Gómez 2020, 14). The very heterogeneity within latinidad(es) allows, through the insistence of difference, one Latinx group to "Other" another. As Aparicio (2007, 45) argues, "There are outright cultural conflicts among Latinas/os, most of which stem from the ways in which we racialize each other. These negative constructions of the national Other are usually fueled and informed by stereotypes and racializations that have been historically shared and internalized, but that also point out differences in behavior that may result from gender and racial subordination and from the larger forces of colonization." Conflicts and prejudices exist not only between Puerto Ricans and Dominicans but also between Mexicans and Central Americans, Cubans and Mexicans, Puerto Ricans and Colombians, and so on. The nuances and intricacies of these inter-Latinx dynamics are fluid, situational, and constantly being

Fig. 4.9 Daya and Ruiz (*left* and *right foreground*) and Aleida and Blanca (*left* and *right background*) set the stage for a confrontation between the Dominican and Puerto Rican inmates.

negotiated. Therefore, engaging in latinidades means addressing the countless ways these dynamics play out.

While Latinx specificity is not in itself an anomaly in mainstream media, it is usually focused on the distinction between Mexicans and other Latin(o) Americans. What makes *OITNB*'s approach to both latinidades and dominicanidad unique is its candid inclusion of the complicated, and often racist, relationship between Blackness and dominicanidad. It is not just the meth addict Leanne who is aware of the confusion and dissonance over Dominican African descent; it is also the writers of the show. Dominican African descent is a tricky topic to address. This is especially true in the US context, as a person with any African ancestry, due to the concept of hypodescent, is understood to be Black. However, although most people from the DR have at least some degree of African descent, they do not typically consider themselves Black. Intrinsic in dominicanidad is a framework that obscures and qualifies Dominican Blackness. In the DR, this framework is related to Haiti, and in the US, it is related to African Americans. There is a great deal of nuance in navigating this ethnoracial framework. One might want to avoid it altogether when creating a media text for a presumed mainstream (i.e., white) audience. However, *OITNB* does not avoid it. Rather, the show directly engages with it in a scene showing the incarcerated women watching a televised soccer match between Haiti and the DR. By juxtaposing US-centric and DR-centric articulations of Dominican

African descent, the show effectively captures some of this complicated nuance ("Power Suit").

> OUIJA AZIZA (PLAYED BY ROSAL COLÓN): These *cocolos* all over the ball like it's a free sandwich.[15]
>
> RUIZ: *Cocolos?* For real? I bet you got cousins darker than they are, *pana*.[16]
>
> OUIJA: They ain't black-black. They indigenous.
>
> RUIZ: Yo, Flores! [whispers while waving Blanca over]. What's up with you? Everyone's already pissed at us. You're acting like an asshole. (speaking Spanish with English subtitles)
>
> BLANCA: It's the World Cup qualifiers! (speaking Spanish with English subtitles)
>
> RUIZ: Never in the history of FIFA has the Dominican Republic qualified (in English). Because they stink. So what the fuck? (speaking Spanish with English subtitles)
>
> BLANCA: It's about national pride. (speaking Spanish with English subtitles)
>
> RUIZ: Fuck national pride.
>
> BLANCA: What is the matter with you? (speaking Spanish with English subtitles)
>
> RUIZ: Their coach is from Cuba! (speaking Spanish with English subtitles)
>
> BLANCA: That's not their fault! (speaking Spanish with English subtitles)
>
> RUIZ: You know it's all bullshit, right? (speaking Spanish with English subtitles) Like, we're all the same, Cuban, Puerto Ricans (in English). We're all *mestizos*, we all eat rice and beans. (speaking Spanish with English subtitles)[17]
>
> BLANCA: Holy shit, when people hear about this, there will be no more war. (speaking Spanish with English subtitles)
>
> RUIZ: Fuck you, Flores (in English). You can't even tell us apart. You thought I was Venezuelan for, like, two months. (speaking Spanish with English subtitles)
>
> BLANCA: I've been here three years getting ignored and shit on. But now? No one's gonna push us around. You hear me? (speaking Spanish with English subtitles)

This humorous exchange takes on several discourses that constitute the negotiation of dominicanidad. It starts with a clear national binary between Haiti and the DR; placing the two countries in literal opposition in a soccer match (fig. 4.10). Through this framing, Haitian African descent is immediately positioned as Other to dominicanidad by Ouija, the inmate who is seen agitating the most for Dominican solidarity in Litchfield. This disavowal of Blackness is then questioned by Ruiz when she criticizes Ouija using the term *cocolos*. In doing so, Ruiz is exposing the tendency to obscure Dominican African descent under the guise of indigeneity. Historically, Dominicans in the DR have explained away their African descent by claiming that their dark brown skin and hair texture came from their Indigenous, not African, origins. As Ruiz redirects the conversation to Blanca,

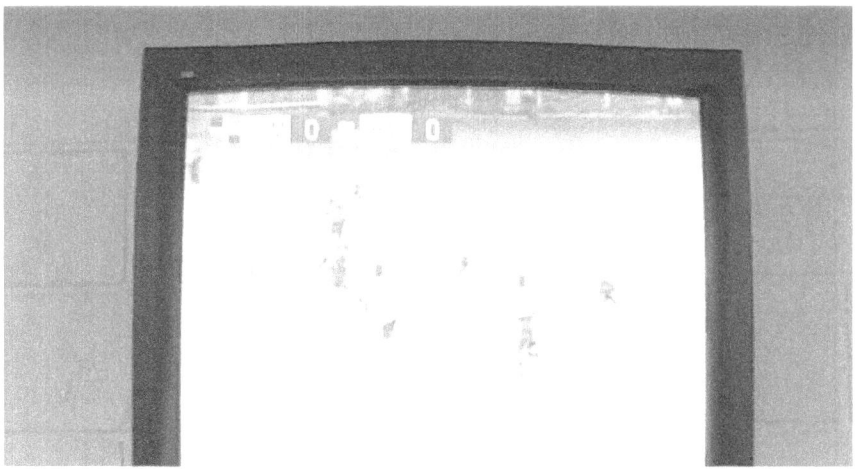

Fig. 4.10 TV in the prison playing a soccer match between the national teams of the Dominican Republic and Haiti.

there is a shift from a debate centered on the Dominican articulation of Haitian Otherness to one that now complicates Spanish Caribbean similarity (fig. 4.11). Ruiz is still clinging to the idea of pan-Latina/o/x unity, while Blanca is suggesting such unity is naive and unhelpful to their situation as incarcerated women. When Ruiz claims that they are all mestizos, she is doing two things: (1) using coded language to acknowledge African descent among herself and other peoples from the Caribbean and (2) demonstrating how national pride can be disruptive among those people who could be seen as sharing a common heritage and identity. Here, in informed and personal terms, each woman engages in a negotiation of dominicanidad and what that looks like for them. Furthermore, this exchange demonstrates how identity categories are both meaningless *and also* intensely significant.

Even if the vehicle for this Latinx specificity is animosity and hostility among Latinx groups, that does not necessarily diminish its significance and authenticity. For many Dominicans, it is imperative that to be understood, they need to be acknowledged as a distinctive group. Conceptualizing dominicanidad as one of the many latinidades, therefore, is a way to not only confirm a Dominican sense of self as distinct from other Latinx groups but also share with those groups a sense of solidarity or alliance. A television show about a women's prison is probably not the platform most Dominicans would have chosen for a televisual dominicanidad that would resonate with them. However, *OITNB*'s fourth season has proven that it is

Fig. 4.11 After celebrating an insult toward the white inmates in the room with Ouija, Blanca (*far left*) turns to Ruiz (*far right*), who is nervous about the interaction.

possible to include the complexities of both latinidades and dominicanidad in a mainstream media text. And when treated with the nuance it requires, dominicanidad can be understood by mainstream audiences while still feeling authentic to Dominican ones.

As part of a larger serial arc, this specificity, and the open and honest discussion it enables, allows all the incarcerated women to not only identify with each other but also resist the authorities that suppress them. In the fourth season, "for the first time, the palpable effects of systemic abuses derived from the lethal intersection between white supremacist governmentality and neoliberal privatization compel characters to see beyond restrictive identity politics and embrace a truly intersectional sense of solidarity" (Hassler-Forest 2018, 374). After the death of the universally beloved character Poussey Washington (Samira Wiley) following a demonstration, led in part by Blanca, against the increasingly brutal treatment of the prison guards, the inmates of Litchfield rebelled.[18] They put factionalism aside and organized a riot to ensure that their demands were met and that the corrections officer who murdered Poussey would be brought to justice. In what seemed to many like a radical move of intersectional alliance politics, the solidarity required to maintain the insurrection had an expiration date. As the uprising descended into a full prison riot, the women, especially those not as invested in justice for Poussey, began to look out for their own interests. The intense but brief moment of solidarity was eroded in the aftermath of the riot it spawned.

Unfortunately, the same was true for *OITNB*'s commitment to latinidades and Latinx specificity. It would not be until the seventh and final season that *OITNB* would renew its engagement with Latinx specificity.

Conclusion: Season 7 and the ICE-ing of Latinidades

As the series ended with its seventh season, most viewers probably expected a resolution to each of the characters' story arcs. And while this was provided for many of them, most notably the initial central character of Piper Chapman, *OITNB*'s writers introduced a new subplot concerning two of the Latinx characters. In what might be seen as a renewed commitment to latinidades, as well as an attempt to enhance its social justice initiative, this plot finds Blanca Flores and Maritza Ramos (played by Colombian American Diane Guerrero) "released" from Litchfield, only to be reinterned in an Immigration and Customs Enforcement (ICE) facility (fig. 4.12). According to one of the series' executive producers and writer of many of season 7's episodes, Guatemalan-born Carolina Paiz (2019), "We hoped our immigration storylines this season would play a similar role in humanizing the immigrant experience to those who see us as subhuman. Maybe I was naive to think this. But I have to believe that stories amount to something."

The story of Maritza is truly heartbreaking. The perpetually optimistic and fan-favorite character finds out that her mother has lied to her about being born in the US. Without the birth certificate that she believed would prove her citizenship, Maritza is handcuffed and deported to Colombia, a country she has never known. As each of the other women deportees disappears from the plane, we see Maritza alone and lost in her pain before she, too, fades away and disappears. When Blanca returns from her preliminary deportation hearing (fig. 4.13), she climbs up to her three-level bunkbed at the ICE facility and turns to see that Maritza is no longer there (fig. 4.14); she has been deported without being able to inform Blanca. Her absence in the bunk next to Blanca reinforces her disposability as an undocumented person in the US. Now there is another interned woman in her bed, another inmate to be disposed of by a system that sees their very existence as criminal.

And what of the Dominican Blanca? Did she share the fates of the other Latinas interned by ICE in *OITNB*—and, of course, the countless other real-life detainees who have had their lives upended, been separated from their children, and been denied even minimal legal and medical attention? Blanca has been one of the cleverest schemers throughout the series, able to use her wits to protect herself, help others, and use whatever leverage she

Fig. 4.12 Establishing shot of the ICE facility Blanca and Maritza are being held in.

Fig. 4.13 Blanca (in red) sits in a courtroom with other scared ICE-detained women as she waits for her turn to speak to the uncaring judge.

could muster to assert a modicum of control over her life. Unlike the others, she does not become one of the faceless and voiceless victims; she manages to mount a legal defense that releases her from ICE custody. Whatever happens next in her life, she has the power to make those choices. The character of Blanca might be seen as analogous to the Dominican experience in the US. She is able to navigate the institutions of oppression and marginalization

Fig. 4.14 Blanca turning to see another detainee in Maritza's bunk after she has unknowingly been deported.

while also having to negotiate her dominicanidad every step of the way. At the same time, her story is individualized. We see the events in her life at every stage when she is the axial character of an episode. She is not a generic figurehead for all Dominicans in the US but an individual who faces the same challenges and experiences many Dominicans face. This chapter began with a discussion of the negotiated dominicanidad of the character of Maria Ruiz; however, it is Blanca's dynamic dominicanidad that it ends with. Her narrative breaks with the conventions of Latinx representations, personalizes the political, and celebrates the power of self-determination.

Notes

1. Quoted in Tabar 2017.
2. Quoted in *HollywoodReporter.com* 2018.
3. To clarify the use of character names in this chapter, I use the name that is most frequently used on the show. As with many inmates, Maria Ruiz is usually referred to by her last name. However, Blanca Flores is most commonly referred to by her first name.
4. For research on televisual streaming, see Sanson and Steirer 2019; Elkins 2018; Barker and Wiatrowski 2017; McDonald and Smith-Rowsey 2016.
5. See Moore 2016 and Silverman and Ryalls 2016.
6. See Angela Davis (2003, 12), "As the US prison system expanded, so did corporate involvement in construction, provisions of goods and services, and use of prison labor . . . in a way that recalls the emergence of the military industrial complex, we began to refer to a 'prison industrial complex." For more on Latinas and the Prison Industrial Complex, see Juanita Diaz-Cotto 1996.
7. bell hooks (1992, 116) states that "all attempts to repress our/black people's right to gaze had produced in us an overwhelming longing to look, a rebellious desire, and oppositional

gaze. By courageously looking we defiantly declared: 'Not only will I stare. I want my look to change reality.' Even in the worse circumstances of domination, the ability to manipulate one's gaze in the face of structure of domination that would contain it, opens up the possibility of agency."

8. See Collins and Bilge 2016.

9. See Sánchez Korrol 1994.

10. Botánicas are shops that sell items for the practice of Santería and other African or Indigenous-derived religions and are usually run by a *santera/santero* (priestess/priest) practitioner.

11. See Goin 2016.

12. See Beltrán 2009.

13. See Scott (2017) and Barak (2016) for a discussion of white otherness in *OITNB*.

14. For a broader discussion of anti-Dominican sentiment among Puerto Ricans, please see Duany 2006; Sagás and Molina 2004; and Duany 1996.

15. *Cocolos* is a Dominican term for Black people from the Caribbean.

16. Dominican and Puerto Rican slang for "friend" or "pal."

17. *Mestizos* is a Spanish term for "mixed" or "mixture." It refers to the hybridization of the population of those places originally colonized by the Spanish. It is the result of ethnic and racial mixture among the colonizing Spanish, the various Indigenous populations, and the enslaved and free Africans.

18. The death of Poussey is one of the most controversial events of the series. It horrified fans and spurred much backlash against the show, specifically for the humanization of the character who murdered her, CO Baxter Bayley (Alan Aisenberg). An adequate discussion of this topic is beyond the scope of this book. For more about the reception and critique of how the show handled Poussey's death, see Brim 2016; Butler 2016; Givens 2016; Houston 2016; Stern 2017.

5

PRODUCING DOMINICANIDAD: *ASÍ SOMOS*/THE WAY WE ARE

Actors, filmmakers, publicists, politicians, journalists, and spectators have filled the United Palace theater—located in the heart of Washington Heights—for the premiere of *El Fantasma de mi Novia* (dir. Disla, 2018) on the first night of the Dominican Film Festival in New York City (DFFNYC). It's an all-hands-on-deck effort for the volunteers, myself included, to seat VIPs, scan tickets, hand out festival schedules, and add to the atmosphere of excitement, fun, and pride. This was a night of entertainment, an opportunity to watch (and maybe even walk) a red carpet, and only one of the countless film events held in New York City (NYC) every year. But for Dominican filmmakers and audiences, this was a night of affirmation. Whatever else the night was about, it was more importantly about demonstrating and celebrating the fact that Dominicans in the US are not only making themselves known but also producing media that can compete with Hollywood itself. For many, this is the "biggest and most important festival pertinent to the Dominican experience."[1] The sense of community in that audience—from the stars of the night to audience members who received free tickets from their employers—was not isolated to a niche film festival. It showcased a community using its creativity to establish a presence in a country that not only is unfamiliar with the Dominican population but also marginalizes Latinx peoples in its mainstream media. As DFFNY creator and director Armando Guareño said, "I wanted people to think of Dominican film as an industry, as a thing. . . . It's something that gets overlooked."[2]

The US media landscape has long been at best homogenous and at worst actively racist and prejudicial. It is controlled by a handful of powerful media conglomerates whose decisions are based on the logic that media must be commercial, media must be mainstream to be commercial, and mainstream means white audiences. This "logic" assumes that mainstream (white) audiences will only engage with media that features people who look like them. In practice, this results in a mass media that overrepresents white bodies and Euro-American norms and underrepresents Others, marginalizing a significant portion of the population (i.e., people of color). As a result, these Other groups are implied to be less important, less central, and even less American than the assumed white Euro-American norm. Anyone knowledgeable about race in media is acutely aware that this creates a barrier to the exclusive media industries. Scholarship on underrepresentation and the relative exclusion of people of color in the media industries abounds (Herrera 2015; Warner 2014; Acham 2012; Molina-Guzmán 2010; Beltrán 2009; Gray 2005; Zook 1999; Noriega and López 1996; hooks 1992). Most of this scholarship invites media-makers of color to "tell their own stories." The previous chapters of this book have examined several specific cases to explore how marginalized Dominican audiences deal with media that gets produced, but it is also imperative that we look to those who are navigating within this industrial environment, even while its "logic" actively works to exclude them.

Dominican media producers and creatives can be found in every sector of the media industry, whether they are visible or not. One needs only to look at the mainstream success of Dominican-born director and writer Osmany "Oz" Rodriguez, whose work on *Saturday Night Live* brought him an Emmy and whose comedy-horror flick *Vampires vs. The Bronx* (2020) was picked up by Netflix. However, due to the homogenization of Latinx people in the US, Dominican cultural specificity not only is often obscured but can also be a further means to their marginalization. As Dominicans do not have what could be called "generic latinidad," they are seen as not fitting into the preconceived notion of what the "normal" Latino should be and look like.[3] This can lead to internal Latinx marginalization, but it also can make Latinx people seem not Latino enough by white industrial gatekeepers (talent agents, studio executives, casting agents, financers, etc.). In the US media industries, Dominicans are rarely allowed to tell their own stories. Therefore, I want to talk about Dominican media production and how certain Dominicans approach their dominicanidad while working within or outside the media industry.

This chapter delves into the work, influences, and objectives of those few Dominican media producers and creatives who are pursuing their place in this fraught industrial environment. I look at the challenges facing

Dominicans working in US media, their goals, and how they pursue mediating their dominicanidad. Through personal interviews, a survey of comments found in journalistic work, and participation in the DFFNYC, a picture of the Dominican experience in the US media industries emerges.[4] Although this chapter focuses primarily on filmmakers, it also looks at Dominicans navigating the US media industries as a whole. While some have found success, many have found it difficult to express and find appreciation for their dominicanidad in an environment with little room for Latinx specificity.

Following a review of the Latinx groups that have created their own unique Latinx cinemas, namely, Chicano and Puerto Rican Cinemas, this chapter outlines how Dominican filmmakers and other media creatives are contributing to an emerging Dominican cinema. Particularly concerned with the themes of responsibility, Latinx solidarity, and Latinx specificity, the Dominican media-makers featured in this chapter share how they have pursued their careers and participated in a growing movement of producing mediated dominicanidad. At the crux of this movement, the DFFNYC is a space for producing dominicanidad as well as for active engagement between media-makers and consumers. The chapter ends with a "circuit of culture" analysis of the film *Veneno, La Primera Caída: El Relámpago de Jack* (dir. Blanchard, 2018). By exploring the various sites of meaning production surrounding a singular media text, this chapter answers the questions: What does producing dominicanidad entail, and how are audiences engaging with it?

Latinx Media Producers and Creatives

To say that Latinx filmmakers, screenwriters, producers, and creatives are underrepresented in the US media industries is an oversimplification of a system that not only undervalues Latinx stories but actively ignores Latinx heterogeneity. Among the interviews I conducted with Dominicans working in the media industries, every person emphasized the importance of supporting Latina/os behind the camera as the most crucial factor in Latinx/Dominican representation. Chicano filmmaker Jesús Salvador Treviño has repeatedly argued, "That's what we need in the industry, people at the top end of it—show runners, creators, producers—people who can create programs and get things going, hire people across the ranks."[5] However, the way the mainstream media industries operate is riddled with nepotism and elitism. Many scholars have pointed to the direct correlation between the symbolic annihilation of Latinx peoples and cultures in mainstream media and the lack of Latinx inclusion among those in behind-the-camera gatekeeping roles (Noriega 2000; Noriega 2004; Piñón 2011; Molina-Guzmán 2016). In fact, while the Latinx population in the US has grown significantly over the past few decades, levels of Latinx involvement in the media industries has remained constant since the 1970s, indicating that "Latinos' presence has decreased, relative to the population, while the power of the media has increased" (Noriega 2004, 106). Therefore, those in the media industries and those who study them pinpoint a "solution" to a myriad of representation problems in US media. But we must also consider the privileging of particular Latinx groups when they are placed in gatekeeping roles. Certain Latinx groups are positioned as the authority on all things Latino in the US media. According to Juan Piñón (2011, 395), "The construction of a sanitized Latinidad by mainstream media corporations has followed the distinctive cultural traits of some groups that are considered economically more valuable than others. The particular media visibility and presence of Puerto Rican, Cuban, and Mexican cultures and traditions are signs of their demographic relevance, whether by their population numbers, purchasing power, or political agendas. This demographic reality has had an impact upon the assumed value of the positioning of specific executives and producers' Latina/o subgroup identity." This indicates that even as the US media industries are beginning to recognize and include certain Latinx gatekeepers, this obscures the deep-rooted marginalization of these "less valuable" Latinx groups, including Dominicans.

Relevant is the legacy of the Latinx groups who have established a mediated space of self-representation. Latinx filmmakers working in Chicano cinema are probably the most successful and well researched.[6] From their origins in the Chicano Rights Movement and the La Raza movement of the 1960s and '70s, they tried to "subvert the discursive parameters for mass media so that Chicano filmmakers could work within and yet against the industry and its conventions" (Noriega 1992, 160). Filmmaker-activists like Francisco X. Camplis wrote manifestos in the 1970s demanding the formation of a Chicano cinema and stressing that this cinema "must by necessity be a weapon! It cannot be anything less" (Camplis 1997, 318). Filmmakers like Moctesuma Esparza, Sylvia Morales, Jesús Salvador Treviño, and Luis Valdez used their filmmaking to reject and confront the way mainstream US media represented Latinx peoples. Their filmmaking was political, confrontational, and empowering. For example, Luis Valdez's *Zoot Suit* (1982) takes the formula of the musical—as well as elements of Greek theater, no less—and turns it on its head to produce a defiant work that is rooted in Chicano sensibility, antiracist politics, and a refusal to let Latinx stories be silenced.

The fulfillment of these lofty ideals may have culminated in the "Decade of the Hispanic" in the 1980s and the "Latin Wave" about a decade later. And while it is certainly true that many Mexican American filmmakers and media producers gained access to mainstream visibility, and even success, it is difficult to see a film like *Selena* (dir. Nava, 1997), for example, as a universal Latinx story. It certainly was a triumph for Gregory Nava to write Mexican Americans into the discourse of the American Dream, make Jennifer Lopez a superstar, and prove his commercial worth to Hollywood. But it did not help US audiences reconsider the portrayal of Latinx peoples or recognize their significant contribution to US society. Nava is a proven talent in Hollywood filmmaking, but that role requires the ability to bend to the industry's will. While it is remarkable that this Chicano filmmaker has been able to not only tell Chicano stories but do so in a way that draws in mainstream (white) audiences, the very fact that he has made films for the mainstream means that his Latinx representations need to be "palatable" and avoid the confrontational politics that has long defined Chicano cinema.[7]

Less commercially successful but more geographically relevant, Puerto Rican cinema emerged around the same time as Chicano cinema. Rooted in the cultural revitalization tied to Puerto Rican political awakening and what Lillian Jiménez (1996) calls the "war of representation," Puerto Rican cinema has connections to the island but is also firmly embedded in the reality of living in NYC. Thinking of filmmaking as a battleground positions Puerto Rican documentarians and storytellers as media guerrillas who, through their multifaceted responses to oppression, work to expose the names and faces previously rendered invisible. Jiménez (1996, 35) asserts that "as we live in a complex and changing world, our special place within the margins allows us to interpret American culture and society in a unique way. We can contribute to the contemporary cultural discourse by producing filmic texts that present the complexity and the innovative and myriad experiences of our survival in an often hostile terrain." Not only do these media texts reflect the dual reality of Puerto Ricans as colonized people with a passion to resist, they also serve as sources of group strength and collectivity and speak to the Puerto Rican condition. For example, filmmaker and academic Frances Negrón-Muntaner, steeped in the tradition of using the camera as a "weapon," has made explicitly political films that reflect the identity struggles of Puerto Ricans in the US and their place within discourses of "American," "Nuyorican," and "Puertorriqueño" subjectivity.[8] Her work takes an intersectional approach to the fraught experience of being pulled by multiple positionalities, the lack of a sense of belonging, and the marginalization of one's voice and existence.

It is important to note the collaborative effort of these early Puerto Rican filmmakers, along with Chicana/o filmmakers, in the production of the 1970s PBS series *Realidades*.[9] The series featured both documentary and narrative content and was executive-produced by Dominican Lou De Lemos. Recordings of this series are part of the audiovisual collection at the City University of New York (CUNY) Dominican Studies Institute Dominican Library and Archives. Of course, this is an early example of pan-Latinx media collaboration, but more importantly, it points to three specific trends in Latinx media regarding Dominicans: (1) Dominicans have been involved in media production as long as and along with the other more visible Latinx groups, (2) Dominicans' geographic proximity to NYC has placed them within a highly active media production space, and (3) Dominicans' involvement in pan-Latinx media-making is often invisible, obscured by their previous demographic minority and the tendencies of Latinx homogenization. Contemporary Dominican filmmakers and media creatives have this legacy to contend with as they fight for their spot in the media industries.

Film as an Expression of Dominicanidad

When asked about their reasons for wanting to work in the media industries, most Dominican producers and creatives tell a story similar to those from people of all backgrounds: They are born to tell stories, making media is an expression of themselves, it allows them to have an impact on the world around them, it provides them a creative outlet, and so on. They share a passion with countless others from all over the world. However, while their various motivations might not be wholly unique, the way those motivations are translated into practice is rooted, often explicitly, in their pursuit of expressing dominicanidad. Even for filmmakers who "simply want to make movies," the films they make, intentionally or not, are rooted in their Dominican experience. According to filmmaker Chris Lopez,

> We have things to say, and it's not always got to be about, "yeah, I'm Dominican." . . . It's not all about me saying I'm Dominican. It's about me

saying, "look what I can do." And it's inherited that I am Dominican. The stories do come from the background that I have. So I don't think you would get the same story if it was some guy in Kansas writing it. So it is all inheritance I think.... And I would love for us to kind of be known as storytellers. And not just a few people that are telling these immigrant stories. I feel like we are just so much more than that.[10]

In other words, Lopez does not have to explicitly address his dominicanidad in his films for his work to be a reflection of it. A film does not have to be a film about Dominicans to express dominicanidad, just as a film does not need to be about the US to express an American worldview. In Lopez's current project, a thriller set in the world of ballet, his Dominican heritage will still influence the film he ultimately creates.

While I contend that dominicanidad is a dominant lens for Dominican filmmakers and media creatives, it is articulated on an individual level. When looking at Latinx filmmakers more broadly, Jonathan Risner (2016, 9) warns, "The relationship between a director's identity (Latina/o or non-Latina/o) and the film's content (Latina/o or non-Latina/o) varies, and each relationship should be approached with an open expectation for how it manifests itself within the film and across different paratexts." Therefore, it would be wrong to assume that every Dominican filmmaker and media creative would share the same relationship and interpretation of their dominicanidad. However, from the interviews I have conducted and those conducted by members of the press, a series of themes emerge. Among them are responsibility, Latinx solidarity, and Latinx specificity. These themes are approached differently by each Dominican working in the media industries, but there is a perceivable sense that they reflect an open and dynamic dialogue between individual media-makers, media-makers and the industry, and media-makers and audiences.

Responsibility

Many of the filmmakers I spoke with shared a sense of responsibility when it came to the media they produced. For Dominican filmmakers and other media creatives, responsibility means not only committing to their own creative vision but also shouldering their inevitable burden of representation. According to filmmaker and actress Soleidy Mendez,

> Generally, anyone working in the media has the power as well as a responsibility to influence how others are seen and portrayed. We should emphasize those qualities that make us who we are without only focusing on

certain aspects. Just as Hispanics, in general, are not a monolith so are not Dominicans. We come in different shapes, forms, and colors. We behave in many different ways and strive for different things in life and all aspects of our idiosyncrasy can be and should be represented so that we are not boxed as this or that but so that people understand us better as a whole and appreciate our differences more.[11]

For Mendez, it is not just about increasing the *quantity* of Dominican representations and stories but also showing their *variety*. Like many mediamakers, Mendez creates films that are deeply personal and dedicated to issues she finds important. And as a Dominican American, whether intentional or not, that means creating through a lens of dominicanidad.

As a colleague of Mendez, Chris Lopez also expressed a sense of expectation and pressure to represent Dominicans and Dominican filmmaking. He told me that he feels as if he is part of an important moment for Dominican filmmaking. And he is right. The Dominican Republic (DR) has released and/or collaborated on around one hundred films in the last five years.[12] Many Dominican filmmakers raised in the US are using their joint citizenship to take advantage of the recent film legislation in the DR that provides support and funding for filmmaking. According to Lopez, these films are part of "a cultural movement . . . this is the whole country, basically. This is us saying, 'this is what we can do.' It's almost like the Olympics for us. Like, we are representing the country, for sure. And we take great pride in that."[13] By capitalizing on recent changes in the DR, along with increasing access to programs like Ibermedia that offer grants and distribution opportunities, those Dominicans who are born, raised, or living in the US are going to the island to make their films when they cannot find the resources here.[14] Not only does this engage in the continuous relationship among the diaspora, it also situates filmmaking as a diasporic phenomenon. The Dominican American transnational experience is being replicated in its filmmaking, which will pave the way for more Dominican films to be screened in US movie theaters—but will it be a step to Hollywood or more profitable filmmaking? The sense of responsibility to other Dominicans might complicate the necessary compromises for entrée into more commercial filmmaking.

National Book Award winner and poet Elizabeth Acevedo, who has recently started writing screenplays for Hollywood, has stated, "I never want to be the only one." This can create pressure on a person to be a perfect representation of a community. She mentions the "pressure that is specifically Dominican, where you have a people that are so invested in being represented carefully."[15] Acevedo's discomfort with being the only Dominican on a production has influenced her professional choices. She leverages her networks to create collaborative projects with other Dominicans, using her capital as a sought-after writer to insist on a strategy that highlights Dominican inclusivity. She describes how an "amazing Dominican production company contacted me. When I talk to producers, I ensure that they work with that production company and shoot in the DR. And to shoot in Spanish when in the DR. We have to collaborate and support those other creatives."[16] In her position, Acevedo wields influence; however, most Dominicans working in the media industries do not have this advantage. They lack the power to demand these types of concessions. Many Dominican filmmakers and media creatives choose to collaborate with other Latinx groups who are better positioned in the media industries.

Latinx Solidarity

Faced with limited resources and recognition, many Dominican mediamakers focus more on leveraging networks through the pan-Latinx paradigm already hegemonic in the media industries than on Latinx solidarity. By tethering media production networks within the pan-Latinx framework, some Dominican filmmakers and media creatives pursue collective clout rather than cultural specificity. For actress and burgeoning screenwriter and producer Katherine Castro, to change representation, actors should use their connections and influence with other Dominicans and Latina/os in the industry to produce their own projects. Castro began her own film project, *Someday* (2018), in response to Hollywood's claim that she was too "ethnically ambiguous" for Latina roles. According to Castro, "I started to create my own creations and I started to get together with people who were also creative and in some way support them."[17] Writing, producing, and starring in *Someday* gave Castro creative control and an opportunity to depict a character the way she wanted. And while this strategy is similar to Acevedo's, Castro's approach is pan-Latinx. For her, Dominicans in the media industries should prioritize their place within the larger Latinx community as a way to find more inclusion and influence. She argues, "We have to support each other, we are a single community. Although within that we have different nationalities, in the end it is a single voice. If it goes well for a Latina, it will go well for all of us . . . I think in this we have to stick together as one voice, as a community."[18] Castro, who internalizes discourses of a unified Latinx imaginary or community, sees Dominicans as intrinsically tied to other groups with Latin American or

Spanish Caribbean heritage. As a model, she points to the work of African American filmmakers and media creatives who "support each other, they help each other out, they cast each other."[19] It would be easy to interpret this strategy as one entrenched in pan-Latino homogeneity, but there is much more to it. By aligning with the broader Latinx community, Dominicans can capitalize on demographic and economic significance. As the largest minority group in the US, Latina/os have more weight and influence than their individual nationality-based groups. Moreover, Latinx consumption of film is disproportionately high, and therefore, they represent a lucrative audience to Hollywood. Drawing on her experience with the complexities of the film industry, Castro recognizes profit as a motivating factor for Latinx solidarity: "The movie industry, it's a business." Castro is willing to prioritize Latinx essentialism over her dominicanidad if it means she must speak a language the industry will listen to. This does not mean, however, that she minimizes her dominicanidad. "Obviously," she says, "highlighting my Dominican-ness, wherever I go, the first thing I say is 'Sure, I'm Dominican, but we [Latina/os] are a community.'"[20] This reveals a savvy approach to an environment that is difficult to navigate as well as a strategy that is primed by Hollywood industrial norms. For those working in a transnational film industry like Spanish-language film, such a tactic would be less effective.

César Rodriguez, a Dominican filmmaker who has done most of his work in the Puerto Rican film industry, carries his dominicanidad into all of his projects, regardless of where he is making them or where the actors and crew are from. Inspired to become a filmmaker after watching Francis Ford Coppola filming scenes for *The Godfather Part II* (1974) while a child in Santo Domingo, Rodriguez has worked on projects in Los Angeles, Miami, New York, Chicago, the DR, Puerto Rico, Colombia, Argentina, Panama, Venezuela, and Brazil. The geographic variety is due, in no small part, to the international reality of Spanish-language media. Yet it also shows Rodriguez's negotiation of where Dominicans might carve out a role for themselves in the international and transnational film industries. Reflecting on how his film *Ruido* (2006)—awarded the Prix de l'Innovation by the Montreal International Film Festival in 2006—was categorized in Canada, Puerto Rico, and the DR, Rodriguez argues that a film made by an entirely Puerto Rican cast and shot in Puerto Rico still counts as a Dominican film because he served as the film's writer and director. "We are still Dominican to the beat of the drum, we may be outside our country, but we never forget our country. We have it here [points to heart], we have it here [points to head]."[21] Rodriguez considers that a work produced by a Dominican living and creating media in Puerto Rico can be both Puerto Rican and Dominican; they are not mutually exclusive. He expressed that his pride in his dominicanidad might connect him to the land of Hispaniola, but his work in Puerto Rico connects him to that land and the people who live there. Rodriquez is a truly transnational filmmaker, yet he does not see that as a threat to his ability to express dominicanidad through his films. He discussed how *Ruido* "winks to the Dominican Republic" at points in the film and was successful in that country.[22] Although he never discussed his work as being explicitly rooted in Latinx solidarity, by placing himself in a community of Latinx and Latin American filmmakers—for example, he exalted in the recent success of Mexican filmmakers in the last decade of the Oscars—he participates in reinforcing the hegemony of pan-latinidad. What I find most revealing about his perspective and experience, however, is his insistence that this equates not to a homogenization of Latinx specificity but to the creation of spaces for Latinx plurality.

Latinx Specificity

Of the three dominant themes (responsibility, Latinx solidarity, and Latinx specificity), it is Latinx specificity that is most explicitly involved in the expression of dominicanidad. As the analysis of Chicana/o filmmakers telling their own stories indicates, "this new way of getting close to the film subjects inverts the filmic practices by dismantling the very formula of otherness" (Meléndez 2016, 41). By foregrounding dominicanidad through a pursuit of Latinx specificity, Dominican filmmakers reject conventions of both mainstream and Latinx media that lead to their mediated invisibility and marginalization. Reflecting on his experiences trying to work in mainstream media, Chris Lopez told me, "When you go to LA, they don't understand what a Dominican is. Yeah, I think the biggest [problem], like industry wide, is that Dominicans aren't considered Latinos . . . we are somehow excluded or we are othered."[23] Essentially, Dominicans not only are invisible in mainstream media but are so marginalized within panethnic latinidad that they are misunderstood by Latina/os and non-Latina/os alike.

As expressed by Soleidy Mendez in her discussion of responsibility, as well as César Rodriguez's insistence on Latinx plurality, the inclusion of dominicanidad in media texts is the result of intention. Mendez told me, "I think the representation issue in the USA is not specific to us [Dominicans] but to Latinos in general and that's what I'd like to see change. Us being represented in proportion to our social presence and contribution in and to this country."[24] She proposes two changes: a greater acknowledgment of Latinx peoples in US society and a better understanding of the various groups that make up the Latinx community. Both changes are essential to improving the underrepresentation and symbolic annihilation of Latina/os, in addition to creating mediated latinidades and, specifically, dominicanidad in US media. Elizabeth Acevedo contends, "In entertainment . . . Latinx people have some of the least representation in terms of writers, producers, directors . . . it is difficult to get into the space, when you get into the space, most people are Mexican. There is nothing wrong with that, but it isn't representative."[25] Acevedo is not suggesting that Mexican and Mexican Americans should not be working in production roles; rather, she believes that their voices are not representative of all Latinx peoples. Many Dominican filmmakers and media creatives are more explicitly invested in Latinx specificity than others and use it as a way to foreground their dominicanidad.

Chris Lopez, whose work does not focus solely on dominicanidad, broadens the perception of Dominicans by casting them in nonstereotypical roles. Lopez, who was inspired to start working on his own projects after years of disappointment as an actor, says, "It was really hard for someone that looks the way I do" to be cast in nonstereotypical roles, where "the roles [he] was going for were like one-liners in *Law & Order*, or rapist, or something weird."[26] His first film as screenwriter and director was the short *The Cure* (2012), in which he cast himself as a neuroscientist. Reflecting on the production, he told me, "I was like, yeah sure, Dominicans can be that. And it wasn't about, like, a Dominican neuroscientist, it's just the actor was Dominican."[27] But that is no simple or meaningless idea. While some might dismiss this as a postracial approach to casting—and that would be a fair assessment—I argue that postracial casting has not led to the inclusion of Dominicans and does not relate to producing mediated dominicanidad. The casting of Dominican actors in nonstereotypical roles is not a practice in Hollywood, Spanish-language films, or mainstream television. Radical by its simple existence, casting Dominicans in nonstereotypical roles is an acknowledgment not only of Latinx specificity but also of the diversity within dominicanidad.

Dominican actors also understand the importance of using their position to creatively express dominicanidad through their performance. Actor Angel Bismark Curiel, who plays Lil' Papi Evangelista on FX's popular television series *Pose*, feels that it is important to draw on his Dominican identity and heritage when playing his role.

> I think I've been very blessed to be able to just really lean into that, right. All the history that I have from my family and their experiences and how it influenced me being a child in America of Dominican parents. And so I get to really bring a lot of that into particularly Papi, right, who is Dominican. So I have all these flavors that I get to play around with when I show up to set. Things like, you know, hold on, how might someone I know say this or what would Mimi say about this plate of food, right? You know, like all this kind of stuff . . . and it becomes this riff that I just get to really enjoy cuz I get to bring that culture aspect of myself that I'm very proud of, you know. I'm proud that my mom is Dominican. I'm proud that my father is Dominican and that I have roots deep into the Dominican Republic.[28]

Although Curiel's experience playing Lil' Papi is self-affirming, it is more of an anomaly in his experience as a working actor in Hollywood. Even after this breakout role, he has struggled with Hollywood casting agents who see his textured hair and slightly-too-brown skin as disqualifying him from most Latinx roles. He described one casting call as entering a "room of Justin Bieber looking individuals. Like, they were all pretty white boys with silky, smooth hair and I was like why am I the only brown dude here with, you know, curly, puffy hair? Are we looking for a Latino or not?"[29] For Curiel, the real problem lies with the (mostly white) executives, producers, and creative decision-makers. With no Latinx people in general and Dominicans in particular in key decision-making roles, the media industry will not change. This motivates Curiel to strive beyond his primary job—performing in front of a camera—to creatively impact the projects he is involved with and to produce projects of his own. He argues that Latinx/Dominican actors must "really just try to push yourself to find out what creating material looks like for you. Cuz that's the one way that we can say, 'no, like we're here and we're gonna make it work.'"[30] And his involvement in projects like the DFFNYC is one way of doing just that.

Celebrating Cinematic Dominicanidad: The Dominican Film Festival

Film festivals have always been places where independent filmmakers can find distribution deals and audiences can gather to explore the possibilities of filmmaking. These festivals connect media-makers to those in the industry, introduce audiences to new approaches to filmmaking, and facilitate the formation of the networks essential to the continued production of new work. Although the number of film festivals increases every year—every niche and city hosting a festival to capitalize on their popularity—some festivals still make a significant impact. This is especially true for marginalized media-makers and audiences who are ignored by mainstream media. And while "Latina/o cinema often possesses an ephemeral cinematic infrastructure... festivals provide a crucial mode of visibility for Latina/o films" (Risner 2016, 11). Consider the significance of the Sundance Film Festival to Robert Rodriguez's meteoric success.[31] Or the unprogrammed premiere of Jordan Peele's directorial debut *Get Out* (2017).[32] The media industry is made and remade at film festivals, and audiences respond with great enthusiasm to the films shown there.

It was in this frenzied environment that the DFFNYC kicked off in 2012. Founded by Dominican-born Armando Guareño, a student of the CUNY City College of New York film school, the festival was created to provide a platform for the exhibition and circulation of Dominican filmmaking. As one of the "most prominent figures in the Latin American cultural scene in the United States," Guareño recognized a void, saying, "Our food and music were everywhere, but where were the arts of ours? I needed an answer for that."[33] Expanding from showing only ten films in its first year to dozens of feature films, special screenings of short film programs, and free-to-the-public workshops and master classes, the DFFNYC has fulfilled many of Guareño's ambitious goals. In fact, it has resulted in a version of the festival held in Montreal, with plans to expand to other cities in the future. Guareño explains, "Eventually, I'd like to bring it all over the world."[34] According to the festival's official website, "DFFNYC is the only official festival that promotes Dominican cinemas and filmmakers in the Diaspora in the USA and Canada. The festival has been recognized by the Speaker of the House of New York City and the Congress of the United States of America" (dominicanfilmfestival.com). Anne del Castillo, director of the NYC Mayor's Office of Media and Entertainment, has said of the festival that "the Dominican community comprises the largest Latino group in New York City and this annual film festival continues to be an important celebration of established and promising talents within this community."[35] Earning its place among the pantheon of highly esteemed film festivals, the DFFNYC is a kind of home for Dominicans in the media industries.

Regarding the filmmakers who see attending the DFFNYC as "coming home," Katherine Castro says that the festival is "very important because it is projecting the work that we, our community, is doing ... if we look at the film industry, there are still not many of us [Dominicans] who are [working] here mostly in Hollywood." In her experience working in Hollywood, Castro has been an outlier, but at the DFFNYC, she and her dominicanidad are seen, appreciated, and understood. Moreover, the festival

> promotes our culture all over the world, and we are presenting to the world that we do know how to make films, that we do understand production. Yes, we have quality products, we are on par with Hollywood. We have so much talent in all areas. In areas of production, areas of acting, in areas of the crew, we have everything, we have so many trained people. If it was not for the festival, I think the film world would not realize that we have all this from the Dominican Republic ... I would always like to be able to participate every year. It will always be my home. And I hope to continue to participate.[36]

Without the DFFNYC, Castro might not have been able to make her passion project, *Someday*. It would have been difficult for her to get the support for its production or find a place to show it. Her experience with the festival resonates with Guareño's goal of "expanding the popular notions of the kinds of art produced and created by those within the Dominican diaspora."[37] Castro is not alone in recognizing the importance of the festival to her career. Comedian Kiki Melendez said, "Our inclusion within the Dominican Film Festival is incredibly exciting and rewarding."[38] Not only does the festival provide a platform to celebrate and get audience feedback, it also facilitates the creation and sustaining of networks that support future work. At the DFFNYC, filmmakers and other media creatives can connect, discuss upcoming projects, get advice, and meet industry professionals who can help them achieve their goals. And while this is not uncommon at other film festivals, those attending the DFFNYC are invested in cultivating Dominican talent and filmmaking.

The DFFNYC has played a significant role in defining what Dominican cinema looks like. Each year's curated list of feature films, shorts, and public events is guided by Guareño's intention to "show films with ideas. I want to show films that people can go see and then think about it when they go home."[39] The festival highlights those making work that resonates with the desire to find a cinema that speaks to dominicanidad. Guareño's object is simple: "make the Dominican culture known through cinematography."[40] According to Chris Lawton (2014) of *Latin Business Today*, "There is such a unique spin of telling a Dominican story and expressing it can be challenging; however, there are minds that can capture the uniqueness in a short or long form film and recognition is needed for that." And it is not just Dominican audiences that are recognizing the potential of Dominican cinema. The Sixth Annual DFFNYC in 2017 debuted with filmmaker José María Cabral's *Carpinteros* (*Woodpeckers*), the first Dominican film to screen at the Sundance Film Festival. Other films have gone on to be showcased at such prestigious festivals as Cannes, Toronto, and the American Film Institute's Latin American Film Festival. Proving that Dominican cinema has reached a pivotal moment, more mainstream festivalgoers are starting to share in the excitement experienced by Dominican audiences.

While the attendance for each film, program of shorts, or talks/panels varies considerably depending on the time, location of venue, and NYC's summer weather, there is usually a respectably sized audience. Not surprisingly, local Dominicans make up most of the viewing audience, but the DFFNYC is now attracting Dominicans from around the US, non-Dominican New Yorkers, and, of course, industry professionals looking to spot new talent. According to Guareño, "Our Dominican films are having an impeccable moment and they are worth sharing on a larger platform."[41] Attendees seem to be aware of annual festival's contribution to showcasing Dominican filmmaking to a wider audience and affirming Dominicans' position as a significant Latinx group in the US. Several audience members spoke of Dominican filmmaking as being "in its infancy" or "too formulaic," or as "copying Mexican or Hollywood films"; however, these comments did not lessen the audience's enjoyment of a cinema that is not only emerging but coming into its own. Reflecting on this current moment in Dominican filmmaking, Chris Lopez told me, "I think the Dominican Renaissance is happening right now. I am really excited to be starting with it, because my film . . . will represent the country anywhere it goes. So I am really excited to have this project, hopefully, be that project that kind of puts us at an international level."[42] Both Guareño's and Lopez's hopes point to a cinema that is on the rise, one that will one day receive the international recognition they feel it deserves.

Lopez's excitement is shared by the attendees of the numerous master classes and talks/panels that the DFFNYC has held for the past few festivals. Free and open to the public, these events are quite popular. Many feature the biggest names in Dominican and US media; actors, filmmakers, academics, and representatives of the new Dominican film studios all interact with attendees in forums of mutual exchange and debate.[43] They facilitate a more intimate engagement between media-makers and their audiences and operate as spaces of shared *dominicanidad*. In attendance are people looking for insight and guidance on entering the media industries, while many others are interested in how media shapes and represents Dominican identity and positionality in the US. These attendees recognize the unifying nature of Dominican media-making and its potential to increase Dominican visibility within US pan-latinidad and the US mainstream. There is an intangible power in telling one's own stories and supporting those filmmakers and media creatives who speak both to and for Dominicans. It is apparent with each year's festival that audiences interested in Dominican cinema are growing in number and strength. As Guareño has said, "We are more than merengue and bachata. We are also cinema."[44]

"This Is What We Can Do": *Veneno, La Primera Caída*

When given the opportunity and industrial support, Dominican filmmakers and media creatives are able to deliver both dominicanidad and high-quality productions. To illustrate this, I examine one film in particular, *Veneno, La Primera Caída: El Relámpago de Jack* (dir. Blanchard, 2018), the first installment of an ambitious three-film project from the young Dominican filmmaker Tabaré Blanchard. The film debuted at the DFFNYC in 2018 and was subsequently picked up first by Showtime *en español* and then by the major streaming services (Amazon, Apple+, Google Play, and YouTube). It stars one of the media industry's most successful Dominicans, Manny Pérez, and tells the story of an icon of Dominican culture, wrestler Jack Veneno. A thoroughly entertaining film, it introduces Blanchard's auteurist style, capitalizes on the star power of Manny Pérez, and uses the nostalgic tie to a beloved figure to delight Dominican audiences.

A Dominican Auteur: Tabaré Blanchard

Starting his career directing music videos and commercials, the Dominican-born Blanchard's first major filmmaking project was the documentary *La montaña* (The Mountain, 2013). Although in many ways a traditional documentary, it has a stylized aesthetic and storytelling approach that is authentically Dominican. Covering the events of the first Dominican expedition to the summit of Mount Everest, the documentary parallels the history-making ascent with the story of three Dominican youths making their own expedition to Pico Duarte, the highest peak in the DR. The message of the film is a bit contrived: Everyone has their own mountain they must climb. Yet, as Dominican film critic José D'Laura (2013) said of the film, "[*La montaña*] deserves to be seen by the greatest number of Dominicans without distinction because we need encouragement in the face of our challenges and because seeing our tricolor flag waving on Everest renews our faith in our future." The narrative approach, visually stunning cinematography, and energetic nondiegetic music establish Blanchard as an auteur, perhaps the first in Dominican cinema. Jaie Laplante (2013), the Miami Film Festival's executive director and director of programming, described *La montaña* as "the first I've seen of what may be a wave of new creative cinematic energy bubbling up in one of the Caribbean's most joyous (and often complicated) cultures... Blanchard brings a sleek photographic sheen and an up-tempo drive to the story. More than many Latin American documentary filmmakers, Blanchard understands an audience's deep emotional identification with heroes." An understanding that would suit him well in his next major project, *Veneno*.

The success of *La montaña* might have brought Blanchard some international recognition, but that does not diminish the cinematic and artistic achievement of his first narrative film project. Having explored what will no doubt become his signature filmmaking aesthetic in *La montaña*, *Veneno, La Primera Caída: El Relámpago de Jack* is not only a thoroughly entertaining and polished work of Dominican cinema but, more importantly, an expression of auteurist filmmaking with marked dominicanidad. I do not use the term *auteur* lightly, nor do I subscribe to its elitist connotations developed by the *Cahiers du Cinéma*'s high-minded François Truffaut and Jean-Luc Godard. The term *auteur* signals a filmmaker's unique style, signature, or narrative approach that characterizes their work as distinctively theirs. Achieving auteur status is not an easy feat, and it is made more difficult by the compromises required of unestablished filmmakers. But by working outside of the dominant centers of filmmaking (e.g., Hollywood), emerging Dominican filmmakers can enjoy a level of creative freedom usually reserved for established directors: Francis Ford Coppola, Guillermo del Toro, Spike Lee, Martin Scorsese, and Quentin Tarantino. Blanchard, however, is taking advantage of this moment in Dominican filmmaking, the newly available resources from the Dominican government, and the hunger for cinematic dominicanidad to secure his spot among the vanguard of Latinx filmmakers.

Based on the rise to fame of Rafael Sánchez—later known as Jack Veneno—and his former partner-turned-archrival, Relámpago Hernández, the nostalgic biopic is not the type of film one would expect from Blanchard. He admitted, "I am not a wrestling fan, I am not a Jack Veneno fan, but I am a fan of telling stories."[45] Blanchard's lack of interest in wrestling is more than made up for by the film's producer and cowriter, Riccardo Bardellino, who says, "I have been a huge fan of Jack my entire life. No one cares more about wrestling than I do."[46] Bardellino approached Blanchard with the idea for the project because he felt that Blanchard was the only filmmaker who could do the story justice. He believed the burgeoning auteur could speak to Dominican sensibilities, brave the required critique of corrupt Dominican institutions, and highlight locations in NYC and the DR as more than mere backdrops. According to Sandra E. Garcia (2018) of the *New York Times*, "*Veneno* also neatly weaves in Dominican culture and folklore, from the fiestas patronales—which are a lot like state fairs—to scenes involving Santeria (which his best friend, the wrestler Relámpago Hernández, hopes will help him in the ring) and corruption ([Hernández] is arrested by progovernment forces). The movie even covers the first time Joaquín Balaguer was elected president, and the response of many Dominicans, who believed Balaguer cheated his way into office but who were too fearful of the government to speak out." The content alone makes it a film rooted in dominicanidad, but it is the production and style of the film that make it so exciting.

Edited in an almost comic book style, the film is fast-paced and even chaotic at times. The ubiquitous superhero movies so popular among international audiences often fail to fully exploit the structure of the comic books they are based on. *Veneno*, similar to the original TV series *Batman* (ABC 1966–68) and Marvel's *Spider-Man: Into the Spider-Verse* (dir. Persichetti, Ramsey, and Rothman, 2018), employs this underused narrative approach to keep the audience in suspense. Complemented by its energetic—almost aggressive at times—soundtrack, the film's look and sound are both fresh and nostalgic. With nods to popular Latin American filmmaking styles, specifically magical realism and *lucha libre* (Mexican wrestling) superheroes, the film also draws on the camp and kitsch of the wrestling world. *Veneno* is peppered with frenetic and acrobatic wrestling and fighting scenes backed by drum-heavy Caribbean music. The acting and cinematography are strong enough to compete with anything mainstream Hollywood has to offer, while keeping the whimsy and spectacle common in the best Latin American films. As stated by one online commentator, "The convincing performances by the cast bring the story to life, treading the line between the absurd and the clever with effortless grace. Scenes of supernatural brujas and over-the-top wrestling matches are accompanied by a serious commentary on the political landscape of Santo Domingo in the '70s. Corrupt policemen, scummy businessmen and mobsters ground the story in historical accuracy."⁴⁷ And what of the man himself? Not only did Jack Veneno have a cameo, but when asked what he thought of the first of the trilogy of films, he said, "I am very proud of this movie," particularly the acting.⁴⁸ If this is what filmmaking in the Dominican diaspora can offer—humor, panache, thrilling stories, and stylish editing—how long will it take the rest of the world to notice?

It has not taken very long for *Veneno* to receive international recognition. It has received numerous film festival awards, including fifteen of the seventeen awards it was nominated for at the 2018 Premio La Silla, granted by the Asociación Dominicana de Profesionales de la Industria del Cine, what one might call the Dominican Academy Awards. A major achievement, considering *Veneno* was competing against the Sundance Film Festival–acclaimed *Carpinteros* (dir. Cabral, 2017). Blanchard said, "I made the film envisioning audiences in the Dominican Republic and in the Dominican Diaspora, but the film has transcended that" through its success in international film festivals. "Sincerely, for me, that has been a big surprise."⁴⁹ However, it was probably not a surprise to the DFFNYC's Armando Guareño or Dominican movie critic Andy Martínez Nuñez, who said it "represents a significant step forward for the Dominican film industry" due to not only its nostalgia and stylized production but also "a talented cast, director, careful editing and a script written with even more care."⁵⁰

The King of Dominican-American Film: Manny Pérez

Starring in *Veneno*'s title role is Dominican American Manny Pérez, who bears a marked resemblance to Jack Veneno and is by far the most versatile and well-known Dominican actor working today. His popularity and success made Pérez the perfect choice to lead the *Veneno* trilogy. The film uses the symbolic capital of Manny Pérez among both mainstream and Dominican audiences to tell the story of the well-known Dominican icon. Without Pérez, the film would still work. But with him, it becomes part of the canon of work highlighting the quality of Dominican film and filmmaking. Saying that he "was born to play this role," Pérez has long strived to play characters that resonated with his own dominicanidad.⁵¹

Currently playing the lead in Amazon Prime's *Big Dogs*—Dominican-American detective Sixto Santiago—Dominican-born Pérez's decades-long career includes appearances in prime-time television: *Luke Cage* (Netflix), *Law & Order: Special Victims Unit* (NBC), *Rescue Me* (FX), *Third Watch* (NBC); US independent cinema: *Coyote Lake* (dir. Seligman, 2019),

Back in the Day (dir. Borghese, 2016), *Love Is Strange* (dir. Sachs, 2014), *The Ministers* (dir. Reyes, 2009), *Rockaway* (dir. Crook Brothers, 2007), *El Cantante* (dir. Ichaso, 2006), *Party Monster* (dir. Bailey and Barbato, 2003), *Washington Heights* (dir. De Villa, 2002); and Spanish-language cinema (mostly produced by Dominican and Puerto Rican filmmakers): *La Isla Rota* (dir. Germán, 2018), *Colao* (dir. Perozo, 2017), *Loki 7* (dir. Alemany, 2016), *Verdad o Reto* (dir. Reyes, 2016), *Ponchao* (dir. Crook, 2013), *El Rey de Najayo* (dir. Baez Mella, 2012), *Yellow* (dir. De Villa, 2006). Any actor with such an impressive résumé not only is busy but also is demonstrating the quality and diversity of Dominican talent. In addition to his starring role in *Veneno*, Pérez is highlighted in this chapter because of his increasingly prolific work as a writer, producer, and director. He was a screenwriter and producer on *Washington Heights*, *La Soga* (dir. Crook, 2009), *Forged* (dir. Wedig, 2010), and *Ponchao*, and he wrote, produced, and directed *La Soga 2* (in postproduction). Like Katherine Castro, Manny Pérez has leveraged his position as a successful actor into not only creative influence but also creative control. He realized there was little hope of finding the roles he wanted, those that he related to and reflected his dominicanidad. Pérez uses his writing and producing to facilitate the career he wants: "That's why I write my stories to make my films as an actor."[52] Regarding others in the industry who have made their mark through creative will, he says, "I believe in the Spike Lee way, in that no one is going to make films about me or for me so it's up to me to create my own and continue doing as I first did with *Washington Heights*."[53]

The best known of his films among Dominicans is, unsurprisingly, *Washington Heights*. It frequently appeared on my interviewees' short lists of Dominican representations in US media. Pérez came up with the concept and was inspired to produce and write the screenplay for the film directed by Mexican director Alfredo Rodriguez de Villa. Although four screenwriters are credited, including his cousin, Pulitzer Prize–winning author Junot Díaz, and de Villa, *Washington Heights* is truly Pérez's story: "My culture is what I know, and I want to write about it."[54] Pérez has worked with de Villa several times throughout his career; the two clearly share a productive relationship. The film stars Pérez as Carlos, a Dominican American comic book illustrator who wants to create his own comics instead of just inking the work of others. However, when his father (played by Cuban-born Tomas Milian) gets shot while working in the bodega he owns, Carlos is forced to step in and put his creative aspirations on the back burner. In running the bodega, a space of community like many Dominican-run bodegas in NYC, he realizes that he must incorporate his experiences and heritage into his comic. This elevates his work and allows him to impress a previously dismissive comic book publisher. While the film includes Latinx characters played by a panethnic cast, it does feature one of the few Dominican actresses to have achieved success in mainstream US media, Judy Reyes (*Scrubs, Devious Maids, Jane the Virgin, One Day at a Time, Claws*). Although it was not a mainstream hit, the film received a great deal of publicity and awards, and Pérez was highlighted as its star.

Whether writing and producing roles for himself or playing one of the few Dominican characters in mainstream US media, Pérez is "trying to show to America that not every Latino is Mexican or Puerto Rican."[55] Latinx specificity is central to his career goals, not simply because he would like to take on roles he can relate to but because he knows how important it is for Dominicans in the US to have representations that resonate with them. Pérez says he has "been fighting this fight for a while"; for nearly three decades, in fact.[56] By embodying a Dominican hero, Jack Veneno, and taking center stage in the tour de force that is the *Veneno* trilogy, Pérez—unlike Zoe Saldana or Alex Rodriguez (see chap. 2)—is perfectly positioned to fulfill the US Dominican community's desperate search for mediated dominicanidad.

Veneno *and Dominican Audiences*

Manny Pérez was not at the DFFNYC premier of *Veneno*—although he has attended several festivals in previous years—but Tabaré Blanchard, Pepe Sierra (who plays Relámpago Hernández), and several cast and crew members were present. The film debuted at the AMC Empire 25 near Times Square, one of NYC's biggest movie theaters. As part of the audience, I felt the palpable excitement of the hundred or so attendees about a favorite Dominican figure from their childhoods and the film's up-and-coming director. The audience that night wanted more than to watch a movie; they wanted to be part of a community that was sharing a culturally resonant experience. Although there are NYC movie theaters in primarily Dominican neighborhoods—and therefore those audiences are mostly part of the Dominican community—people rarely get the opportunity to be part of an audience that is watching a Dominican film. Filmgoers' investment in an uncommon experience was apparent as they talked before the film, engaged with the film throughout the showing through gestures and callouts, and enthusiastically participated in the Q&A that followed.

Observing audience reception in real time is rare among media reception scholarship, and my chance to do this provides a unique perspective that informs my interpretation of how the Dominican audience engages with Dominican filmmaking. For example, at DFFNYC 2018, *Veneno* received a standing ovation. Several films received a similar response, but not all of them did. There are nuances in knowing that a film ends with a standing ovation and understanding the atmosphere that is produced by it. For some audiences, applause and a standing ovation was an act of respect, an acknowledgment of the paucity of Dominican films and an opportunity to engage with them as part of a community. In other audiences, these same behaviors signaled excitement and pride regarding a film they saw as accomplishing something special. That year's premiere of *Veneno* was one of those latter occasions.

One of the most poignant elements of this screening was the Q&A with Tabaré Blanchard and Pepe Sierra. The audience and Blanchard and Sierra seamlessly flowed between Spanish and English, highlighting the diasporic nature of the DFFNYC. Often excited and quite expressive, many in the audience wanted to know more about the making of the film. Who came up with the concept? What kind of research was done into Veneno's background, and did he like the film? Why was this a narrative film instead of a documentary like Blanchard's acclaimed *La montaña*? What will the second film in the trilogy be about? And where can they find the film so they can watch it again and show other Dominicans? They discussed music choice with Blanchard and asked him what types of films influenced him. They asked Sierra what it was like working as an actor in Hollywood, especially because he does not necessarily "look like the average Latino." Those few hours spent in a large auditorium in NYC's center of theater and entertainment, watching and discussing a film that meant something special to everyone in attendance, served as a microcosm of the relationship between Dominican media production and the navigation of dominicanidad.

My experience with all types of filmmaking across historical and global scopes made my participation in this event an exciting opportunity for me. However, I realize that my education and status as a professor set me apart from this audience and also influenced how I interpreted their reception of the film. Moreover, the elements of the film that impressed me might not have stood out to the Dominicans in the audience. I attended the screening for a very different reason than they did. This is why I did not participate in the postscreening Q&A. I didn't want to have any influence over the direction of the questions and conversations. However, through informal conversations with audience members, careful observation of viewers' real-time reactions to the film, and documenting the Q&A, I left that auditorium feeling that I understood not only this film but, more importantly, this audience.

The real-time audience reception was not the only indicator of how Dominican audiences reacted to the film; I also observed the online community's enthusiasm. Some examples of posts include: "*Veneno* is a game-changer for Dominican cinema," "This movie gave me joy. I want more please," "This must be one of the best Dominican films produced as of yet."[57] Blanchard and his team had hoped to reach an audience that was old enough to remember the fanfare and excitement of Jack Veneno's career. The film was primarily made for people who grew up in the DR during that time or for the many US-raised Dominicans who returned to the island every summer. Sometimes referred to on the island as "Dominicanyorks," US-born and US-raised Dominican-Americans are one of the main reasons the Dominican diaspora remains so tightly knit. Furthermore, it was quite significant for this group to see Dominican icons, representations, and heroes while on the island because the media they consumed in the US was completely void of them. According to artist and designer M. Tony Peralta, whose personal work engages in the hybridity of Dominican and NYC culture, *Veneno* "took me back. Jack Veneno is the closest thing to a superhero that we have. As a Dominican American I don't see representation of my culture and people that look like me in the American media, but in the Dominican Republic we have Jack Veneno and Relámpago Hernández."[58] This nostalgic sentiment was echoed by others online; for example, one of the film's reviewers on Amazon.com said, "Great Story! This took me back in time when I was growing up in the Dominican Republic and I used to look up to the incredible Jack Veneno character as an example of courage and valor to assimilate." Another reviewer said, "They absolutely nailed the essence and the feeling of the earlier years of Jack Veneno. I vividly remember witnessing one of those lucha libre matches en el parque Eugenio Maria de Hostos as a child with dad, uncle, and cousins."[59]

Much of the online reception reflects the thrill of seeing a movie about a childhood hero. Yet these comments do not make up the majority of what Dominicans are saying about *Veneno*. Instead, they express pride in the film's high production value, celebrate its unique storytelling aesthetic, and express excitement for what it means for the future of Dominican filmmaking. One poster on the film discussion site Letterboxd.com left the following review:

> *Veneno* is simply the best Dominican film that I've ever seen. Period. Everything from the dialogue, acting, cinematography—it was great. Its technicalities were simply astounding for the current standards of Dominican film.
>
> The performances from Manny Perez and Pepe Sierra were mesmerizing. Going back to view footage of the real [wrestlers] (Jack Veneno, Relampago Hernandez) I was very impressed with the level of performance put on by these two.
>
> The film's best asset had to be its use of production design and editing. Being Dominican, witnessing so many locales of the country back in the 1970s felt oddly nostalgic (even though I never lived to see any of it). The way everything paced and flowed within the sets felt natural—felt real. It made the viewer feel more immersed with the picture. Not only that but the editing was quick, snappy and stylish—everything that editing should be (with some specific exceptions).
>
> If you want to watch the best that Dominican cinema has to offer—this right here is the one for you. I'll for sure keep my eye out on Tabaré Blanchard's future work, guy's got something going here.

Another review on Amazon.com declares, "Any Dominican kid born in the 70's or 80s knows of Jack Veneno. The fact that this movie finally presents something of a back story but also presents the rise of Relámpago Hernández already makes it great. But the production value, the details regarding the political situation that took place in Dominican Republic during the 70s (student riots) and the striking resemblance of the main actors takes this movie above and beyond." This is a film that shares *their* memories, tells *their* stories, and expresses *their* dominicanidad. Dominicans cannot find this kind of gratification from mainstream US media or the Spanish-language media industries. Dominicans are all but invisible in both. Most Dominican Americans felt they would just have to accept this invisibility and hope for change in the future.

Conclusion

Veneno does not solve the problems of Dominican mediated invisibility and marginalization, but it does prove that Dominicans do not have to be content with the status quo. As demonstrated by the reception to this film, there is a yearning for media that feels representative, reflective, and authentic to one's sense of dominicanidad. As one online reviewer posted,

"It feels amazing being a Dominican and finally seeing a movie that I can relate to in such a high extent, something I never knew I wanted so badly. This movie blew my mind and made my hairs stand, at how well the portrait of Dominican culture was set in place."[60] What is clear is that Dominican audiences in the US are invested in the pursuit of a mediated dominicanidad, and Dominican filmmakers and other media creatives are just as invested in making media that speaks to that.

It is difficult to predict the impact of this particular moment in Dominican filmmaking. The larger call by audiences for more Black, Indigenous, and people of color (BIPOC) inclusiveness in the media industries is bound to provide some access that has eluded Dominican media-makers. The Dominican filmmakers and media creatives I spoke with are optimistic about what is to come for them and other Dominicans who want to work in the media industries. But generic inclusion is not necessarily the same thing as creative freedom and control. While Dominican creatives might find work, they still have an uphill battle against the forces of Latinx homogenization and the marginalization of their voices. There has yet to emerge a Dominican Spike Lee, Gregory Nava, or Ava DuVernay. Moreover, Dominican audiences have yet to develop the economic clout of the larger US Latinx community that is proving so lucrative to mainstream media industries. Furthermore, internal marginalization of subgroups is not uncommon among BIPOC. Media industrial "logic" and the politics of pan-latinidad seem to have no incentive to prioritize dominicanidad. And why would they? It does not serve their interests or inclinations. Possibly more significantly, increased and nuanced inclusion of Dominican representation threatens to disprove entrenched ethnoracial thinking that pervades every institution in the US. The fact of Dominican multiraciality might be contentious among Dominicans, both on the island and in the diaspora, but it is a direct assault on the contrived and orderly categories that sustain US ethnoracial hegemony.

Notes

1. See ESENDOM.com 2017.
2. Quoted in McQueen 2017.
3. Generic latinidad can be understood as the way mainstream US society conceptualizes a Latinx norm that usually includes an adherence to the "Latin look" and an implied Mexican origin (Goin 2016).
4. Many of the interviews and press statements included in this chapter were originally in Spanish or a mixture of Spanish and English. Because this chapter does not focus on language, the author has translated all Spanish into English.

5. Quoted in Berumen 2003, 26.
6. For a more extensive discussion of Chicano cinema, see Noriega 1992.
7. See Beltrán 2009 for a discussion of palatable latinidad in Hollywood.
8. See Rivero 2009.
9. See Jiménez 1993.
10. Interview conducted on January 28, 2021, by author.
11. Interview conducted on December 25, 2020, by author.
12. See Garcia 2018.
13. Interview conducted on January 28, 2021, by author.
14. See Ibermedia's website at https://www.programaibermedia.com/ for more details about the organization.
15. Interview conducted by José R. García, Dominican Studies Association Conference, December 2020.
16. Interview conducted by José R. García.
17. Interview conducted by DFFNY, October 2020.
18. Interview conducted by DFFNY.
19. Interview conducted by DFFNY.
20. Interview conducted by DFFNY.
21. Interview conducted by DFFNY.
22. Interview conducted by DFFNY.
23. Interview conducted on January 28, 2021, by author.
24. Interview conducted on December 25, 2020, by author.
25. Interview conducted by José R. García.
26. Interview conducted on January 28, 2021, by author.
27. Interview conducted on January 28, 2021, by author.
28. Interview conducted by DFFNY.
29. Interview conducted by DFFNY.
30. Interview conducted by DFFNY.
31. Robert Rodriguez entered his $7,000 film school project, *El Mariachi* (1992) and signed a deal with Universal Studios to be the film's distributor.
32. Jordan Peele, half of the comedy duo Key and Peele, would later go on to win an Academy Award for best screenplay for the film.
33. See Hidalgo-Ayala 2017; Quoted in Lawton 2014.
34. Quoted in McQueen.
35. Quoted in LatinxToday.com 2020.
36. Interview conducted by DFFNY.
37. See McQueen.
38. Quoted in Lawton.
39. Quoted in McQueen.
40. Quoted in Hidalgo-Ayala 2017.
41. Quoted in Feeney 2014.
42. Interview conducted on January 28, 2021, by author.
43. See LatinxToday.com 2020.
44. Quoted in McQueen.
45. Quoted in Garcia.
46. Quoted in Garcia.
47. Quoted in Letterboxd.com discussion posts on *Veneno*.
48. Quoted in Garcia.
49. Interviewed by *Siendo Honestos* in June 2019.
50. Quoted in Garcia.
51. Quoted in Garcia.

52. Quoted in *San Diego Union Tribune* 2014.
53. Quoted in Haas 2008.
54. Quoted in Salamone 2010.
55. Quoted in Tavarez 2005.
56. Quoted in Patta 2020.
57. Quoted in Letterboxd.com and Amazon.com reviews.
58. Quoted in Garcia.
59. Quoted in Amazon.com reviews.
60. Quoted in IMDb.com.

CONCLUSION

"Mi raza es dominicana": Dominicanidad as a Unique Lens for Approaching US Racial Hegemony

I never expected to face so much ambivalence toward the term *Dominican-American*, but among the many Dominicans I spoke with in New York City (NYC), the term seemed to have little resonance. In the US, it is common to refer to various established immigrant groups along this hyphenated framework (German-American, Jewish-American, Greek-American, etc.), but for Dominicans in the US, this terminology represents an assimilation process that might be standard practice for other immigrant communities, but it is incompatible with how they form their identities. The term *Dominican-American* was used to help explain their nationality in ways that I, the interviewer, was familiar with. But, for them, this term does not appropriately address their identities as Dominicans in the US. Of course, some aspects of their identity were easily connected to an "American" sensibility; however, each of these intersections is rooted in a sense of the Dominican imaginary that appears to be uniquely cultivated in this community. Dominican intersectional identity challenges the boundaries of national identity and what that means for Dominicans living in the US. By doing so, the negotiation of *dominicanidad* in the US is in a state of flux and constant becoming.

Dominicans in the US are positioned under a panethnic Latinx umbrella, which tends to reduce their cultural specificity and national heritage. Certainly, Dominicans claim a Latino/Hispanic identification; however, this identification is more appropriative or assimilationist than organic. Their association with this identity category is more nuanced than current articulations of "Latino" allow for and results in a desire to qualify where they fit within this panethnic conglomeration. Juan Flores (2009) addresses a similar dilemma in his discussion of (Afro-)*Antillanismo*, contending that what separates "*caribeños*" (those who situate their identities within the Spanish Caribbean) from Latinx panethnicity is Blackness and an Afro-Atlantic imaginary. He suggests that as the three countries (Puerto Rico, Cuba, and the Dominican Republic [DR]) engage with US notions of Blackness, nationally created racial ideologies, and constructions of race articulated through pan-Caribbean/Antillean discourses, each one faces very real and persisting challenges to how they shape their national identities. This is a critical component in the current state of the NYC Dominican community, but it does not fully represent the complexities of existing identity negotiations. From the themes that have emerged over the course of my research, I have identified some of these particularities of Dominican construction of self, or dominicanidad, within the US that are not well covered in the academic literature.

This conclusion attempts to recenter dominicanidad as it is understood by Dominicans living in the US. The media influences both negotiations of dominicanidad and Dominican-American expressions of it, but the real discursive work of identity struggle can be best understood through the voices of my interviewees: Dominicans living in NYC whose everyday lived realities are embedded within a US-fashioned dominicanidad. One cannot truly understand Dominican-American dominicanidad through the glimpses at Dominican subjectivity in US mainstream media or the Dominican-centric films created by US Dominicans trying to self-represent. Such an abstract notion can only begin to be conveyed on the individual level. This book is a testament to the complex and problematic ways in which media attempt to engage with discourses of identity. But it was not until I heard the voices of my interviewees that I was able to conceptualize Dominican-American dominicanidad outside of the discursive frameworks that I unwittingly carried into the field. Dominicans in the US challenge hegemonic paradigms that aim to label, categorize, and neatly situate them within ideologies that they are finding increasingly difficult to maintain. Consequently, I conclude this study with a discussion of those themes of the Dominican experience in the US most salient among the NYC Dominicans who are living them.

Rethinking the Dominican Relationship with Blackness

While not the only reason she was criticized for not authentically representing dominicanidad, the fact that Zoe Saldana has played Black/

African American characters in so many films suggests a certain racialized component within the Dominican American audience reception of her star text. Many of the negative comments directed at her by my interviewees and online posters would not have been made about a lighter-skinned Dominican American. For example, even though both Saldana and Alex Rodriguez have been criticized for being overly Americanized, the topic of race has only been mentioned in connection with Saldana. The claim that Rodriguez has become Americanized implicitly suggests that he has whitewashed his image and is therefore seen as "wanting to be white"; however, race was explicitly addressed in people's discussions of Saldana. Ultimately, this speaks to the contentious relationship between Blackness and dominicanidad that is rooted in Dominican history and its complicated relationship with African descent.

My interviewee Tina told me, "When Dominicans say they are not Black they mean that they are not 'African American,' not that they are not of African descent." When Saldana plays African American characters, she is accused of not being Dominican enough by the Dominican American community, even if this reasoning happens on an unconscious level. This highlights the complicated relationship between dominicanidad and Blackness playing out through Dominican media reception in the US.

Many scholars, including myself, have reduced Dominican racial identification to a process of denial wherein Dominicans are seen as refusing to acknowledge their seemingly obvious African descent. And while I hold that this is an observable truth, it is still only a partial truth. Among Dominicans in the US who are exposed to the academic discourse that labels them racial deniers, there exists a desire to rearticulate this phenomenon through their own framework. The claim that Dominicans reject their Blackness oversimplifies a system of racial thinking based on notions of *mestizaje* (mixture) and the blending of separate heritages. In an interview that shifted my perspective on Dominican racialized thinking, Luis asked me, "Why should we claim one part of our racial heritage at the cost of ignoring the others?" Luis is denying not the existence of Blackness within his dominicanidad but its centrality. Even while analyzing the conflicting constructions of racialization between the US and the DR, I was influenced by US-based hegemonic notions of Blackness rooted in the logic of the one-drop rule. It is all too easy for US academics to read the body and identify it as Black and to subsequently blame those who do not read their bodies the same way as rejecting the obvious. However, this way of thinking is grounded in a logic that positions race as a biological property, a way of thinking that is not articulated in the same way in the DR. To step out of this mindset, I use the interviews of two Dominicans living in NYC to resituate this discourse in a way that is not affected by my racialized dispositions.

Luis, a US-born Dominican in his late twenties, insisted that the argument that Dominicans have historically denied their African descent does not fully explain the situation. He claimed that although outsiders might not see the influence of African heritage in Dominican culture, it is nevertheless there. Luis told me that in the DR, Blackness is viewed differently than how it is commonly represented in the US, and that it is actually celebrated through Dominican cultural expression. "We do embrace it," he said of the African cultural heritage of the island. Rather than taking the view that the DR's population is primarily of African descent, Luis claims that it is actually a more accurate reflection of how the US mythically characterizes itself: a melting pot. "You live through it almost every day, and we joke about it. It is not that we don't highlight it, it is just part of who we are as much as the European and Indian.... We can't disentangle one part from the others." For Luis to say that he is of African descent is not completely accurate, just as if he were to say that he is of Indigenous descent. He is all of these things at once.

Emmanuel, a Dominican-born member of the US Army, expressed a similar sentiment. When discussing the *Black in Latin America* (PBS 2011) series produced by Henry Louis Gates, Emmanuel was very critical of it, saying, "It was a travesty. At least when it came to the Dominican Republic. It didn't help Dominicans to be explained to the general public because they showed us as denying our African heritage. But there is nothing to deny. What we have done is reinvented something new." He was offended by how the series portrayed Dominicans as deniers of their Blackness. He said, "We do not deny it, we have re-invented a new thing that is Dominican and it goes way beyond that." He wanted to defend Dominican racialized thinking as not a mindset but an evolving process of identification that reflects both current and historical realities of Dominican identity. Emmanuel saw the identifier *Dominican* as already connoting African descent, and so it was both redundant and unrepresentative to claim Blackness as well.

By challenging the discourses that label Dominicans as racial deniers, both Emmanuel and Luis insist on an alternative identity paradigm, one that is not beholden to erroneous conceptualizations of race as biologically determined in a way that makes any degree of African descent *the* deciding racial factor. Similar to how Ella Shohat and Robert Stam (1994) expose how critiques of Eurocentrism ironically work to recenter it, scholars who insist Blackness is central to the discussion of Dominican ethnoracial reality obscure the fact that these criticisms are simply rehashing the biological determinism that critical race theorists have fought so hard to discredit. I find Rachel Afi Quinn's (2021) theorization of Dominican mixed-race ambiguity and flexibility a much more compelling way to frame the relationship between dominicanidad and Blackness. Through her research on the "surrealist aesthetic" imbued within Dominican visual culture, Afi Quinn argues that the Dominican surrealist aesthetic parallels notions of the racialized self as being able to be both Black and non-Black. Moreover, dominicanidad is able to sustain a continuation of cultural tradition while simultaneously rejecting it. This idea is not about contradiction but rather the pursuit of trying to express the experience of both *being* and *not being*. Afi Quinn theorizes that because dominicanidad is articulated in a transnational and ongoing process, it fluctuates, or "oscillates," due to its inherent ambiguity. Dominicans are able to claim that they are not Black and that they are Black by conceptualizing their African descent as a "thin and impermeable packaging under which blackness is able to gleam, without one having to truly encounter blackness itself" (Afi Quinn 2021, 117).

Dominicanidad: A Dominican Paradigm of Identity Negotiation

Concerns about representation and the importance of "authentic" dominicanidad were central to how Dominicans responded to MTV's *Washington Heights*. It seems, however, that the show's main issue was its failure to translate dominicanidad as a paradigm of identification within the network's identity project, one that was already entrenched in more normative frameworks of US identification. Diego told me, "The ideal Dominican-American is from the Heights for most people," but the show was unable to convey that Dominican-American-ness both televisually and discursively. Instead of reflecting the fluidity of identity characteristic of the Dominican imaginary, *Washington Heights* aimed to root its cast members geographically. This process of tethering Dominican Americans to the neighborhood of Washington Heights detaches them from the diaspora and the imaginary that are central to how they construct their subjectivities.

No one is saying that being a Dominican in NYC is the same as being a Dominican in the DR. Yet the same could be said about a Dominican in Santo Domingo versus one in Santiago. A vibrant and growing immigrant community, Dominicans in the US position their notions of self firmly within an understanding of a transnational and diasporic Dominican imaginary. This nationally aligned imaginary is based not on geography but on a sensibility that grounds their construction of self through connections to Dominican culture and worldview. Dominicans reject US-based frameworks of identification, insisting that they should not have to conform to preexisting US ideologies concerning their race, ethnicity, class, and so on. Claiming the right to identify themselves outside of these paradigms, Dominicans in the US assert their identity beyond the established and institutionalized Black/white binary, choosing to embrace the cultural paradigms that resonate with them. Dominicans in the US do not merely replicate ideologies from the island, however. Rather, they engage with these ideologies alongside US ones to negotiate more situated notions of self.

Situated within a society that interprets race in terms of a Black/white binary, the US racial landscape was frequently mentioned and criticized during my interviews. Junior told me, "Being Dominican is all about the way you act and you speak, it is not really about how you look, anyone can be Dominican." This young man meant that there is no one standard Dominican "look" and that people cannot easily identify someone's Dominican heritage just by looking at them. Most of my interviewees mentioned that non-Dominicans struggled to identify their race or ethnicity, but among Dominicans, their identity was never ambiguous. Like Mary Beltrán's (2009) concept of "cultural racialization"—a process through which an individual is ethnoracialized based on perceived cultural factors—Dominicans identify cultural characteristics in other Dominicans in order to recognize them as part of their in-group. Dominican audiences of *Washington Heights* desperately searched for these instances of cultural racialization, elements they could recognize as representative of dominicanidad. Most people agreed with Ciel, who told me that she "just wished the show had more Dominican culture."

The most important of these recognizable elements of dominicanidad is the use of Dominican Spanish. Dominican Spanish, different from the standardized Spanish variant in Spanish-language media, has its own speed, syntax, and slang. When these elements are combined with the accent, it is easy to identify someone speaking Dominican Spanish as Dominican. And in a community that has prioritized cultural retention, speaking this type of Spanish is crucial to that retention. Tina, when discussing why she thought *Washington Heights* did not adequately represent dominicanidad, told me, "We don't talk like that, more use of Spanish language among the cast would have made it more authentic." Most of the Dominicans I met in NYC spoke Spanish fluently regardless of their immigrant generation or fluency with English. There is clearly a perception that Dominican culture is so inextricably linked to Dominican Spanish that the loss of one would cause the loss of the other. *Washington Heights*, unlike the celebrities of Dominican heritage who sparked feelings of disapproval and betrayal among my interviewees, embodied the threat of the potential loss of Dominican Spanish among Dominicans living in the US.

Hyphenated Identity, Hyphenated Existence: The Notion of Being Both "Here" and "There"

As an example of the complexity of immigration and the resulting negotiation of a hyphenated identity, Silvia Spitta (1997) describes Cuban, Cuban-American, and "hyphenated" conceptualizations of identity. Seeing Cuban-American positionality as one that is split between the "there" and the "here," Spitta (1997, 164) contends that Cuban-Americans "theorize Cuba and the Caribbean from the hyphen that both connects the Cuban to the 'American' and separates the Cuban from the 'American.'" Spitta suggests that those living in the space of the hyphen have constructed two distinct yet overlapping modes of conceptualizing the border, one that is oppositional, explosive, and politically engaged, and one that internalizes the border. Subsequently, the border comes to represent a choreographed dance as well as a war zone. Although not the same as the tension caused by the hyphen between *Dominican* and *American*, similar examples of the impact of hyphenated identity are evident among many of the interviews in this book. It is by sustaining online communities and producing their own media that many Dominicans in the US negotiate their experience with hyphenated subjectivity.

Dominican-Americans maintain a sense of being two places at once: both "here" and "there." This is not unique to Dominicans in the US, as many other immigrant communities have shared similar sentiments. I argue, however, that even those Dominicans among the second and third immigrant generations retain a strong connection to the island in a way that is unique to their community. Facilitated by ever-advancing communication technology, frequent return visits, and the concentration of culture obliged by an enclave reality, Dominicans in the US have avoided the traditional assimilation path that most US immigrant groups have followed. Instead, Dominican-Americans have not only a "hyphenated identity" but also a hyphenated existence. The most pronounced example of this was found among those who hesitated using the label "Dominican-American" opting instead to identify themselves as simply "Dominican." Luis asked me, "Is it really indicative of the actual Dominican experience?" It seems surprising that Dominicans born and raised in the US felt more connected with their parents' or grandparents' country than to the place they had lived their entire lives. For many Dominicans, in both the US and the DR, NYC is just another Dominican city regardless of its actual geographic location. Those living in NYC are able to vote in Dominican elections, speak Dominican-style Spanish, and purchase the same items found in the stores on the island. Furthermore, most US Dominicans have family in both countries and maintain close relationships that seem to be unaffected by the physical distance. As a result, Dominican-Americans/Dominicans in the US are able to be present in two places at once.

Dominicans in the US were often described to me as having two simultaneous identities. They have developed a sensibility that allows them to feel like they are part of both places at once by sharing a common Dominican imaginary, seeing their US self and their DR self as overlapping and intertwined. Emmanuel referenced a lyric by singer José Peña Suazo that he saw as emblematic of the immigrant experience for many groups in the US: "*Estoy aqui pero mi menta esta allá* [I am here but my mind is there]." But for Emmanuel, this concept is a thing of the past. He is able to be "here" and "there" at the same time. "My mind is here *and* it is there. . . . You are here yeah, but by living here you can actually follow every aspect of Dominican life. Especially through the web." Unlike the experience of Cuban-Americans discussed by Spitta, Dominicans in the US are able to live and identify with the hyphen and both of its parts simultaneously.

According to my interviewees, engaged internet use greatly influences Dominican-Americans' ability to be both "here" and "there" regarding their experiences of hyphenated identity. Alma told me that she "lives on the island through Facebook." Dania suggested that "websites that use videos as part of their platform" have the opportunity to foster a "promising internet Dominican community." I found one such digital Dominican community that shows how this hyphenated existence is maintained. ESENDOM.com—the name comes from an abbreviation of *Esencia Dominicana* (Dominican Essence)—is a celebration of Dominican culture, but one that is clearly marked by the realities of US

Dominican biculturalism and bilingualism. The website operates as both a news source and a platform for distributing Dominican-centric content. ESENDOM covers current events about Dominicans diasporically and promotes upcoming cultural events (mostly in NYC). The site also includes various reviews of recent Dominican/Dominican-American cultural products such as music, films, and prominent academic and popular publications. ESENDOM serves as a reservoir of explicit documentation of the changing trends in Dominican culture in the US and the Dominican diaspora more broadly.

Launched in 2009 by two undergraduate classmates, Nelson Santana and Emmanuel Espinal, the original inception of ESENDOM was meant to be a magazine targeting Dominicans living in the US. ESENDOM was created to fill a void felt by Santana and Espinal, who wanted to report on stories, events, and cultural content that were being ignored by other media platforms. Santana told me, "We believe there is a market and we wanted to bring together Dominicans and non-Dominicans alike through content: Dominican history, popular culture (music, arts, performance, etc.), sports, feature restaurants in DR and in the US, feature different places such as the different provinces, towns, etc. Overall, we wanted to promote the Dominican Republic, the Dominican people, bring them together, etc. Since we did not have the funds (and were actually rejected for a bank loan) we decided to create the website instead, which was part of the original plan to complement the magazine."[1] Although ESENDOM's current home is online, its founders hope to transition the site into a print magazine, like other marginalized groups that try to break into the mainstream media market. However, as a website, ESENDOM can provide audiovisual content, publish and update quickly, and foster a more engaged audience.

Due to the structure of the website and the nature of its content, ESENDOM's audience consists mostly of New Yorkers who are interested and invested in the Dominican cultural experience within the US. Much of the website's focus is on music, probably because both Santana and Espinal are interested in Dominican music. Much of the music-related content consists of photos, interviews, and recordings of performances, which has attracted the attention of the *merengue tipico* fan community.[2] ESENDOM also provides a space where people interested in Dominican cultural events can find information about upcoming concerts, lectures, workshops, and film festivals. The website featured a short-lived podcast that was relatively successful but ultimately ended when Santana started graduate school and had less time to devote to the site.

Among a worldwide audience, most users come from the DR, the US, and Spain—however, the site also has a presence in Brazil, India, and Japan. ESENDOM's audience is mostly made up of bilingual and Spanish speakers, but there are some English-only speakers. The website is set up to accommodate non-Spanish speakers; stories are written in both Spanish and English, some English-only content is available, and (as most of the audiovisual content is music-related) one does not need to speak Spanish to appreciate much of the website's content.

ESENDOM is unique because of its offline presence within the NYC Dominican community. Most of the audience feedback has been given in person (as opposed to a string of comments at the end of an article or video). Visitors who frequent the site share their appreciation for ESENDOM directly with Santana and Espinal and use it to engage with the different ways that dominicanidad is expressed and experienced in NYC. The site aims to be a hub for this very purpose and has connected with many Dominican public figures (media representatives, musicians, celebrities, politicians, academics, etc.). ESENDOM's positive reception over its tenure is reflected in the exclusive music content provided by artists and the interviews and event coverage that are not available to other media representatives. The result is the cultivation of a community of NYC cultural figures. One might dismiss ESENDOM as relatively insignificant, like a small fish in the vast online ocean. Indeed, the site's content is clearly influenced by the advanced academic background of its creators, potentially making it less accessible. However, as the Dominican community in NYC becomes more established and their numbers continue to grow, a forum that highlights the vibrancy of Dominican cultural life in NYC and provides intellectual conversations becomes all the more relevant. The concept of dominicanidad—what it means, how it is expressed, and how it is negotiated and constituted—is being discussed in the digital domain created by ESENDOM and many other similar websites emerging every day.

Websites like ESENDOM can both reflect and cultivate hyphenated subjectivity as foundational to US dominicanidad. Unlike the failure of *Washington Heights* and the celebrities of Dominican heritage to translate dominicanidad in a salient and authentic fashion for Dominicans in the US, online spaces are not beholden to a mainstream audience or the barriers to access that often exclude different perspectives from more traditional media industries. In digital spaces, dominicanidad can align with the Dominican imaginary and reflect the complex relationship between "here" and "there."

The same goes for spaces like the Dominican Film Festival in NYC. The festival is diasporic in mindset, and Dominican cinema is diasporic by industrial design. The center for exhibiting films made in the DR is not in that country but in NYC. Because so many Dominican filmmakers and media-makers have dual citizenship, their creative output embodies the simultaneous "here" and "there." The audiences who watch these films and attend the festival are also participating in a concurrent "here" and "there."

Revisiting *In the Heights*

And if not me, who keeps our legacies?
Who's gonna keep the coffee sweet with secret recipes?
Abuela, rest in peace, you live in my memories
But Sonny's gotta eat, this corner is my destiny

Abuela, I'm sorry
But I ain't goin' back because I'm telling your story
And I can say goodbye to you smilin', I found my island
I been on it this whole time
I'm home!
(*In the Heights*, lyrics by Lin-Manuel Miranda, 2021)

At the end of *In the Heights*, Usnavi (Anthony Ramos) realizes that his longing to return to the DR is surpassed by the life he envisions building with his love interest, Vanessa (Melissa Barrera Martínez), and his desire to help his cousin Sonny (Gregory Diaz IV) with his struggle for citizenship. Through this change in priorities, he realizes that his "home" and his "island" do not have to be the DR—that he can fulfill his deepest desires and still hold on to his dominicanidad on Manhattan Island. In Washington Heights, he can pursue the elusive American Dream, stay connected to Dominican sensibility, and engage in the US-based Latinx community identity. He has created a version of his idealized DR that can fit in with his NYC bodega and Washington Heights barrio. He no longer has to pine for "there" from "here"; his "here" in Washington Heights has become intertwined with his "there" of the DR. Usnavi does not have to sacrifice his "American" or "Dominican" selves; the dominicanidad of Washington Heights lets him live on the hyphen.

The film's upbeat, and decidedly saccharine-sweet, conclusion is intended to be relatable to the millions of viewers who, at some point in their ancestral history and regardless of where in the world those ancestors came from, have experienced the same thing. Navigating the tensions between the "here" and the "there" has been a hallmark of the American experience. Subsequently, comparing the Dominican-American experience to that of other immigrant groups mitigates the specificity of the Dominican experience in the US. However, it also places Dominican-Americans in a context where dominant society finds common ground, a common ground that has the potential to lead to further conversations and acceptance. The film sparked a media explosion by fulfilling a Latinx-dominated mainstream cultural product and because of the many criticisms of how it failed expectations of certain Latinx audiences. In doing so, it has opened up broader mainstream discussions on the issues of latinidad, afrolatinidad, and dominicanidad—even if people were unaware these were the concepts they were discussing—and the challenges of representation.

Implications and Final Thoughts

Dominicans in the US, whether they identify as Dominican-American, whether they associate with Blackness or latinidad, or whether they are just lost in the maelstrom of transcultural ethnoracial identity negotiation, serve as a critical interjection into how discourses and the ideologies they support are understood. By connecting to a Dominican imaginary that is partially constituted and substantiated through media, dominicanidad is articulated on an individual basis and is therefore almost impossible to generalize into a presentable form. Due to academic conventions and my role as a researcher interested in dominicanidad's impact on how ethnoracial discourses are conceptualized and explored in both the academic and popular realms, I must still strive to explain the breadth of research presented in this book. Therefore, I conclude with what I consider to be the most important contributions of this research: (1) the limitations of "authentic" representations of dominicanidad within US media due to the inadequacies of framing ethnoracial discourses to accommodate for US Dominicans, (2) the productive tensions produced through hyphenated expressions of identity that reveal, through the media that try to explain them, the ability to sustain a complex, fluid, and conflicting dominicanidad, and (3) the influence of hegemonic ethnoracial constructs that force Dominicans in the US to describe the indescribable, to explain the unexplainable, and to show that which cannot be shown.

My analysis of the criticism toward Zoe Saldana and Alex Rodriguez as inauthentic representatives of dominicanidad, along with the audience reception to MTV's *Washington Heights* suggesting that the show's representation of dominicanidad was unrecognizable to most Dominicans living in the US, indicates that US mainstream media is fundamentally ill-equipped to conscientiously represent dominicanidad. Even when the mainstream *Orange Is the New Black* tried to do so with nuance and care, it could not consistently maintain its commitment to either latinidades or dominicanidad. The US mainstream media's failure to understand Latinx specificity, and the ideological frameworks that constitute the meaning-making abilities of the media as a sociohistorical institution in the US, is preventing the effective presentation of Dominican perspectives to a wider mainstream audience. Through its contradiction with dominant US ethnoracial paradigms, dominicanidad can only be precariously placed within the construct of what is perceived as "American" and must therefore be diluted into a more acceptable form. However, the resilience of the Dominican community in the US to demand mediated acknowledgment is ready to challenge how race and ethnicity are understood in this country.

As has long been argued by intersectionality scholars, identity as a social force is not easily anchored, nor is it a simple process of categorization. The question "What is Dominican/dominicanidad?" is not a game of arbitrary semantics; it is a process that uses media spaces as the arena for its struggle. In the internet era, digital spaces allow people to discuss and express dominicanidad, including those who value its legitimacy and those who prefer to overlook it. The various online discussion forums mentioned in this book demonstrate the importance of the internet as a space for discourse.

Finally, this research speaks to the difficulty of navigating ideological frameworks that thrive on the eradication and delegitimization of dominicanidad as an alternative paradigm of identification. Dominicans, invested in preserving their connections to a Dominican imaginary, are forced to contend with a level of critical self-awareness that most people never have to consider. They cannot merely abandon Dominican-centric cultural signification, as that would cut their ties with the Dominican imaginary—and, subsequently, their dominicanidad—they so desperately want to maintain. However, they cannot simply ignore the deep-rooted systems in US institutions that support ideologies of white supremacy, which undermine their culture and language, limit their opportunities for success, and emphasize their Otherness in the pursuit of maintaining the status quo. As I try to understand these various conflicts, something Emmanuel said to me continues to return to my mind: "You in America might not know we are here . . . yet. But soon we will make ourselves known, we will have our day."

It seems that we will just have to watch and wait.

Notes

1. Interview conducted by author with cofounder and cochief editor Nelson Santana in January 2015.

2. *Merengue tipico* is a traditional Dominican music genre that is becoming increasingly popular in the US.

REFERENCES

Aceto, Michael. 2002. "Ethnic Personal Names and Multiple Identities in Anglophone Caribbean Speech Communities in Latin America." *Language in Society* 31 (4): 577–608.

Acevedo, Elizabeth. 2020. Interview conducted by José R. García, Dominican Studies Association Conference.

Acham, Christine. 2012. "Blacks in the Future: Braving the Frontier of the Web Series." In *Watching While Black: Centering the Television of Black Audiences*, edited by Beretta E. Smith-Shomade. Rutgers University Press.

Affuso, Elizabeth. 2009. "'Don't Just Watch It, Live It'—Technology, Corporate Partnerships, and *The Hills*." *Jump Cut: A Review of Contemporary Media* 51. https://www.ejumpcut.org/archive/jc51.2009/Hills-Affuso/index.html.

Afi Quinn, Rachel. 2019. "Spinning the Zoetrope: Visualizing the Mixed-Race Body of Dominican Actress Zoe Saldaña." *Latin American and Latinx Visual Culture* 1 (3): 44–59.

Afi Quinn, Rachel. 2021. *Being La Dominicana: Race and Identity in the Visual Culture of Santo Domingo*. 1st ed. University of Illinois Press.

Aguilar, Carlos. 2019. "Melinna Bobadilla on Playing a Maya K'iche' Immigrant on 'OITNB': Not All Latinos Are Mestizo." Remezcla. https://remezcla.com/features/film/melinna-bobadilla-oitnb-maya-kiche-television-academy-panel/.

Alvarez-Monzoncillo, Jose Maria. 2011. *Watching the Internet: The Future of TV?* FormalPress/Media XXI.

Anderson, Benedict. (1983) 1991. *Imagined Communities: Reflections on the Origin and Spread of Nationalism*. Verso.

Andrejevic, Mark. 2002. "The Kinder, Gentler Gaze of Big Brother: Reality TV in the Era of Digital Capitalism." *New Media Society* 4 (2): 251–70.

Ang, Ien. 1996. "On the Politics of Empirical Audience Research." In *Living Room Wars: Rethinking Media Audiences for a Postmodern World*. Routledge.

Aparicio, Frances R. 2007. "(Re)constructing Latinidad: The Challenge of Latina/o Studies." In *A Companion to Latina/o Studies*, edited by Juan Flores and Renato Rosaldo. Wiley-Blackwell.

Aparicio, Frances R. 2019. *Negotiating Latinidad: Intralatina/o Lives in Chicago*. University of Illinois Press.

Aparicio, Frances R., and Susana Chávez-Silverman, eds. 1997. *Tropicalizations: Transcultural Representations of Latinidad*. University Press of New England.

Appadurai, Arjun. 1996. *Modernity at Large: Cultural Dimensions of Globalization*. University of Minnesota Press.

Arreola, Cristina. 2013. "Prince Royce Teams Up with Carlito Olivero on 'The X Factor'." *Latina*, December 19.
Avatar. 2009. Directed by James Cameron. 20th Century Fox.
Báez, Jillian M. 2018. *In Search of Belonging: Latinas, Media, and Citizenship*. University of Illinois Press.
Baltes, Paul. 1991. "Semantic Variation in the Connotations of Personal Names." In *Proceedings of the Deseret Language and Linguistics Society 1991 Symposium*. Brigham Young University.
Barker, C., and M. Wiatrowski, eds. 2017. *Age of Netflix: Critical Essays on Streaming Media, Digital Delivery and Instant Access*. McFarland.
BBC.com. 2020. "Zoe Saldana Apologises for Playing Nina Simone: 'She Deserved Better.'" https://www.bbc.com/news/entertainment-arts-53676550.
Beltrán, Mary. 2002. "The Hollywood Latina Body as Site of Social Struggle: Media Constructions of Stardom and Jennifer Lopez's 'Cross-over Butt.'" *Quarterly Review of Film & Video* 19:71–86.
Beltrán, Mary. 2009. *Latina/o Stars in U.S. Eyes: The Making and Meanings of Film and TV Stardom*. University of Chicago Press.
Beltrán, Mary, and Camilla Fojas, eds. 2008. *Mixed Race Hollywood*. New York University Press.
Bernardi, Daniel. 1997. "'Star Trek' in the 1960s: Liberal-Humanism and the Production of Race." *Science Fiction Studies* 24 (2): 209–25.
Berumen, Enrique. 2003. "From Aztlán to Hollywood . . . and Back: A Conversation with Filmmaker Jesus Treviño." *Journal of Film and Video* 55 (2/3): 22–28.
Black in Latin America. PBS. 2011.
Blackwell, Maylei, Floridalma Boj Lopez, and Luis Urrieta Jr. 2017. "Special Issue: Critical Latinx Indigeneities." *Latino Studies* 15:126–37.
BMN News Team. 2010. "A-Rod: Baseball's Bad Boy." *Brand Maker News*. http://brandmakernews.com/celebrity-brand/2141/a-rod-baseball%E2%80%99s-bad-boy.html.
Bobo, Jacqueline. 1995. *Black Women as Cultural Readers*. Columbia University Press.
Bonfante, Julissa. 2013. "Washington Heights: Where's the 'Dominicanness' in MTV Reality Show?" Huffington Post, January 10, 2013.
Brennan, Denise. 2007. "Love Work in a Tourist Town: Dominican Sex Workers and Resort Workers Perform at Love." In *Love and Globalization: Transformations of Intimacy in the Contemporary World*, edited by Mark B. Padilla, Jennifer S. Hirsch, Miguel Munoz-Laboy, Robert E. Sember, and Richard G. Parker. Vanderbilt University Press.
Brim, Shanice. 2016. "This Season of *Orange Is the New Black* Walks the Line of Exploitation." Philadelphia Printworks. https://philadelphiaprintworks.com/blogs/news/this-season-of-orange-is-the-new-black-walks-the-line-of-exploitation-spoilers.
Brown, Jeffrey A. 1997. "'They Can Imagine Anything They Want . . .': Identification, Desire, and the Celebrity Text." *Discourse* 19 (3): 122–43.
Brown, Kennaria. 2010. "West Side Story Read from Below: Young Puerto Rican Women's Cultural Readings." *Communication Review* 13:193–215.
Bucholtz, Mary, and Kira Hall. 2003. "Language and Identity." In *A Companion to Linguistic Anthropology*, edited by Alessandro Duranti. Blackwell.
Buckwild. 2013. MTV.
Burgos, Adrian Jr. 1997. "Playing Ball in a Black and White 'Field of Dreams': Afro-Caribbean Ballplayers in the Negro Leagues, 1910–1950." *Journal of Negro History* 82 (1): 67–104.
Burgos, Adrian Jr. 2005. "Baseball Should Follow the Flag: Latinos, the Color Line, and Major League Baseball's Globalization Strategies." Paper presented at the Conference on Globalization and Sports in Historical Context, University of California San Diego, March 2005.

Busis, Hillary. 2014. "Orange Is the New Black Recap: Gloria's Flashback." *Entertainment Weekly*. https://ew.com/recap/orange-is-the-new-black-season-2-episode-5/.

Butler, Bethonie. 2016. "Let's Talk About That Heartbreaking Death on *Orange Is the New Black*." *Washington Post*. https://www.washingtonpost.com/news/arts-and-entertainment/wp/2016/06/23/lets-talk-about-that-heartbreaking-death-on-orange-is-the-new-black/.

Calderon, Jose. 1992. "'Hispanic' and 'Latino': The Viability of Categories for Panethnic Unity." *Latin American Perspectives* 19 (4): 37–44.

Caminero-Santangelo, Marta. 2007. *On Latinidad: U.S. Latino Literature and the Construction of Ethnicity*. University Press of Florida.

Campbell, Alex. 2006. "The Search for Authenticity: An Exploration of an Online Skinhead Newsgroup." *New Media & Society* 8 (2): 269–94.

Camplis, Francisco X. 1997. "Towards the Development of a Raza Cinema." In *Chicanos and Film: Essays on Chicano Representation and Resistance*, edited by Chon A. Noriega. Garland.

Candelario, Ginetta E. B. 2007. *Black Behind the Ears: Dominican Racial Identity from Museums to Beauty Shops*. Duke University Press.

Capellán Pichardo, Moraima. 2015. "What Maria Montez Means for Dominican Identity, Hollywood and the Marginalized." The High Screen, January 17. https://thehighscreen.com/show-dont-tell/2015/01/17/maria-montez-means-dominican-identity-hollywood-marginalized.html.

Carnelio-Mari, E. M. 2017. "Digital Delivery in Mexico: A Global Newcomer Stirs the Local Giants." In *The Age of Netflix: Critical Essays on Streaming Media, Digital Delivery and Instant Access*, edited by C. Barker and M. Wiatrowski. McFarland.

Castañeda, Mari. 2008. "The Importance of Spanish-Language and Latino Media." In *Latina/o Communication Studies Today*, edited by Angharad N. Valdivia. Peter Lang.

Castells, Manuel. 1997. *The Information Age: Economy, Society and Culture, Vol. II: The Power of Identity*. Blackwell.

Castillo, Amaris. 2013. "Zoe Saldaña Reveals Her Favorite Sex Position." *Latina*, July 17. http://www.latina.com/entertainment/buzz/zoe-saldana-favorite-sex-position.

Castro, Katherine. 2020. "Katherine Castro: A Dominican Actress in Hollywood: The Journey to Tinseltown." Interview conducted by Dominican Film Festival in NYC, October.

Center Stage. 2000. Directed by Nicholas Hytner. Columbia Pictures.

Cepeda, María Elena. 2008. "Survival Aesthetics: U.S. Latinas and the Negotiation of Popular Media." In *Latina/o Communication Studies Today*, edited by Angharad N. Valdivia. Peter Lang.

Cepeda, María Elena. 2010. *Musical ImagiNation: U.S.-Colombian Identity and the Latin Music Boom*. New York University Press.

Chun, Allen. 2001. "Diasporas of Mind, or Why There Ain't No Black Atlantic in Cultural China." *Communal/Plural* 9 (1): 95–109.

Cobo, Leila. 2010. "Aventura: The Billboard Cover Story." *Billboard*, April 26. https://www.billboard.com/music/music-news/aventura-the-billboard-cover-story-958477/.

Cobra Woman. 1944. Directed by Robert Siodmak. Universal Pictures.

Colombiana. 2011. Directed by Olivier Megaton. TriStar Pictures.

Collins, Patricia Hill, and Sirma Bilge. 2016. *Intersectionality*. Polity.

Cruz-Janzen, Marta I. 2010. "Latinegras: Desired Women—Undesirable Mothers, Daughters, Sisters, and Wives." In *Afro-Latin@ Reader: History and Culture in the United States*, edited by Miriam Jiménez Román and Juan Flores. Duke University Press.

Curiel, Angel Bismark. 2020. "Angel Bismark Curiel: A Dominican Actor in Hollywood: On Being Lil Papi from FX's Acclaimed Series, *Pose*." Interview conducted by Dominican Film Festival in NYC, October.

Curnutt, Hugh. 2013. "You Can't Handle My Truth: Reality TV's Trompe-l'oeil Effect and the (Im)possible Reality of Its Participants." *Psychoanalysis, Culture & Society* 18 (3): 295–312.

Curtin, Michael. 2007. "Introduction: Media Capital in Chinese Film and Television." In *Playing to the World's Biggest Audience: The Globalization of Chinese Film and TV*. University of California Press.

Dagbovie, Sika Alaine. 2007. "Star-Light, Star-Bright, Star Damn Near White: Mixed-Race Superstars." *Journal of Popular Culture* 40 (2): 217–37. https://doi.org/10.1111/j.1540-5931.2007.00376.x.

Dávila, Arlene. 1998. "El Kiosko Budweiser: The Making of a 'National' Television Show in Puerto Rico." *American Ethnologist* 25 (3): 452–70.

Dávila, Arlene. 2000. "Mapping Latinidad: Language and Culture in the Spanish TV Battlefront." *Television & New Media* 1 (1): 75–94.

Dávila, Arlene. 2001. *Latinos, Inc.: The Marketing and Making of a People*. University of California Press.

Davis, Angela. 1997. "Interview with Lisa Lowe, Angela Davis: Reflections on Race, Class, and Gender in the USA." In *The Politics of Culture in the Shadow of Capital*, edited by Lisa Lowe and David Lloyd. Duke University Press.

Davis, Angela. 2003. *Are Prisons Obsolete?* Seven Stories.

Dayan, Colin. 1995. *Haiti, History, and the Gods*. University of California Press.

Death at a Funeral. 2010. Directed by Neil LaBute. Screen Gems.

Delgado, Fernando. 2005. "Golden but Not Brown: Oscar De La Hoya and the Complications of Culture, Manhood, and Boxing." *International Journal of the History of Sport* 22 (2): 196–211.

Del Río, Esteban. 2017. "Authenticity, Appropriation, Articulation: The Cultural Logic of Latinidad." In *The Routledge Companion to Latina/o Media*, edited by María Elena Cepeda and Dolores Inés Casillas. Routledge.

Demers, Jason. 2017. "Is the Trojan Horse an Empty Signifier? The Televisual Politics of *Orange Is the New Black*." *Canadian Review of American Studies* 47 (3): 403–22.

Diaz-Cotto, Juanita. 1996. *Gender, Ethnicity, and the State: Latina and Latino Prison Politics*. SUNY Press.

D'Laura, José. 2013. "La montaña: La dominicanidad en el punto más alto del planeta." http://josedlaura.blogspot.com/2013/11/la-montana-la-dominicanidad-en-el-punto.html.

Domino Rudolph, Jennifer. 2020. *Baseball as Mediated Latinidad: Race, Masculinity, Nationalism, and Performances of Identity*. Ohio State University Press.

Drumline. 2002. Directed by Charles Stone III. 20th Century Fox.

Duany, Jorge (1994) 2008. *Quisqueya on the Hudson: The Transnational Identity of Dominicans in Washington Heights*. Dominican Studies Institute.

Duany, Jorge. 1996. "Transnational Migration from the Dominican Republic: The Cultural Redefinition of Racial Identity." *Caribbean Studies* 29 (2): 253–82.

Duany, Jorge. 2006. "Racializing Ethnicity in the Spanish-Speaking Caribbean: A Comparison of Haitians in the Dominican Republic and Dominicans in Puerto Rico." *Latin American and Caribbean Ethnic Studies* 1 (2): 231–48.

Duffett, Mark. 2009. "'We Are Interrupted by Your Noise': Heckling and the Symbolic Economy of Popular Music Stardom." *Popular Music and Society* 32 (1): 37–57.

Dyer, Richard. (1979) 1998. *Stars*. New ed. BFI.

Dyer, Richard. (1986) 2005. *Heavenly Bodies: Film Stars and Society*. Routledge.

Dyer, Richard. 1997. *White: Essays on Race and Culture*. Routledge.

Elkins, E. 2018. "Hulu: Geoblocking National TV in an On-Demand Era." In *From Networks to Netflix*, edited by D. Johnson. Routledge.

ESENDOM.com. 2017. "6th Dominican Film Festival Is More Than Merengue and Bachata: 'We Are Cinema.'" https://esendom.com/cine/2017/7/24/6th-dominican-film-festival-is-more-than-merengue-and-bachata-we-are-cinema.

Fabian, Monika. 2013. "Opinion: On MTV's 'Washington Heights,' a Stylized Image Trumps Authenticity." ABC News, January 9, 2013. https://abcnews.go.com/ABC_Univision/mtvs-washington-heights-jersey-shore/story?id=18171800.

Feeney, Michael J. 2014. "Dominican Film Festival Rolls into Washington Heights." *New York Daily News*, June 2014. https://www.nydailynews.com/2014/06/17/dominican-film-festival-rolls-into-washington-heights/.

Fernandez, Maria Elena. 2019. "Why *Orange Is the New Black* Brought the Immigration Crisis to Litchfield." *Vulture*, July 2019. https://www.vulture.com/2019/07/orange-is-the-new-black-immigration-storyline-bts.html.

Finnigan, Bob. 1994. "Winter-League Baseball—Winter Ball Helps Rodriguez Discover His Dominican Roots." *Seattle Times*, December 14. https://archive.seattletimes.com/archive/19941214/1947289/winter-league-baseball—winter-ball-helps-rodriguez-discover-his-dominican-roots—mariner-shortstop-alex-rodriguez-could-have-taken-the-winter-off-or-played-baseball-elsewhere-but-opted-to-go-h.

Flores, Juan. 2000. *From Bomba to Hip-Hop: Puerto Rican Culture and Latino Identity*. Columbia University Press.

Flores, Juan. 2009. *The Diaspora Strikes Back: Caribeño Tales of Learning and Turning*. Routledge.

Frida. 2002. Directed by Julie Taymor. Miramax Films.

Garcia, Sandra E. 2013. "Washington Heights Half-Welcomes MTV Series." *Uptowner*, January 7.

Garcia, Sandra E. 2018. "A Dominican Wrestling Hero Gets a Biopic to Match His Star Power." *New York Times*, May 27. https://www.nytimes.com/2018/05/27/movies/jack-veneno-dominican-republic-wrestling.html.

García-Peña, Lorgia. 2016. *The Borders of Dominicanidad: Race, Nation, and Archives of Contradiction*. Duke University Press.

Garsd, Jasmine. 2011. "Romeo Santos: Taking Bachata Mainstream." NPR, November 18. https://www.npr.org/2011/11/19/142514062/romeo-santos-taking-bachata-mainstream.

Gates, Racquel. 2013. "Keepin' It Reality Television." In *Watching While Black: Centering the Television of Black Audiences*, edited by Beretta E. Smith-Shomade. Rutgers University Press.

Gay, Jason. 2009. "A-Rod: Confessions of a Damned Yankee." *Details*, April.

Giannino, Steven S. 2013. "Guidos and Guidettes: Exploring Editorial News Media Frames of Italian-Americans on *Jersey Shore*." *Review of Journalism and Mass Communication* 1 (1): 1–13.

Giles, David. 2000. *Illusions of Immortality: A Psychology of Fame and Celebrity*. Macmillan.

Giles, David. 2002. "Parasocial Interaction: A Review of the Literature and a Model for Future Research." *Media Psychology* 4 (3): 279–305.

Ginsburg, Faye D., Lila Abu-Lughod, and Brian Larkin, eds. 2002. *Media Worlds: Anthropology on New Terrain*. University of California Press.

Givens, Orie. 2016. "About the Unbearable Whiteness Behind *Orange Is the New Black*." *Advocate*, July 21. https://www.advocate.com/arts-entertainment/2016/7/21/about-unbearable-whiteness-behind-orange-new-black.

Godreau, Isar P. 2006. "Folkloric 'Others': Blanqueamiento and the Celebration of Blackness as an Exception in Puerto Rico." In *Globalization and Race: Transformations in the Cultural Production of Blackness*, edited by Kamari Maxine Clark and Deborah A. Thomas. Duke University Press.

Goin, Keara. 2009. *Communicating Identity: Gendered Representation and the Influence of the Megadiva*. Master's thesis, University of South Carolina.

Goin, Keara. 2016. "Marginal Latinidad: Afro-Latinas and U.S. Film." *Latino Studies* 14 (3): 257–75. https://doi.org/10.1057/s41276-016-0006-2.

Goin, Keara. 2017. "Zoe Saldana or Zoë Saldaña?: Cinematic *dominicanidad* and the Hollywood Star." *Celebrity Studies* 8 (1): 34–50. https://doi.org/10.1080/19392397.2016.1172974.

Gómez, Laura E. 2020. *Inventing Latinos: A New Story of American Racism*. New Press.

Gonzalez-Barrera, Ana. 2022. "About 6 Million U.S. Adults Identify as Afro-Latino." Pew Research Center, May 2. https://www.pewresearch.org/fact-tank/2022/05/02/about-6-million-u-s-adults-identify-as-afro-latino/.

Gray, Herman S. 2005. *Cultural Moves: African Americans and the Politics of Representation*. University of California Press.

Guardians of the Galaxy. 2014. Directed by James Gunn. Marvel Studios.

Guardians of the Galaxy Vol. 2. 2017. Directed by James Gunn. Marvel Studios.

Guess Who. 2005. Directed by Kevin Rodney Sullivan. Columbia Pictures.

Guidotti-Hernandez, Nicole M. 2007. "Dora the Explorer, Constructing 'Latinidades' and the Politics of Global Citizenship." *Latino Studies* 5:209–32.

Gupta, Akhil, and James Ferguson. 1992. "Beyond 'Culture': Space, Identity, and the Politics of Difference." *Cultural Anthropology* 7 (1): 6–23.

Gupta, Akhil, and James Ferguson. 1997. "Discipline and Practice: 'The Field' as Site, Method, and Location in Anthropology." In *Anthropological Locations: Boundaries and Grounds of a Field Science*, edited by Akhil Gupta and James Ferguson. University of California Press.

Haas, Lupe. 2008. "Manny Perez's Pride and Glory." Cinemovie.tv.

Hall, Stuart. 1993. "Cultural Identity and Diaspora." In *Colonial Discourse and Post-Colonial Theory: A Reader*, edited by Patrick Williams and Laura Chrisman. Harvester Wheatsheaf.

Hall, Stuart. 1996. "New Ethnicities." In *Black British Cultural Studies: A Reader*, edited by Houston A. Baker, Manthia Diawara, and Ruth H. Lindeborg. University of Chicago Press.

Hall, Stuart. 1997a. "The Local and the Global." In *Culture, Globalization and the World System: Contemporary Conditions for the Representation of Identity*, edited by Anthony B. King. University of Minnesota Press.

Hall, Stuart. 1997b. *Representation: Cultural Representations and Signifying Practices*. The Open University and Sage.

Halterman, Jim. 2012. "Interview: Head of MTV Programming David Janollari." The Futon Critic, October 16, 2012.

Harkins, Anthony. 2004. "Introduction: Race, Class, and the 'Hillbilly.'" In *Hillbilly*. Oxford University Press.

Hassler-Forest, Dan. 2018. "'Life Isn't Some Cartoon Musical': Neoliberal Identity Politics in *Zootopia* and *Orange Is the New Black*." *Journal of Popular Culture* 51 (2): 356–78. https://doi.org/10.1111/jpcu.12658.

Here Comes Honey Boo Boo. 2012–14. TLC.

Hernandez, Lee. 2013. "Zoe Saldaña Is Latina's May 2013 Cover Girl!" *Latina*, April 2. http://www.latina.com/zoe.

Hernández, Ramona, Francisco L. Rivera-Batiz, and Sidie S. Sisay. 2022. *Dominicans in the United States: A Socioeconomic Profile 2022*. CUNY Dominican Studies Institute.

Hernández, Ramona, and Utku Sezgin. 2010. "Second-Generation U.S. Dominicans and the Question of Transnational Orientation." *Camino Real* 2 (3): 59–87.

Herrera, Brian Eugenio. 2015. *Latin Numbers: Playing Latino in Twentieth-Century U.S. Popular Performance*. University of Michigan Press.

Heyman, Jon. 2014. "Alex Rodriguez's Downfall Is One of Saddest Baseball Stories Ever Told." CBSSports.com, January 11, 2014.

Hidalgo-Ayala, Ximena. 2017. "Entrevista Exclusiva con Armando Guareño, Fundador de Festival de Cine Dominicano." *Impacto Latino*. https://impactolatino.com/entrevista-exclusiva-con-armando-guareno-fundador-de-festival-de-cine-dominicano/.

Hoffnung-Garskof, Jesse. 2008. *A Tale of Two Cities: Santo Domingo and New York After 1950*. Princeton University Press.

Hollywood Reporter.com. 2018. "'OITNB' Star Opens Up About Tackling 'Dangerous' Immigration Storyline." The Hollywood Reporter. https://www.hollywoodreporter.com/tv/tv-news/oitnb-season-6-what-immigration-storyline-means-season-7-laura-gomez-interview-1131193/.

Holmes, Su. 2005. "'Starring . . . Dyer?': Re-visiting Star Studies and Contemporary Celebrity Culture." *Westminster Papers in Communication and Culture* 2 (2): 6–21.

Holmes, Su, and Deborah Jermyn, eds. 2004. *Understanding Reality Television*. Routledge.

hooks, bell. 1992. *Black Looks: Race and Representation*. South End.

Houston, Shannon M. 2016. "How *Orange Is the New Black* Used, and Then Failed the Black Lives Matter Movement." *Paste*. https://www.pastemagazine.com/tv/orange-is-the-new-black/how-orange-is-the-new-black-used-and-then-failed-t/.

Howard, David. 2001. *Coloring the Nation: Race and Ethnicity in the Dominican Republic*. Signal Books.

Ignacio, Emily N. 2004. *Building Diaspora: Filipino Cultural Community Formation on the Internet*. Rutgers University Press.

In the Heights. Directed by John M. Chu. Warner Bros. Pictures. 2021.

Jersey Shore. 2009–12. MTV.

Jiménez, Lillian. 1993. "Puerto Rican Cinema in New York: From the Margin to the Center." *Jump Cut: A Review of Contemporary Media* 38:60–66.

Jiménez, Lillian. 1996. "Moving from the Margin to the Center: Puerto Rican Cinema in New York." In *The Ethnic Eye: Latino Media Arts*, edited by Chon A. Noriega and Ana M. López. University of Minnesota Press.

Jiménez Román, Mariam, and Juan Flores. 2010. "Introduction." In *Afro-Latin@ Reader: History and Culture in the United States*, edited by Miriam Jiménez Román and Juan Flores. Duke University Press.

Jones, Steve. 2005. "MTV: The Medium Was the Message." *Critical Studies in Media Communication* 22 (1): 83–88.

Julien, Isaac, and Kobena Mercer. 1988. "Introduction: De Margin and De Centre." *Screen* 29 (4): 2–11.

Kalogeropoulos Householder, April, and Adrienne Trier-Bieniek, eds. 2016. *Feminist Perspectives on Orange Is the New Black: Thirteen Critical Essays*. McFarland.

Kearney, Michael. 1995. "The Local and the Global: The Anthropology of Globalization and Transnationalism." *Annual Review of Anthropology* 24:547–65.

Keene, Allison. 2013. "Washington Heights: TV Review." *Hollywood Reporter*, January 9.

Khanna, Nikki. 2010. "'If You're Half Black, You're Just Black': Reflected Appraisals and the Persistence of the One-Drop Rule." *Sociological Quarterly* 51:96–121.

Klein, Allan. 1991. *Sugarball: The American Game, the Dominican Dream*. Yale University Press.
Klein, Amanda. 2009. "Postmodern Marketing, Generation Y, and the Multiplatform Viewing Experience of MTV's *The Hills*." *Jump Cut: A Review of Contemporary Media* 51. https://www.ejumpcut.org/archive/jc51.2009/HillsKlein/index.html.
Klein, Amanda. 2011. "The Hills, *Jersey Shore*, and the Aesthetics of Class." *Flow: Television and Media Journal* 13 (12). https://www.flowjournal.org/2011/04/the-hills-jersey-shore-and-the-aesthetics-of-class/.
Klein, Amanda. 2013. "MTV Reality Programming & the Labor of Identity Construction." *Judgmental Observer: Media/Popular Culture/Higher Ed*, January 11.
Klein, Amanda. 2021. *Millennials Killed the Video Star: MTV's Transition to Reality Programming*. Duke University Press.
Kraszewski, Jon. 2010a. "Coming to a Beach Near You! Examinations of Ethnic and State Identity in *Jersey Shore*." *Flow: Television and Media Journal* 11 (8). https://www.flowjournal.org/2010/02/coming-to-a-beach-near-you-examinations-of-ethnic-and-state-identity-in-jersey-shore-jon-kraszewski-seton-hall-university/.
Kraszewski, Jon. 2010b. "Multiracialism on *The Real World* and the Reconfiguration of Politics in MTV's Brand During the 2000s." *Popular Communication* 8:132–46.
Kraszewski, Jon. 2014. "Branding, Nostalgia, and the Politics of Race on VH1's *Flavor of Love*." *Quarterly Review of Film and Video* 31 (3): 240–54.
Krohn-Hansen, Christian. 2013. *Making New York Dominican: Small Business, Politics, and Everyday Life*. University of Pennsylvania Press.
Laguna Beach. 2004–6. MTV.
Laplante, Jaie. 2013. "A New Wave of Creative Cinematic Energy from Dominican Republic? (Surprise!)." *Miami Film Festival Blog*. https://miamifilmfestival.com/a-new-wave-of-creative-cinematic-energy-from-dominican-republic-surprise/.
LatinoRebels.com. 2013. "MTV's 'Washington Heights:' Just Another Lost Opportunity for Latinos." https://www.latinorebels.com/2013/01/10/mtvs-washington-heights-just-another-lost-opportunity-for-latinos/.
Latinxtoday.com. 2020. "Dominican Film Festival in New York Will Present More Than 70 Films." http://www.latinxtoday.com/6467_hispanos/7074171_festival-de-cine-dominicano-en-nueva-york-presentara-mas-de-70-peliculas.html.
Lawton, Chris. 2014. "Into the Dominican Film Festival's World." *Latin Business Today*. https://www.latinbusinesstoday.com/into-the-dominican-film-festivals-world/.
Levin, Jordan. 2013. "Dominican-American Pop Star Prince Royce Opens Up About His Cross-Cultural Inspiration and His New Album 'Soy El Mismo.'" *Miami Herald*, October 11.
Lines, Gill. 2010. "Villains, Fools or Heroes? Sports Stars as Role Models for Young People." *Leisure Studies* 20 (4): 285–303.
López, Ana M. 1991. "Are All Latins from Manhattan? Hollywood, Ethnography, and Cultural Colonialism." In *Unspeakable Images: Ethnicity and the American Cinema*, edited by Lester D. Friedman. University of Illinois Press.
López, Gustavo, and Ana Gonzalez-Barrera. 2016. "Afro-Latino: A Deeply Rooted Identity Among U.S. Hispanics." Pew Research Center. https://www.pewresearch.org/fact-tank/2016/03/01/afro-latino-a-deeply-rooted-identity-among-u-s-hispanics/.
Maestas, Adriana. 2013. "Authenticity of MTV's 'Washington Heights' Questions." Politic360.com, January 16.
Mankekar, Purnima. 1999. *Screening Culture, Viewing Politics: An Ethnography of Television, Womanhood, and Nation in Postcolonial India*. Duke University Press.
Martin, Pete. 1945. "Dominican Dynamite." *Saturday Post*, July 29.

Martinez, Marissa. 2019. "What Yalitza Aparicio's Role Means for Indigenous Representation." *Daily Northwestern*, February 19. https://dailynorthwestern.com/2019/02/19/lateststories/martinez-what-yalitza-apariciosrole-means-for-indigenous-representation/.

Mayer, Vicki. 2003. *Producing Dreams, Consuming Youth: Mexican Americans and Mass Media*. Rutgers University Press.

Mayer, Vicki. 2004. "Please Pass the Pan: Retheorizing the Map of Panlatinidad in Communication Research." *Communication Review* 7 (2): 113–24.

McDonald, K., and D. Smith-Rowsey. 2016. *The Netflix Effect: Technology and Entertainment in the 21st Century*. Bloomsbury.

McFarland, Melanie. 2019. "Orange Is the New Black Gives the Immigration Crisis a Familiar Face." Salon, July 29. https://www.salon.com/2019/07/29/orange-is-the-new-black-gives-the-immigration-crisis-a-familiar-face/?fbclid=IwAR34JmGzlOTsq_ewnhiGSQzDxScnA_hHaYDaVm2KN5WWLNaRDM2Gqtv4ipE.

McIntosh, Peggy. 1989. "White Privilege: Unpacking the Invisible Knapsack." *Peace and Freedom*, July/August.

McQueen, Gregg. 2017. "A New Rhythm in Reel." *Manhattan Times*. https://www.manhattantimesnews.com/a-new-rhythm-in-reelun-nuevo-ritmo/.

Melanie. 2011. "Another Former WWE Diva Linked to an A-Lister." *Diva Dirt*. https://www.diva-dirt.com/another-former-wwe-diva-linked-to-an-a-lister/.

Meléndez, A. Gabriel. 2016. "No Longer Hidden: Bless Me, Última and Recent Chicana/o-Latina/o Cinema." *Chiricú Journal: Latina/o Literatures, Arts, and Cultures* 1 (1): 39–52.

Méndez, Danny. 2018. "María Montez: The Unnatural Actress and the Consumption of the Early Dominican Diva." *Small Axe* 56:115–27. https://doi.org/10.1215/07990537-6985807.

Messina, Elizabeth. 2004. "Psychological Perspectives on the Stigmatization of Italian Americans in the American Media." In *Saints and Rogues: Conflicts and Convergence in Psychotherapy*, edited by R. Marchesani and M. Stern. Haworth.

Miller, Daniel, and Don Slater. 2003. "Ethnography and the Extreme Internet." In *Globalisation: Studies in Anthropology*, edited by Thomas Hylland Eriksen. Pluto.

Miranda, Lin-Manuel. 2021. *In the Heights* (lyrics). AllMusicals. https://www.allmusicals.com/i/intheheights.htm.

Mitra, Amanda, and Eric Watts. 2002. "Theorizing Cyberspace: The Idea of Voice Applied to the Internet Discourse." *New Media & Society* 4 (4): 479–98.

Molina-Guzmán, Isabel. 2010. *Dangerous Curves: Latina Bodies in the Media*. New York University Press.

Molina-Guzmán, Isabel. 2013a. "Zoë Saldana: The Complicated Politics of Casting a Black Latina." *Flow: Television and Media Journal* 17 (5). https://www.flowjournal.org/2013/01/zoe-saldana-the-complicated-politics-of-casting-a-black-latina/.

Molina-Guzmán, Isabel. 2013b. "Commodifying Black Latinidad in US Film and Television." *Popular Communication* 11:211–26.

Molina-Guzmán, Isabel. 2016. "#OscarsSoWhite: How Stuart Hall Explains Why Nothing Changes in Hollywood and Everything Is Changing." *Critical Studies in Media Communication* 33 (5): 438–54.

Molina-Guzmán, Isabel, and Angharad N. Valdivia. 2004. "Brain, Brow, and Booty: Latina Iconicity in U.S. Popular Culture." *Communication Review* 7:205–21.

Moore, Anne. 2016. "Anatomy of a Binge: Abject Intimacy and the Televisual Form." In *Feminist Perspectives on Orange Is the New Black: Thirteen Critical Essays*, edited by April Kalogeropoulos Householder and Adrienne Trier-Bieniek. McFarland.

Mora, Adolfo R., and Viviana Rojas. 2016. "Latinas'/os' Facebook Usage: An Inter-Ethnic and Inter-Generational Exploration of Their Engagement with a Social Networking Site." In *The Routledge Companion to Latina/o Media*, edited by María Elena Cepeda and Dolores Inés Casillas. Routledge.

Morley, David. 1992. *Television, Audiences, and Cultural Studies*. Routledge.

Morley, David. 2009. "For a Materialist, Non-Media-Centric Media Studies." *Television & New Media* 10 (1): 114–16.

Moslimani, Mohamad, Luis Noe-Bustamante, and Sono Shah. 2023. "Facts on Hispanics of Dominican Origin in the United States, 2021." Pew Research Center, August 16. https://www.pewresearch.org/fact-sheet/us-hispanics-facts-on-dominican-origin-latinos/.

Nakamura, Lisa. 2008. "Mixedfolks.com: 'Ethnic Ambiguity,' Celebrity Outing, and the Internet." In *Mixed Race Hollywood*. New York University Press.

Nakashima, Cynthia. 1992. "An Invisible Monster: The Creation and Denial of Mixed Race People in America." In *Racially Mixed People in America*, edited by Maria P. P. Root. Sage.

Negra, Diane. 2001. *Off-White Hollywood: American Culture and Ethnic Female Stardom*. Routledge.

Nina. 2015. Directed by Cynthia Mort. Ealing Studios.

Nishime, LeiLani. 2010. "Aliens: Narrating U.S. Global Identity Through Transnational Adoption and Interracial Marriage in *Battlestar Galactica*." *Critical Studies in Media Communication* 28 (5): 450–65.

Noriega, Chon A. 1992. "Between a Weapon and a Formula: Chicano Cinema and Its Contexts." In *Chicanos and Film: Essays on Chicano Representation and Resistance*, edited by Chon A. Noriega. Garland.

Noriega, Chon A. 1994. "U.S. Latinos and the Media: Theory and Practice." *Jump Cut: A Review of Contemporary Media* 39:57–58.

Noriega, Chon A. 2000. *The Future of Latino Independent Media: A NALIP Sourcebook*. UCLA Chicano Studies Research Center.

Noriega, Chon A. 2004. "Strategies for Increasing Latinos' Media Access." *Harvard Journal of Hispanic Policy* 16:105–9.

Noriega, Chon A., and Ana M. López, eds. 1996. *The Ethnic Eye: Latino Media Arts*. University of Minnesota Press.

Nuun, Heather, and Anita Biressi. 2010. "'A Trust Betrayed': Celebrity and the Work of Emotion." *Celebrity Studies* 1 (1): 49–64.

Oboler, Suzanne. 1995. *Ethnic Labels, Latino Lives: Identity and the Politics of (Re)Presentation in the United States*. University of Minnesota Press.

Ono, Kent A. 2010. "Postracism: A Theory of the 'Post-' as Political Strategy." *Journal of Communication Inquiry* 34:227–33.

Orange Is the New Black. 2013–19. Netflix.

O'Sullivan, Shannon. 2016. "Who Is Always Already Criminalized? An Intersectional Analysis of Criminality on *Orange Is the New Black*." *Journal of American Culture* 39(4): 401–12.

Ouellette, Laurie. 2010. "Reality TV Gives Back: On the Civic Functions of Reality Entertainment." *Journal of Popular Film and Television* 38 (2): 66–71.

Paiz, Carolina. 2019. "Opinion: We Put ICE Detention Centers Into Orange Is The New Black. Now I'm Heading Back to One." BuzzFeed News. https://www.buzzfeednews.com/article/carolinapaiz/ice-detention-centers-orange-is-the-new-black.

Palomares, Sugey. 2012. "The Nina Simone Bio-Flick Controversy: What Does It Say About Race?" *Latina*, September 13.

Patta, Gig. 2020. "Manny Perez on Playing Tough Latino in a Cop Show with Big Dogs [Exclusive Interview]." LRM Online. https://lrmonline.com/news/manny-perez-interview/.
Peña Ovalle, Priscilla. 2008. "Framing Jennifer Lopez: Mobilizing Race from the Wide Shot to the Close-Up." In *The Persistence of Whiteness: Race and Contemporary Hollywood Cinema*. Routledge.
Peña Ovalle, Priscilla. 2011. "Dolores Del Rio Dances Across the Imperial Color Line." In *Dance and the Hollywood Latina: Race, Sex, and Stardom*. Rutgers University Press.
Pérez Firmat, Gustavo. 1994. *Life on the Hyphen: The Cuban-American Way*. University of Texas Press.
Perse, Elizabeth, and Rebecca Rubin. 1988. "Audience Activity and Satisfaction with Favorite Television Soap Opera." *Journalism Quarterly* 65:368–75.
Piñón, Juan. 2011. "Ugly Betty and the Emergence of the Latina/o Producers as Cultural Translators." *Communication Theory* 21:392–412.
Premium. 2006. Directed by Pete Chatmon. Codeblack Entertainment.
PR Newswire. 2013. "Prince Royce le Canta a una Audiencia de Fanáticas Emocionadas Durante su Primer Concierto 'Terra Live Music.'" https://www.prnewswire.com/news-releases/prince-royce-le-canta-a-una-audiencia-de-fanaticas-emocionadas-durante-su-primer-concierto-terra-live-music-236586091.html.
Ramírez Berg, Charles. 1992. *Cinema of Solitude: A Critical Study of Mexican Film, 1967–1983*. University of Texas Press.
Ramírez Berg, Charles. 2002. "'Introduction' and 'A Crash Course in Hollywood's Latino Imagery.'" In *Latino Images in Film: Stereotypes, Subversion, and Resistance*. University of Texas Press.
RealClearSports.com. 2013. "TOP 10 MOST HATED PEOPLE IN SPORTS 9. Alex Rodriguez." http://www.realclearsports.com/lists/most_hated_people_in_sports/alex_rodriguez_yankees.html.
Real Housewives. 2006–Present. Bravo.
Risner, Jonathan. 2016. "Taking Stock: Recent and Emerging Lines of Study in U.S.-Latina/o Cinema." *Chiricú Journal: Latina/o Literatures, Arts, and Cultures* 1 (1): 7–16.
Rivera, Raquel Z. 2003. *New York Ricans from the Hip Hop Zone*. Palgrave Macmillan.
Rivero, Yeidy M. 2009. "Diasporic and Marginal Crossroads: The Films of Frances Negrón-Muntaner." *Latino Studies* 7:336–56.
Road Rules. 1995–2007. MTV.
Roberts, Shari. 1993. "'The Lady in the Tutti-Frutti Hat': Carmen Miranda, a Spectacle of Ethnicity." *Cinema Journal* 32 (3): 3–23.
Rodriguez, América. 1999. *Making Latino News: Race, Language, Class*. Sage.
Rodriguez, Cesar. 2020. "Cesar Rodriguez Dominicans in the Diaspora: Directing in Hollywood." Interview conducted by Dominican Film Festival in NYC, October.
Rodriguez, Clara E. 1997. *Latin Looks: Images of Latinas and Latinos in the U.S. Media*, edited by Clara E. Rodriguez. Westview.
Rodriguez, Clara E. 2000. *Changing Race: Latinos, the Census and the History of Ethnicity*. New York University Press.
Rodriguez, Clara E. 2004. *Heroes, Lovers, and Others: The Story of Latinos in Hollywood*. Smithsonian Books.
Rojas, Viviana. 2007. "Chusmas, Chismes, y Ecandolos: Latinas Talk Back to El Show de Cristina and Laura en America." In *From Bananas to Buttocks: The Latina Body in Popular Film and Culture*, edited by Myra Mendible. University of Texas Press.
Rojek, Chris. 2001. *Celebrity*. Reaktion Books.

Román, Miriam Jiménez, and Juan Flores, eds. 2010. *Afro-Latin@ Reader: History and Culture in the United States.* Duke University Press.

Rose, Lacey. 2014. "MTV Chief on 'Real World's' Future, a 'Saturday Night Live' Past and Reality TV's 'Reality' Problem (Q&A)." *Hollywood Reporter,* April 9. https://www.hollywoodreporter.com/news/general-news/mtv-chief-real-worlds-future-694321/.

Roth, Wendy D. 2012. *Race Migrations: Latinos and the Cultural Transformation of Race.* Stanford University Press.

Rúa, Merida M. Maria. 2005. "Latinidades." In *The Oxford Encyclopedia of Latinos and Latinas in the United States,* edited by Suzanne Oboler and David González, vol. 2. Oxford University Press.

Sagás, Ernesto. 1985. "Spanish-Language Print Media Use As an Indicator of Acculturation." *Journalism Quarterly* 62 (4): 734–62.

Sagás, Ernesto. 2000. *Race and Politics in the Dominican Republic.* University Press of Florida.

Sagás, Ernesto, and Sintia Molina. 2004. *Dominican Migration: Transnational Perspectives.* University Press of Florida.

Salamone, Gina. 2010. "Manny Perez's 'La Soga' Is Reflection of His Washington Heights Life." *Daily News,* August 6.

Sánchez Korrol, Virginia E. 1994. *From Colonia to Community: The History of Puerto Ricans in New York City.* University of California Press.

San Diego Union Tribune. 2014. "Dominican Actor Manny Pérez Pleased with the Support of the Latino Public." https://www.sandiegouniontribune.com/en-espanol/sdhoy-complacido-actor-dominicano-manny-perez-con-apoyo-2014jun19-story.html.

Sanson, Kevin, and Gregory Steirer. 2019. "Hulu, Streaming, and the Contemporary Television Ecosystem." *Media, Culture & Society* 41 (8): 1210–27.

Santana, Nelson. 2010. "The Great Dominican Ignorance Toward Alex Rodriguez." ESENDOM.com, August 4.

Santana, Nelson. 2013. "Baseball's Steroids Era and Its Dominican Scapegoats." *Flow: Television and Media Journal* 18 (6). https://www.flowjournal.org/2013/09/baseball%E2%80%99s-steroids-era/.

Santana, Nelson. 2015. Personal correspondence.

Schein, Louisa. 2002. "Mapping Hmong Media in Diasporic Space." In *Media Worlds: Anthropology on New Terrain,* edited by Faye D. Ginsburg, Lila Abu-Lughod, and Brian Larkin. University of California Press.

Scott, Jessica. 2017. "Hillbilly Horror and the New Racism: Rural and Racial Politics in *Orange Is the New Black.*" *Journal of Appalachian Studies* 23 (2): 221–38.

Shadow and Act. 2012. "MTV Takes Viewers to 'Washington Heights' w/ New Docu-Series Premiering January." December 7. http://blogs.indiewire.com/shadowandact.

Shadow and Act. 2014. "Zoe Saldana/Nina Simone Bio-Pic Shopped to Distributors at Cannes Film Market as Director Files Lawsuit." May 15. http://blogs.indiewire.com/shadowandact.

Shohat, Ella, and Robert Stam. 1994. *Unthinking Eurocentrism: Multiculturalism and the Media.* Routledge.

Shpigel, Ben. 2010. "The Man Baseball Loves to Hate." *New York Times,* April 23.

Siendo Honestos. 2019. "Siendo Honestos: Tabaré Blanchard Parte 1/4." https://www.youtube.com/watch?v=5JOtYcoTVwg.

Silverman, Rachel E., and Emily D. Ryalls. 2016. "'Everything Is Different the Second Time Around': The Stigma of Temporality in *Orange Is the New Black.*" *Television & New Media* 17 (6): 520–33.

Simmons, Kimberly E. 2005. "'Somos una Liga': Afro-Dominicanidad and the Articulation of New Racial Identities in the Dominican Republic." *Wadabagei* 8 (1): 51–64.

Simmons, Kimberly E. 2008. "Navigating the Racial Terrain: Blackness and Mixedness in the United States and the Dominican Republic." *Transforming Anthropology* 16 (2): 95–111.

Smith, Carol A. 1996. "Myths, Intellectuals, and Race/Class/Gender Distinctions in the Formation of Latin American Nations." *Journal of Latin American Anthropology* 2:148–69.

Snookie & Jwoww. 2012–15. MTV.

Sommers, Laurie Kay. 1991. "Inventing Latinismo: The Creation of 'Hispanic' Panethnicity in the United States." *Journal of American Folklore* 104 (411): 32–53.

Spitta, Silvia. 1997. "Transculturation, the Caribbean, and Cuban-American Imaginary." In *Tropicalizations: Transcultural Representations of Latinidad*, edited by Frances R. Aparicio and Susana Chávez-Silverman. University Press of New England.

Spivak, Gayatri Chakravorty. 2010. "Can the Subaltern Speak?" In *Reflections on the History of an Idea*, edited by Rosalind C. Morris. Columbia University Press.

Staiger, Janet. 2005. *Media Reception Studies*. New York University Press.

Stern, Marlow. 2017. "Samira Wiley on Poussey's Powerful—and Controversial—OITNB Death and Living Out Loud." Daily Beast. https://www.thedailybeast.com/samira-wiley-on-pousseys-powerfuland-controversialoitnb-death-and-living-out-loud.

Stevens-Acevedo, Anthony, Tom Weterings, and Leonor Alvarez Francés. 2013. *Juan Rodriguez and the Beginnings of New York City*. CUNY Dominican Studies Institute.

Sullivan Barak, Katie. 2016. "Jenji Kohan's Trojan Horse: Subversive Uses of Whiteness." In *Feminist Perspectives on Orange Is the New Black: Thirteen Critical Essays*, edited by April Kalogeropoulos Householder and Adrienne Trier-Bieniek. McFarland.

Symes, Katerina. 2017. "Orange Is the New Black: The Popularization of Lesbian Sexuality and Heterosexual Modes of Viewing." *Feminist Media Studies* 17 (1): 29–41. https://doi.org/10.1080/14680777.2017.1261836.

Tabar, Alex. 2017. "Laura Gómez—Dreamer, Actress and Activist." https://www.latinasinmedia.com/laura-gomez-blanca-flores-oitnb/.

Tavarez, Jessica. 2005. "Manny Pérez: His Take on Being a Sex Symbol." *Dominican Times Magazine* 17. https://latintrends.com/manny-perez-his-take-on-being-a-sex-symbol/.

The Hills. 2006–10. MTV.

The Losers. 2010. Directed by Sylvain White. Warner Bros. Pictures.

The Pauley D. Project. 2012. MTV.

The Real World. 1992–Present. MTV.

The Show with Vinny. 2013. MTV.

Thrift, Nigel. 1997. "'"US" and "Them"' Re-imagining Places, Re-imagining Identities." In *Consumption and Everyday Life*, edited by Hugh Mackay. Sage.

Torres-Saillant, Silvio. 1998. "The Tribulations of Blackness: Stages in Dominican Racial Identity." *Latin American Perspectives* 25 (3): 126–46.

Torres-Saillant, Silvio. 2010. *Introduction to Dominican Blackness*. CUNY Dominican Studies Institute.

Torres-Saillant, Silvio, and Ramona Hernández. 1998. *The Dominican Americans*. Greenwood.

Torres-Santos, Raymond. 2013. *Juan Luis Guerra and the Merengue: Toward a New Dominican National Identity*. CUNY Dominican Studies Institute.

Tuchman, Gaye. 1978. *Making News: A Study in the Construction of Reality*. Free Press.

Valdivia, Angharad N. 2000. *A Latina in the Land of Hollywood: And Other Essays on Media Culture*. University of Arizona Press.

Valdivia, Angharad N. 2004. "Latinas as Radical Hybrid: Transnationally Gendered Traces in Mainstream Media." *Global Media Journal* 3 (4): online.

Valdivia, Angharad N. 2007. "Is Penelope to J. Lo as Culture Is to Nature? Eurocentric Approaches to 'Latin' Beauties." In *From Bananas to Buttocks: The Latina Body in Popular Film and Culture*, edited by Myra Mendible. University of Texas Press.

Valdivia, Angharad N. 2010. *Latino/as in the Media*. Polity.

Valdivia, Angharad N. 2020. *The Gender of Latinidad: Uses and Abuses of Hybridity*. Wiley Blackwell.

Valdivia, Angharad N., and Ramona Curry. 2000. "Can Latin Americans Be Blonde or Can the US Tolerate a Latin American." In *A Latina in the Land of Hollywood: And Other Essays on Media Culture*. University of Arizona Press.

Vargas, Diana. 2020. "Dominican Film Festival in New York Performs Its Ninth Edition Virtually." Cinelatinoamericano. http://cinelatinoamericano.org/texto.aspx?cod=28337.

Vargas, Lucila. 2008. "Media Practices and Gender Identity Among Transnational Latina Teens." In *Latina/o Communication Studies Today*, edited by Angharad N. Valdivia. Peter Lang.

Veneno, La Primera Caída: El Relámpago de Jack. 2018. Directed by Tabaré Blanchard. Frío Frío.

Wallace, Benjamin. 2013. "Diamond in the Mud: The Death of Buckwild Star Shain Gandee and the Search for Authenticity in Reality TV." Vulture, September 15.

Warner, Kristen J. 2011. "'Who Gon Check Me Boo': Reality TV as a Haven for Black Women's Affect." FLOW. https://www.flowjournal.org/2011/08/who-gon-check-me-boo/.

Warner, Kristen J. 2014. "The Racial Logic of Grey's Anatomy: Shonda Rhimes and Her 'Post-Civil Rights, Post-Feminist' Series." *Television & New Media*. https://doi.org/10.177/1527476414550529.

Warner, Kristen J. 2015. "They Gon' Think You Loud Regardless: Ratchetness, Reality Television, and Black Womanhood." *Camera Obscura* 30 (1): 129–53. https://doi.org/10.1215/02705346-2885475.

Washington Heights. 2002. Directed by Alfredo Rodriguez De Villa. AsDuesDon.

Washington Heights. 2013. MTV.

Weber, Patrick. 2013. "Discussions in the Comments Section: Factors Influencing Participation and Interactivity in Online Newspapers' Reader Comments." *New Media & Society* 16 (6): 941–57.

White, Amanda. 2013. "Washington Heights—A Show Abandoned." *Mandy's Blog*, March 17.

Wood, Raymond F. 1981. "Anglo Influence on Spanish Place Names in California." *Southern California Quarterly* 63 (4): 392–413.

Zook, Kristal Brent. 1999. *Color by Fox: The Fox Network and the Revolution in Black Television*. Oxford University Press.

INDEX

Acevedo, Elizabeth, 166-67, 170
Afi Quinn, Rachel, 63, 72, 191
African American, xi, 37, 38, 62, 68
Afro-Latina/o/x, 4, 33, 37, 38, 40, 42, 44, 61, 62
Afrolatinidad(es), 4
Aparicio, Frances, 34, 138, 150; and Susana Chávez-Silvermann, 41
Aventura, 88-90

baseball: and Dominicans, 2, 77-79, 111; and race, 81, 83
Báez, Jillian, 10, 128-29
Beltrán, Mary, 192
Blackness: Black/white binary, 9, 37, 39-40, 62, 192; category of, xi; Dominican Blackness, 37-39, 151-53, 188-91; negrophobia, 35, 36, 44
Blanchard, Tabaré, 175-78, 181, 182; director of *La montaña* (The Mountain, 2013), 175-76
Blanqueamiento, 43
Burden of representation, 53-54, 58, 65, 88, 106, 118, 119, 165

Candelario, Ginetta E. B., 10, 34, 38, 68
Chicano cinema, 162-163
Curiel, Angel Bismark, 170-171

Dominican Film Festival New York City, 159, 171-75, 197
Dominican filmmakers: Chris Lopez, 164-65, 166, 169, 170, 174; Soleidy Mendez, 165, 166, 169-70; Katherine Castro, 167-68, 172-73; César Rodriguez, 168-69
Dominican imaginary, 24, 187, 191-92, 194, 196, 198, 199
Dominican media studies, 9

Dominican Republic: diaspora, 2; history of, 6-9; *Indio*, 36; and immigration, 7-9, 18; Quisqueya, 6
Dominican Spanish, 13, 14, 15, 17, 18, 19, 21, 62, 87, 89, 90, 97, 111-12, 121, 127-28, 181, 192-93, 194
Duany, Jorge, 8, 120, 128

Ernesto, Sagás, 7
ESENDOM.com, 194-96

Flores, Juan, ix, xi, 144, 187-88; and Miriam Jiménez Román, 4

García-Peña, Lorgia, 34, 39, 44
Gómez, Laura (actor), 134, 137
Gómez, Laura E. (author), ix
Guareño, Armando, 172, 173, 174, 175

Haiti, 6; *antihationaismo*, 6, 7, 35, 44; Haitians, 35, 151-52; Revolution, 6
Hispanic, xi
Horizontal hierarchies, 34, 42, 44, 87, 150
Hyphenated identity, 87-88, 193-97, 198
Hypodescent, 37-38, 151

In the Heights (2021) (film), 33-34, 34, 45-49, 197-98; and colorism, 49
In the Heights (play), 33

Klein, Amanda, 97, 99, 100, 104, 117, 129

Latin(o) American, xi
Latina/o media studies, 10
Latina/o/x (s), definition of, x; origins of, ix, x; usage of, x;
Latine, x

Latinidad(es), 4, 39-45, 137-138, 150; Marginal *Latinidad*, 147; Pan-latinidad, 64-65
Latino imaginary, ix, 138
Latinx specificity, 138, 148-149, 150, 151, 169-71, 180

Mestizaje, 42-43
Miranda, Lin-Manuel, 32-33
Molina-Guzmán, Isabel, 24, 66, 71, 74
Montez, María, 52-53
MTV: branding, 97-101; *Buckwild* (2013), 106-107; *Jersey Shore* (2009-2012), 104-106; *The Hills* (2006-2010), 114-117

Pan-Caribbean casting, 147-148
Pimentel, Jessica, 137
Polanco, Dascha, 47, 145
Puerto Rican cinema, 163-64
Pérez, Manny, 178-80; and *Washington Heights* (2002), 179-80

Reyes, Judy, 180
Rodriguez, Alex, 75-85
Royce, Prince, 90-92

Saldana, Zoe, 58-75; and blackness, 67-68, 188-89; and *Center Stage* (2000), 60-61; and *The Losers* (2011), 61; and *Nina* (2016), 73-74
Santana, Nelson, 81, 82, 195
Spectacle of containment, 101-104
Strategic ethnoracial flexibility, 60, 71-72

Torres-Saillant, Silvio, 35, 67
Trujillo, Rafael, 7, 35-36

Valdivia, Angharad N., x, 40, 70, 87
Veneno, La Primera Caída: El Relámpago de Jack) (2018), 175-83; and Pepe Sierra, 181

Washington Heights (neighborhood), 45, 47-49, 108-11, 120-123

KEARA K. GOIN is Associate Professor and Director of Undergraduate Programs in the Department of Media Studies at the University of Virginia.

For Indiana University Press

Tony Brewer, Artist and Book Designer
Allison Chaplin, Acquisitions Editor
Anna Garnai, Production Coordinator
Sophia Hebert, Assistant Acquisitions Editor
Samantha Heffner, Marketing Production Manager
Katie Huggins, Production Manager
Alyssa Nicole Lucas, Marketing and Publicity Manager
David Miller, Lead Project Manager/Editor
Dan Pyle, Online Publishing Manager
Leyla Salamova, Artist and Book Designer